D1559174

This award-winning book, co-authored by AAP Founding Partner, Dr. Aaron Conley, received the 2023 Skystone Partners Prize for Research on Fundraising and Philanthropy.

Philanthropy Fundamentals
for
Academic Leaders

AAP offers this custom major gifts training program for deans, department chairs, center directors, and other faculty. All participants receive a copy of this book in advance.

Recent Clients

The American University in Cairo
California State University Long Beach
Georgia State University
Purdue University Fort Wayne
St. Mary's University (TX)
Texas State University
University of Massachusetts Amherst
University of Southern California
University of Texas at San Antonio
Western Kentucky University

Save time and travel costs by bringing this research-intensive experience to your campus.

Gift officers are encouraged to attend with their academic leaders to strengthen collaboration.

Visit our website for program details.

Philanthropy and Education

Series Editor
Noah Drezner, Department of Organization and Leadership, Teachers
College, Columbia University, New York, USA

This series highlights first-rate scholarship related to education and philanthropy, attracting the top authors writing in the field. Philanthropy is broadly defined to include time, talent, and treasure. In addition to traditional forms and definitions of philanthropy, the series highlights philanthropy in communities of color as well as philanthropy among women and LGBT communities. Books in the series focus on fundraising as it is an integral part of increasing philanthropy and has an ever-increasing market.

More information about this series at
http://www.palgrave.com/gp/series/14553

Aaron Conley · Genevieve G. Shaker

Fundraising Principles for Faculty and Academic Leaders

palgrave
macmillan

Aaron Conley
Lilly Family School of Philanthropy
Indiana University
Indianapolis, IN, USA

Genevieve G. Shaker
Lilly Family School of Philanthropy
Indiana University
Indianapolis, IN, USA

Philanthropy and Education
ISBN 978-3-030-66428-2   ISBN 978-3-030-66429-9   (eBook)
https://doi.org/10.1007/978-3-030-66429-9

This Palgrave Macmillan imprint is published by the registered company Springer Nature
Switzerland AG
The registered company address is: Gewerbestrasse 11, 6330 Cham, Switzerland

PREFACE

This is not your typical book of fundraising insights written for those who are (or seeking to be) in academic leadership roles. Our motivation for this book was to write as academics for academics. Most prior works on this subject are authored by fundraising practitioners, many of whom migrated successfully into consulting roles and chose to share their experiences of what worked, and what did not, in their fundraising endeavors with deans, department chairs, and other academic leaders.

While the publication of a book is a worthy pursuit and practice-based insights can be especially valuable, most of these prior works rely extensively on subjective and anecdotal observations from the fundraiser's perspective. While we have been successful fundraisers, we also earned doctoral degrees in higher education. We teach. We publish. We commit to disciplinary service through academic and professional societies. We approach these responsibilities with an abiding belief in the importance of higher education and philanthropy and a personal and professional responsibility to contribute in both areas.

During our fundraising careers, we relied on academic research about philanthropy, interpreting and applying the field's critical concepts and findings to our practice. A great joy of higher education development for us was engaging with faculty members across the academic spectrum in fundraising and other engagement activities. Many faculty colleagues appreciated learning about the growing body of research on philanthropy, and that we embraced its applications to our work. This book is an extension of our fundraising approach and pedagogy.

The following pages provide guidance and insights for deans and department chairs, research center directors, and presidents and provosts. Wherever possible, we ground this guidance with research-based evidence. Additionally, we reference even more resources for those interested in exploring philanthropic studies more generally, and support for higher education particularly.

This book is not intended as a comprehensive tome containing every fundraising principle, activity, or potential scenario academic leaders will experience. Instead, we believe the book's sections contain fundamental knowledge that academic leaders need to be effective and successful in fundraising.

Part I is *Core Fundraising Concepts for the Non-fundraiser* and includes chapters on key operational matters, as well as historical insights on the role of philanthropy in American higher education. Another chapter considers the language of fundraising, with an emphasis on distinct words and phrases that should (and should never) be used with donors, prospective donors, and internally among faculty and staff.

Part II is *Research Insights to Drive Fundraising* and includes thought-provoking chapters on research behind donor motivations and giving, with a special focus on high net worth (HNW) individuals. We expect this section will challenge assumptions and provide new information to readers about raising major gifts. We also provide a framework for applying this knowledge to engagement activities with HNW individuals. We do not dwell extensively on the ideal approaches to "making the ask" and take a different approach than many other texts on this subject. As the evidence will make clear, HNW individuals are influenced by much more powerful forces than face-to-face solicitations or extensive and colorful written proposals.

Part III includes three chapters around the theme, *Operational Strategies and Tactics for the Academic Unit*. The chapters on working with partners, developing an annual plan, and focusing the leader's energies on a select set of tasks were chosen as critical areas where academic leaders often struggle. Understanding the importance of these topics allows leaders to make vital contributions to the unit's fundraising success in ways no one else can.

Part IV integrates the concepts and findings from the earlier sections into *Executing Fundraising Plans and Initiatives*. The chapters here focus on aligning strategic plans with existing and potential philanthropic support, understanding campaigns, and measuring impact in ways beyond simply counting dollars raised.

Two additional features are included in this book to make it a more relevant and valuable resource. A brief case study highlights and reinforces the content of one chapter in each of the four sections. These case studies are real stories of academic units that found success in some aspect of their engagement and fundraising activities and are intended to inspire ideas and strategies translatable to other institutions.

The other feature is the book's final part, written by a contributing author. David Perlmutter, a dean at Texas Tech University, wrote a seven-part series for *The Chronicle of Higher Education* between 2013 and 2016 entitled, *Don't Fear Fund Raising*. These articles, written specifically for academicians, provide a valuable perspective for experienced and uninitiated academic fundraising leaders alike, and reinforce many of the principles cited throughout the book. We are grateful to Dean Perlmutter for the opportunity to publish the series in its entirety and for contributing a new foreword.

Philanthropic support has never been more important to our institutions of higher learning. Faculty and academic leaders are playing an increasingly critical role in partnership with their institutional development and alumni professionals. We hope this book both guides and inspires even greater collaboration to further benefit the advancement of knowledge through our colleges and universities.

Aaron Conley
Academic Advancement Partners
Dallas, USA

Genevieve G. Shaker
Indiana University Lilly Family School
of Philanthropy at IUPUI
Indianapolis, USA

CONTENTS

ABOUT THE AUTHORS

Aaron Conley, Ed.D. is a faculty member for The Fund Raising School in the Indiana University (IU) Lilly Family School of Philanthropy at IUPUI and founder of the consulting practice, Academic Advancement Partners. He consulted previously with Grenzebach Glier and Associates where he led the teaching and coaching practice. He also held senior development roles including vice chancellor for advancement at the University of Colorado and vice president for development and alumni relations at the University of Texas at Dallas. He previously held school-based leadership roles at the University of Pittsburgh, Florida State, and Purdue.

Conley has contributed book chapters on philanthropy to *Achieving Excellence in Fundraising* (Wiley, 2016) and *Privatization and Public Universities* (IU Press, 2006) as well as research articles in a number of journals on philanthropy and nonprofit management. He earned an Ed.D. in higher education from IU.

Genevieve G. Shaker, Ph.D. is associate professor of philanthropic studies in the IU Lilly Family School of Philanthropy at IUPUI and adjunct professor of liberal arts and women's studies. She is also a faculty member of The Fund Raising School. She was an advancement officer for 20 years, most recently as associate dean for development and external affairs for the IU School of Liberal Arts.

Professor Shaker's research focuses on fundraising and fundraisers; higher education advancement; and, philanthropy in the workplace. She was named the Association of Fundraising Professionals' Emerging Scholar for 2015 and is a fellow of the TIAA Institute. She is the editor of *Faculty Work and the Public Good* (Teachers College Press, 2015) and author of multiple research articles and practice-oriented resources. She earned a Ph.D. in higher education from IU.

LIST OF FIGURES

LIST OF TABLES

PART I

Core Fundraising Concepts for the Non-fundraiser

CHAPTER 1

Fundraising for Academicians

Fundraising, like it or not, has become an expectation not only for presidents and deans, but also for department chairs, center directors, and any other faculty members with ambitious plans or needs that cannot be met through existing institutional resources. While donors have supported American higher education since the founding of Harvard College in 1636, the importance of private contributions has not been embraced in all corners of academe until recent decades, especially among public institutions and community colleges.

This reality is reflected in statements on educational philanthropy across four decades: "Voluntary support is becoming the only source of real discretionary money and in many cases is assuming a critical role in balancing institutional budgets" (Leslie & Ramey, 1988, pp. 115–116); "Private philanthropy is an important, probably essential, ingredient in making the American research university the extraordinarily successful institution it is" (Rothschild, 1999, p. 423); and, "Philanthropy was once used exclusively as a margin of excellence for American higher education. Today, it is central to the mere existence and daily function of academe" (Drezner, 2010, p. 195).

The good news for the uninitiated is that fundraising can be, for many academic leaders, one of the most enjoyable and rewarding activities among the litany of responsibilities they oversee. A longtime dean

© The Author(s), under exclusive license to Springer Nature
Switzerland AG 2021
A. Conley and G. G. Shaker, *Fundraising Principles for Faculty
and Academic Leaders*, Philanthropy and Education,
https://doi.org/10.1007/978-3-030-66429-9_1

at Harvard University, Henry Rosovsky, shared this perspective in the foreword of a book on fundraising for deans:

> Fund raising is fun, and many of us have come to enjoy the game. Most donors treat institutions and their representatives with love and respect, and more often than not, donors are interesting people with valuable insights. There is also considerable value in testing one's ideas with people outside your institution; fund raising gave me the opportunity to learn about my own institution while making many friends. Like everyone else, I encountered my share of no's delivered with varying degrees of emotion, but no one ever threw me out of their office or home. In general, I would have to say that alumni and other potential donors treat deans with greater courtesy than do professors or students. (Hall, 1993, p. xiii)

Those who hold similarly positive perspectives of fundraising share two key attributes. They have realistic expectations regarding the rate of growth that is possible for increased support for their unit. And, they have embraced the understanding that the process of raising a major gift from a donor is not transactional in the same way a wealthy person decides to buy a car, a house, or other major purchase. Rather, they understand that philanthropic giving at this level is relational and that either they, or others in their institution, can personally help donors feel the transformational power of giving.

THINKING DIFFERENTLY ABOUT FUNDRAISING

It is important to note in this opening chapter that academicians who are accomplished fundraisers have also learned to set aside biases or perceived truths about philanthropy and the inner workings of charitable giving. Faculty members currently in academic leadership roles, as well as those who envision one in their future, have already spent many years committed to learning, teaching, research, and service. They are looked upon as an expert in their given field and have the academic credentials and record of scholarly activity to back it up.

For such faculty, when it comes to seeking philanthropic support either for their own work, or on behalf of a department, center, or school, it would seem to be a fairly straightforward process of meeting with individuals interested in the subject matter or project and asking them for support. This observation is only partly correct.

Inserting personal assumptions about how donors think without first attempting to understand their motives for giving is dangerous. Dismissing the advice and counsel of experienced development staff often makes matters worse. Academicians who struggle with fundraising may have compelling opportunities worthy of donor support. But they may also view fundraising as a simple, linear process, "*We have needs – our alumni are loyal – so they should give.*" The same logic is often applied to fundraising from corporations, "*We generate skilled future employees and conduct research that is relevant to XYZ Corporation's bottom line, so they should support us.*"

This book includes extensive research about how donors think, as well as how to strengthen empathy skills to better understand donors' perspectives. This is truly one of the most critical skills of an effective fundraiser. An important area to understand first and long before thinking about soliciting gifts is philanthropic trends generally and in higher education particularly.

FUNDAMENTAL GIVING DATA AND RESOURCES TO KNOW AND SHARE

When academicians are immersed in their expertise area, they are comfortable and adept with the theory and data (often while recognizing that there is always more to learn). On the other hand, when one engages others in an unfamiliar field, uneasiness and apprehension can easily arise. A key fact to remember when engaging potential major donors is that high net worth individuals may be equally uninformed about philanthropy and may also need baseline information.

As evidence of this, only 4% of 1,600 wealthy study participants considered themselves philanthropy "experts" according to the biennial *U.S. Trust Study of High Net Worth Philanthropy*, the largest and longest ongoing study about high net worth individuals' philanthropic perspectives and behaviors (Bank of America, 2018). About half (52%) reported feeling "knowledgeable" and a remarkable 44% rated themselves as "novices" about philanthropy. In the study, the average household income was $331,000 and average net worth (excluding home value) was $16.8 million. Having philanthropic capacity does not equate to philanthropic expertise, by wealthy individuals' own self-assessments.

This finding is further reinforced in a 2017 study partially funded by the Bill and Melinda Gates Foundation (The Philanthropy Workshop, 2017). In this study, 80% of the 219 survey participants held a net worth of $10 million or more, and 20 qualitative interviews supplemented the survey results. This group was similarly candid. As the study noted, "Regardless of starting point, the vast majority of respondents showed they want to understand how to practice philanthropy, and pursued relationship-based as well as more technical approaches to learning" (p. 15). The technical approaches included attending conferences and engaging financial professionals, and the relationship-based activities included speaking openly with personal acquaintances of similar wealth about how they decide what to support.

Academic leaders can feel more at ease based on these findings and in knowing that they are engaging potential donors in an educational capacity. For example, it is entirely likely that prospective donors have limited understanding of the technical details of endowed scholarships or chairs. Similarly, most alumni, parents, and other individual constituents do not fully realize how philanthropic support helps colleges, departments, and other units deliver on their educational mission. One of the most effective ways for an academic leader to overcome apprehension toward fundraising is not to think of themselves as a fundraiser, but to look at fundraising as an extension of the teaching skills they already possess.

An initial step to becoming an effective teacher about philanthropy is to be familiar with national giving data and trends. This is critical, as the US Trust study reveals that high net worth individuals give to an average of seven organizations annually (Bank of America, 2018). Being aware of trends and influences across the philanthropic spectrum enables academic leaders to talk about more than just the urgent, pressing needs of their own institutions. For donors who give to organizations across multiple sectors, this presents welcome opportunities to discuss their interests broadly, potentially allowing strong listeners to learn more about donors' giving history and patterns. Such insights can be invaluable in planning future interactions that may lead to successful gift solicitations (More on this in Chapter 7).

Giving USA

A major source documenting national trends in philanthropic giving is the annual report, Giving USA. This study, released each June, provides an estimate of total charitable giving in the USA with specific details on giving by source and the designation of gifts to nine subsectors of nonprofit organizations. The report shows that giving in 2019 reached more than $449.6 billion, rising more than 4% (2.4% adjusted for inflation) over the prior year (Giving USA, 2020).

The annual release of Giving USA draws substantial media attention, so donors may be familiar with the total amount given. However, despite what appears to be an ever-increasing level of generosity in America, there are three vital trends behind these numbers that are helpful in "teaching" wealthy constituents about philanthropy.

First, while total giving is going up over time, the total number of individuals who give is declining. This means a smaller proportion of donors are giving, and they are giving larger gifts. In 2018, total giving among those who donated $1,000 or more to nonprofit organizations increased 2.6% over the previous year, while revenue from mid-level donors ($250–999) fell 4.0% and general donors (less than $250) declined 4.4%. The total number of mid-level and general donors also fell (Nilsen, 2019). Data from donors who itemized their taxes further illustrates the dominance of high net worth individuals. In 2015, three-quarters of all itemized donations came from taxpayers who earned more than $100,000. Those earning above $200,000 accounted for more than half of the donations (Lindsay, 2017).

Individuals able to make larger donations are becoming an increasing priority to nonprofits of all kinds. This is important for high net worth individuals to know, especially those who may be potential first-time donors to a school or unit. Colleges and universities are viewed with envy in the nonprofit sector because of an inherent advantage. While other organizations must expend considerable effort to build a prospective donor base, higher education institutions come with a built-in base through their alumni. Many institutions have 100,000 or more living alumni, so it is natural to assume that needs can be met by simply looking to a large number of alumni to contribute small and medium gifts. But, higher education is not immune to the trend of upward growth through bigger gifts from fewer donors as evidenced by decades of declining alumni participation rates (Blackbaud, 2018; Council for Advancement and Support of Education, 2020). Academic leaders may need to teach key donors and potential donors that the reality is not what they thought when it comes to higher education's inherent advantage.

Second, another teaching point related to Giving USA is that while giving totals generally appear to increase, another measure shows that giving remains at a near constant in relative terms. For more than 50 years, total charitable giving measured as a percentage of the gross domestic product (GDP) has remained at approximately two percent (Soskis, 2017). In general terms, this means that even though greater wealth is being created in the USA, a greater share is not given to charitable causes from year to year—despite periodic, concerted marketing and public-awareness efforts to give more (Perry, 2017).

The Giving USA study includes the sources of charitable dollars, also good information to talk about with donors. In 2019, individuals gave the largest share at 69% ($309.66 billion), followed by foundations at 17% ($75.69 billion), bequests at 10% ($43.21 billion), and corporations at 5% ($21.09 billion). The third key point and teaching opportunity here lies in recognizing the reality of corporate giving.

Large companies, especially those located near a university, are often assumed to be inclined to contribute to the institution. But nationally, corporate giving comprises the smallest proportion of the total dollars given. Corporate giving today is highly strategic, and companies rarely give simply to be upstanding community members. It could be argued companies hardly give at all when measured against their profits. Corporate giving as a percent of pre-tax profits has historically remained below one percent and has not been above this level since 2003, even though corporate profits have more than doubled over this same period (McCambridge, 2019).

This shift toward more strategic giving began in the early 1980s, resulting in "...a major change away from corporate philanthropy to giving that is designed to build alliances and partnerships or downright commercial relationships" (Burlingame & Dunlavy, 2016, p. 96). The two main vehicles emerging from this shift included gifts through sponsorships and cause-related marketing efforts, in addition to focused initiatives driven by employees.

Teaching moments for academic leaders also occur in relation to faculty members and in discussions of overall fundraising strategies for schools, departments, and research centers. In searches for external research funding, faculty members will find linkages (real or imagined) between their research and company missions. Solicitations to companies should always be coordinated with unit gift officers or the institutional development office. Chances are, there is already an established relationship between the institution and the company. Moreover, most companies have specific policies and protocols for the submission of requests for corporate gifts, including a common practice of accepting only one submission per nonprofit organization each year.

The larger lesson is to emphasize that individuals, not corporations, are the donor population with the best major gift potential. As the Giving USA figures illustrate, 69% of total US charitable giving comes from individuals and another 10% is received from individuals through bequests. Plus, approximately half of the 17% from foundations comes from family foundations, which could arguably be considered as individuals. This makes the total percent of giving driven by individuals more than 87%.

Thinking back to the finding that indicates high net worth individuals support an average of seven organizations annually, the odds are more favorable to be considered among a handful of other organizations for an individual's charitable dollars, rather than against hundreds, or possibly thousands, of charitable requests to a corporation. Financial support from companies can be important and viable in particular circumstances, however it is also not as easy to fundraise from corporations as is commonly believed.

Voluntary Support of Education

The Voluntary Support of Education (VSE) survey, conducted by the Council for Advancement and Support of Education (CASE), is an annual report focused specifically on higher education charitable giving. Like the Giving USA study, the VSE provides baseline data to be aware of and potentially share in discussions with donors. The study noted a record $49.6 billion raised during the 2018–2019 fiscal year, up 6.1% over the previous year and the tenth consecutive year of giving growth (Council for Advancement and Support of Education, 2020). Although this is an estimate of all giving, the 913 survey participants raised 88.3% of total voluntary support for US institutions of higher education.

A notable trend of the VSE is that the largest source of charitable giving to higher education is foundations, which has been the case since 2007. Totals from the other categories in the VSE study include alumni at $11.2 billion (23%), non-alumni at $8.3 billion (17%), corporations at

$6.8 billion (14%), and other organizations at $6.3 billion (13%). Foundations accounted for 34% of all giving ($17 billion), although alumni may indirectly give the most, as more than 47% of this total came from family foundations, where there are likely to be alumni connections.

NACUBO-TIAA Endowment Study

One final resource to know is an annual study of endowments conducted by the National Association of College and University Business Officers and TIAA (2020). This study reports the market value of more than 700 US and Canadian college and university endowments, along with the total percentage change in market value over the previous year.

This is a valuable resource for knowing where an institution's endowment size ranks among peers. The annual data tables are made available publicly, which also allows for the calculation of accurate rates of growth over many years. This resource can be utilized, for example, to set challenging, but realistic goals as part of a campaign or a long-term strategic plan. By examining the five- or ten-year compound annual growth rates of peer institutions, an objective benchmark can be established. Then the specific strategies and tactics necessary to reach a new endowment goal can be determined. While these figures represent institutional endowments and not individual academic units, the growth rates still provide an objective starting point to contemplate new goals.

The Costly Obsession with Alumni Giving Participation

This introductory chapter closes with an imperative to address the topic of alumni giving. As the VSE study confirms, gifts from alumni are a substantial portion of the total amount given. As many gift officers can attest, however, there is an unfounded and unrealistic expectation among institutional leadership and the professoriate that a far greater proportion of their alumni should be giving something annually to their alma mater.

Commonly expressed as the alumni giving ratio or participation rate, the percentage of all alumni who are donors during the fiscal year is often used as a key performance indicator for the effectiveness of a development program, at the unit and institutional levels. It is also a common target for improvement, with presidents and deans often announcing grand goals to double alumni participation in just two or three years but making little or no investment in activities to generate this volume of new donors. These same leaders would likely not announce similar goals for student enrollment, graduation rates, or faculty research income without committing additional resources.

This misplaced obsession is driven largely by the annual rankings by *U.S. News & World Report*, where the alumni giving ratio is included as a criterion in the ranking methodology. Data reported are only for undergraduate alumni, and the rationale for including this measure, according to *U.S. News*, is that it is a reflection of alumni satisfaction with their educational experience (Morse & Brooks, 2020). Overlooked by some who push for unrealistic increases is that this criterion traditionally accounts for only 5% in the overall ranking criteria. The weighting of alumni giving dropped to just 3% in the 2021 rankings methodology. The highest, at 22%, is graduation and retention rates. Two other criteria are weighted at 20%; faculty resources and a peer reputational rating labeled as expert opinion.

The pressure to increase alumni giving participation for the sake of rankings can invite questionable and unethical fundraising practices and has the potential to damage public confidence. This occurred in 2019 when the University of Oklahoma (OU) acknowledged that it had provided alumni giving rates to *U.S. News* that were significantly overstated during the past 20 years. As a result, *U.S. News* stripped the university of its ranking (Jaschik, 2019) and one student filed a class-action lawsuit (on behalf of all graduates since 1999) claiming that OU misled them through a falsely inflated ranking (Kirker, 2019).

Current and future academic leaders would benefit from a stronger understanding of giving participation among alumni. The most important fact to know is that participation, which was likely never as high as some imagine, has been dropping steadily for decades. Two studies show that this is the case.

The aforementioned VSE study has documented alumni participation since the 1970s. Figures 1.1 and 1.2 illustrate the four-decade period from 1979 to 2019 and the downward participation trend that began in the early 1990s and has continued unabated.

In 2018, another study showed a similar declining trend. This study tracked participation over five years at 123 public and 102 private institutions in the USA and Canada. Median alumni giving participation at the public institutions dropped steadily from 5.9% in 2013 to 4.8% in 2017. Private institutions saw a decline from 19.5 to 17% (Blackbaud, 2018).

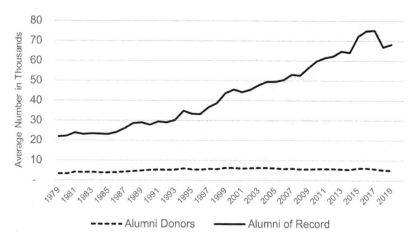

Fig. 1.1 Components of alumni giving participation, 1979–2019 (Council for Advancement and Support of Education, 2020)

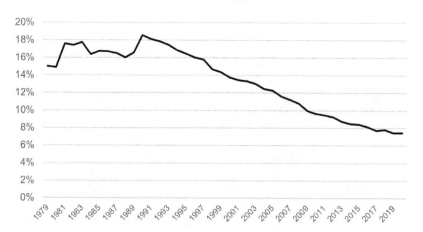

Fig. 1.2 Alumni giving participation, 1979–2019 (Council for Advancement and Support of Education, 2020)

The evidence of this trend is only part of the reason for focusing on this topic in this opening chapter. Blame for the failure to increase alumni participation or meet unrealistic, short-term goals is often placed squarely on institutional development teams and can distract from other, potentially more fruitful, fundraising concerns. While execution certainly matters, larger influences affecting higher education are also contributing to this trend and are far beyond the influence of the development office. Four examples follow.

1. Growth in Degrees Awarded

As noted in Fig. 1.1, the annual number of new graduates has risen dramatically over the past 40 years. During the most recent decade for which data are available, the number of bachelor's degrees awarded rose from 1,601,368 in 2008–2009 to 1,976,116 in 2017–2018 (The Chronicle of Higher Education, 2011, 2020). At many institutions, the number of new alumni every year is exponentially greater than any gains in the number of new alumni donors. For institutions with rapid enrollment growth, it is nearly impossible to generate enough new alumni donors to even maintain a flat alumni giving ratio from year-to-year.

2. Better Technology

Advances in database management now allow institutions to keep better track of their alumni. The start of the downward decline of alumni participation in the early 1990s reflected in Fig. 1.2 coincides with widespread technology improvements and software upgrades implemented by many institutions for better database records management. The result of this was far fewer "lost" alumni. These alumni had not been included previously in giving ratio calculations since they could not be reached by telephone or mail to receive gift solicitations.

3. Greater Competition

During this same time period, the number of nonprofit organizations in the USA increased dramatically. The latest figures available indicate there were 1.54 million nonprofits registered with the Internal Revenue Service in 2016 (Urban Institute and National Center for Charitable Statistics, 2020). However, this figure is far larger since religious congregations and organizations with less than $5,000 in gross receipts are not required to register with the IRS. Charitable dollars are subject to the same economic forces as other expendable income, and more nonprofits means more places for alumni to choose from when giving, in addition to their alma mater.

4. Student Debt

The data behind rising tuition and student debt are troubling far beyond the impact on alumni giving. However, it must be recognized by institutional leadership that graduates who are facing years or decades of repaying student loans will be among the most challenging constituencies for development offices to engage. Successfully encouraging these alumni to give back to their alma mater through an annual gift, even at the smallest amount, can be very difficult when they feel they have little to give.

CONCLUSION

The downward trend of alumni participation in giving and the broader trend of larger donors increasingly driving US overall giving are concerning and linked. While larger gifts certainly have larger impact, the donors who make them often begin as small, annual donors. A striking example of this is the great alumni benefactor to Johns Hopkins University, Michael Bloomberg. He had already given more than $1 billion to his alma mater when he announced a new commitment of $1.8 billion devoted to undergraduate financial aid (Johns Hopkins University, 2018). He earned a bachelor's degree there in 1964 and made his first annual fund gift in 1965, donating five dollars. If he had not made that initial, small gift (and others), there is the possibility that he would not have made the mega-gifts either.

As an academic leader engaged in fundraising, it is imperative to embrace the perspective that all gifts matter. Small, annual fund gifts may not address the most critical needs, and new estate commitments and other types of deferred gifts will likely not be realized during a single leadership tenure. However, these types of gifts, along with the prized major gifts of immediate cash, collectively demonstrate the outcomes of a high-performing advancement program.

For academic units that struggle with achieving higher levels of philanthropic support, academic leaders can be a catalyst for change. By approaching philanthropy and working with donors as akin to teaching and education and using data as a guide, academic leaders can overcome some of the concerns hampering their success. By knowing the reality of alumni giving, based on broader research, academic administrators can better lead fundraising teams and counter misconceptions among faculty and potential donors. The chapters of this book, and the case studies within them, provide more guidance, resources, and inspiration to help effectively integrate impactful advancement activities into academic leadership roles.

Actionable Strategies

1. Read the most recent Giving USA and VSE report announcements to become familiar with national trends and issues of charitable giving, especially for higher education. Compare your institution's fundraising results. What are the biggest similarities and differences between your institution's fundraising and these national trends?
2. Review the most recent NACUBO endowment study. Find your institution's entry, and look up five other institutions you consider to be academic peers. Compare how much higher, or lower, your endowment is compared to these peers, as well as the percentage growth over the previous year. If you did not previously know the rate of growth for your institution, how close were your expectations to reality?
3. With the help of your advancement office, review your institution's overall alumni giving ratio, as well as the ratio of alumni who gave last year to your school or department. If possible, review these figures for the past 10 years. Discuss this data among your fellow academic leaders and with faculty, along with the trends cited in this chapter, to ensure a realistic viewpoint of alumni giving participation.

Section I Case Study: A Culture of Philanthropy Catches up to a Top Business School

U.S. News & World Report's list of the nation's top MBA programs is populated, as expected, with elite private institutions and many public flagship universities. Less expected is the inclusion of a business school that is less than 50 years old and that evolved at a predominantly commuter student institution. The Jindal School of Management (JSOM) at the University of Texas at Dallas (UT Dallas) provides an example of how philanthropy can empower academic units even at institutions with a limited history of giving.

UT Dallas was established in 1969, but only offered graduate-level degrees in its early years. The management school was created in 1975, the same year that undergraduate juniors and seniors were allowed to enroll at the university. It was not until 1990 that freshmen and sophomores were admitted, and just nine enrolled in management that year (University of Texas at Dallas, n.d.a.).

JSOM first entered the *U.S. News* ranking of graduate business schools in 2010, placing 50th overall, and moving up to 40th the next year. It has remained in the top 40 ever since and reached 33rd place overall and 12th among publics in the 2021 ranking (U.S. News & World Report, n.d.).

Comparatively limited endowment resources are a disadvantage for schools aspiring to elevate their ranking to this top level. Among the top 40 business schools in the 2021 *U.S. News* ranking, only two are at universities with endowments of less than $1 billion (National Association of College and University Business Officers, 2020). These are Arizona State University and UT Dallas. The average endowment market value for the rest of the group is more than $7 billion, and the median is nearly $5 billion. The endowments of the business schools at these institutions likely account for a significant share of the overall total, with some above $1 billion and the rest in the hundreds of millions (Bonsoms, 2016).

As illustrated in Fig. 1.3 with data provided by UT Dallas, JSOM's endowment market value remained under $10 million through 2010 and comprised less than 20 funds. In less than a decade, it increased to more than $70 million with 231 funds. The book value, representing the actual amount of dollars designated to the endowment by donors, grew at a compound annual rate of 23.6% from 2005 to 2019.

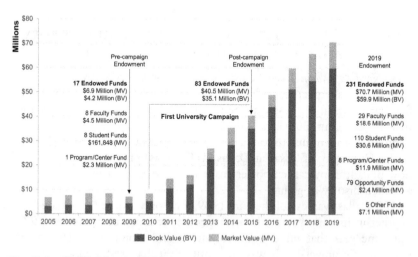

Fig. 1.3   Jindal School of Management endowment, 2005–2019

Despite its location in a major metropolitan area with a majority of alumni remaining there, JSOM's fundraising totals had historically struggled to surpass $1 million annually in gifts and pledges. In the 2010 fiscal year, which was the initial year of the university's first comprehensive fundraising campaign, JSOM raised $1,215,571 from 346 gifts. Over the course of the five-year campaign, these numbers exploded. The campaign closed on December 31, 2014 with more than $53.4 million, surpassing the school's $50 million goal. A confluence of events contributed to the rapid growth in private support including:

In 2009, the state of Texas initiated the Texas Research Incentive Program (TRIP), which provided matching funds for gifts made to a number of emerging public research universities in the state, including UT Dallas. Gifts had to be designated to help build the research capabilities of the schools through faculty support, graduate student support, or research facilities. The University of Texas System later followed with a similar matching gift program, called UTRIP, for its member institutions that were eligible for TRIP. In addition to UT Dallas, these included UT Arlington, UT El Paso, and UT San Antonio. By the conclusion of the campaign in 2014, qualifying gifts to JSOM resulted in TRIP matching funds totaling $15.3 million and UTRIP matching funds of $10.4 million.

In 2011, two transformational alumni gift commitments triggered the school's philanthropic momentum. In a joint announcement, a $20 million commitment from an MBA alumnus from Delhi, India, resulted in the naming of the school. And a $10 million commitment from an alumni couple in Houston resulted in the naming of the honors program. The two gifts qualified for matching gifts through both TRIP and UTRIP.

Also in 2011, UT Dallas began offering donors a new endowment gift option called Opportunity Funds (Univesity of Texas at Dallas, n.d.). These could be established with a minimum gift of $10,000 and designated to support any school, department or unit for unrestricted purposes. Donors may change their fund in the future to a restricted purpose, such as a scholarship, provided the fund's principal reached the minimum established amount for that purpose. By 2019, more than 120 funds had been established, with the largest number (79) designated to JSOM.

Key Lessons

- **Confidence and stability in leadership**. JSOM has been led by the same dean, Dr. Hasan Pirkul, since 1996 and many of the associate deans have served in their roles for a decade or more. The leadership team was highly visible, traveling on a regular basis locally, nationally and globally to engage alumni and corporate partners in long-lasting relationships.

- **Investment in staff and outreach programming.** In 2009, JSOM had only one dedicated development position and limited formal structures for engaging alumni. In partnership with the university's development office, JSOM created new positions dedicated to major gifts, corporate relations, alumni relations, and communications. Regular events, publications, and on-campus programming became part of JSOM's advancement activities that help drive fundraising.
- **Application of a long-term perspective.** JSOM and UT Dallas leadership understood that fundraising transformation would take multiple years. Nevertheless, they also realized exponential growth rates were possible compared to other institutions, especially privates, where comprehensive development programs had been in place for many decades and growth rates were far lower (Rogers & Strehle, 2007).

REFERENCES

Bank of America. (2018). *The 2018 U.S. Trust study of high net worth philanthropy.* Retrieved May 14, 2020, from https://scholarworks.iupui.edu/handle/1805/17667.

Blackbaud. (2018). *2017 donorCentrics annual report on higher education giving.* Retrieved June 23 2020, from https://www.blackbaud.com/industry-insights/resources?&pager=5.

Bonsoms, D. J. (2016, May 2). *The boom in business school endowments.* Retrieved June 22, 2020, from https://poetsandquants.com/2016/05/02/boom-business-school-endowments/.

Burlingame, D. F., & Dunlavy, S. (2016). Corporate giving and fundraising. In E. R. Tempel, T. L. Seiler, & D. F. Burlingame (Eds.), *Achieving excellence in fundraising* (4th ed., pp. 85–99). Hoboken, NJ: Wiley.

Council for Advancement and Support of Education. (2020, February 5). *2019 voluntary support of education.* Retrieved May 14, 2020, from https://www.case.org/resources/voluntary-support-education-key-findings-2018-19.

Drezner, N. D. (2010). Fundraising in a time of economic downturn: Theory, practice and implications. *International Journal of Educational Advancement, 9*(4), 191–195.

Giving USA. (2020, June 16). *Giving USA 2020: Charitable giving showed solid growth, climbing to $449.64 billion in 2019, one of the highest years for giving on record*. Retrieved August 20, 2020, from https://givingusa.org/giving-usa-2020-charitable-giving-showed-solid-growth-climbing-to-449-64-billion-in-2019-one-of-the-highest-years-for-giving-on-record/.

Hall, M. (1993). *The dean's role in fund raising*. Baltimore: The Johns Hopkins University Press.

Jaschik, S. (2019, May 28). Oklahoma gave false data for years to 'U.S. News,' loses ranking. *Inside Higher Ed*. Retrieved May 14, 2020, from https://www.insidehighered.com/admissions/article/2019/05/28/university-oklahoma-stripped-us-news-ranking-supplying-false.

Johns Hopkins University. (2018, November 18). *Michael Bloomberg makes largest ever contribution to any education institution in the United States*. Retrieved May 14, 2020, from https://releases.jhu.edu/2018/11/18/michael-bloomberg-makes-largest-ever-contribution-to-any-education-institution-in-the-united-states/.

Kirker, S. (2019, May 29). Former student files lawsuit against OU for providing false data to US news & world report, inflating university's ranking. *OU Daily*. Retrieved May 14, 2020, from http://www.oudaily.com/news/former-student-files-lawsuit-against-ou-for-providing-false-data-to-us-news-world-report/article_9325c8b8-823a-11e9-94dc-3fb5fdfd19c3.html.

Leslie, L., & Ramey, G. (1988). Donor behavior and voluntary support of higher education institutions. *Journal of Higher Education, 59*(2), 115–132.

Lindsay, D. (2017, October 3). Fewer Americans find room in their budgets for charity, chronicle data shows. *The Chronicle of Philanthropy*. Retrieved May 15, 2020, from https://www.philanthropy.com/article/Share-of-Americans-Who-Give-to/241345.

McCambridge, R. (2019, June 18). Giving USA 2019: Most nonprofits will need to work harder for their money. *Nonprofit Quarterly*. Retrieved May 15, 2020, from https://nonprofitquarterly.org/giving-usa-2019-most-nonprofits-will-need-to-work-harder-for-their-money/.

Morse, R., & Brooks, E. (2020, September 13). *How U.S. News calculated the 2021 best colleges rankings*. Retrieved September 25, 2020, from https://www.usnews.com/education/best-colleges/articles/how-us-news-calculated-the-rankings.

National Association of College and University Business Officers and TIAA. (2020). *2019 NACUBO-TIAA study of endowments*. Retrieved from https://www.nacubo.org/Research/2020/Public-NTSE-Tables.

Nilsen, M. (2019, February 25). *Fundraising effectiveness project quarterly fundraising report for Q4 2018*. Retrieved May 14, 2020, from http://afpfep.org/blog/fundraising-effectiveness-project-quarterly-fundraising-report-for-q4-2018/.

Perry, S. (2017, June 17). The stubborn 2% giving rate: Even as more fundraisers seek donations, Americans don't dig deeper. *The Chronicle of Philanthropy.* Retrieved May 15, 2020, from https://www.philanthropy.com/article/The-Stubborn-2-Giving-Rate/154691.

Rogers, F., & Strehle, G. (2007). *Strategies for increasing endowment giving at colleges and universities.* Commonfund Institute. Retrieved June 9, 2020, from https://apps.carleton.edu/campus/treasurer/assets/Commonfund___Strategies_for_Increasing_Endowment_Giving_at_Colleges_and_Universities.pdf.

Rothschild, M. (1999). Philanthropy and American higher education. In C. T. Clotfelter & T. Ehrlich (Eds.), *Philanthropy and the nonprofit sector in a changing America* (pp. 413–427). Bloomington, IN: Indiana University Press.

Soskis, B. (2017, Fall). Giving numbers: Reflections on why, what, and how we are counting. *Nonprofit Quarterly.* Retrieved May 15, 2020, from https://store.nonprofitquarterly.org/products/giving-numbers-reflections-on-why-what-and-how-we-are-counting-fall-2017.

The Chronicle of Higher Education. (2011). Almanac of Higher Education 2011–12. *58*(1).

The Chronicle of Higher Education. (2020). Almanac of Higher Education 2020–21. *66*(36).

The Philanthropy Workshop. (2017). *Going beyond giving: Perspectives on philanthropic practices of high and ultra-high net worth donors.* Retrieved May 15, 2020, from http://www.philanthropy-impact.org/.

U.S. News & World Report. (n.d.). *2021 best business schools.* Retrieved June 9, 2020, from https://www.usnews.com/best-graduate-schools/top-business-schools/mba-rankings.

University of Texas at Dallas. (n.d.a). *40 years, 40 memories.* Retrieved June 9, 2020, from https://jindal.utdallas.edu/jsom40/timeline.php.

Univesity of Texas at Dallas. (n.d.b). *Endowments / opportunity funds.* Retrieved June 11, 2020, from https://www.utdallas.edu/development/endowments/opportunity-funds/.

Urban Institute and National Center for Charitable Statistics. (2020). *The nonprofit sector in brief 2019.* Retrieved August 19, 2020, from https://nccs.urban.org/publication/nonprofit-sector-brief-2019#the-nonprofit-sector-in-brief-2019.

CHAPTER 2

Historical Perspectives on Academic Fundraising

The full history of philanthropy in higher education is not a subject in which fundraisers must be especially well-versed in order to perform their role. However, knowledge of some significant historical events and trends can be useful to provide context to potential donors, especially when discussing the importance of endowments and other gifts intended to support institutions in perpetuity.

Academicians in particular can benefit by expanding their knowledge of philanthropic history, especially within their own institution. When cultivating relationships with potential donors, academic leaders and faculty members alike are in an enviable position compared to development staff. They are able to speak with direct authority and first-hand experience about philanthropy's impact within their own unit, on their students, and even on their own career. They can personally articulate the impact of recent gifts, as well as gifts made decades ago that are still serving critical purposes or allowing for ambitious plans into the future.

Being conversational in recent and long-term historical information about philanthropic support is a skill that can help faculty members build stronger constituent relationships. Rather than appearing simply as a solicitor, historical narratives clearly reflect the potential impact and outcomes of gifts in relation to the academic mission. As cited in Chapter 1,

© The Author(s), under exclusive license to Springer Nature Switzerland AG 2021
A. Conley and G. G. Shaker, *Fundraising Principles for Faculty and Academic Leaders*, Philanthropy and Education,
https://doi.org/10.1007/978-3-030-66429-9_2

evidence indicates high net worth individuals want to gain better understandings of philanthropy to help inform their own giving. An awareness of key historical linkages in educational philanthropy could be a useful teaching tool to help potential donors visualize the immediate and long-term effects of their giving. One of the most interesting and relevant linkages comes from this nation's oldest higher education institution.

HARVARD AND THE FIRST FUNDRAISERS

The founding of Harvard College in 1636 brought the first formal structure of higher learning to the British colonies of North America. The relationship between these two lands also facilitated the first example of an organized fundraising effort to advance a higher education institution in this country. Remarkably, several core aspects of this effort still endure in the fundraising activities of US colleges and universities to this day.

A summary of the account from the landmark book, *Fund Raising in the United States* (Cutlip, 1965 [1990]) notes just five years after the founding of Harvard College, the fledgling seminary hired three local clergymen to travel to England on a fundraising mission. The effort also resulted in the equivalent of the first fundraising brochure, described as a 26-page pamphlet originally written in Massachusetts, but later published in 1643 in London as a book entitled, *New Englands First Fruits*. The passage that recounts the first gifts, which led to the institution's founding, is particularly enlightening, especially to potential donors seeking insights into educational philanthropy:

> And as we were thinking and consulting how to effect this great work, it pleased God to stir up the heart of one Mr. Harvard (a godly gentleman and a lover of learning, there living among us) to give the one-half of his estate (it being in all about £700) toward the founding of a college, and all his library. After him, another gave £300; others after them cast in more; and the public hand of the state added the rest. (1643, pp. 23–24)

This brief passage, summarizing an act of generosity nearly 400 years ago, serves as a notable teaching tool for faculty members and development staff alike. Its value is reflected in two fundamental concepts of educational fundraising.

The first concept addresses the importance of recognizing that a donor's motives for giving, especially for very large gifts, are often grounded in emotion and values. The words in the passage, "...*it pleased God to stir up the heart of one Mr. Harvard...*" reinforce the idea that the gift was not made simply because Mr. Harvard could give a large amount.

Potential major donors are too often considered "potential" first and foremost based on their wealth, and secondarily on their connection to the institution. Experienced development staff understand the importance of acquiring knowledge of a prospective donor's personal interests, passions, and values, while the academic leaders they support may view this process with less urgency. The common failure here is viewing the process of soliciting a major gift in the same way as a small, annual fund gift. Unlike small gifts, major gifts are not transactional.

The second concept illustrated in the Harvard passage is the core principle of a successful fundraising campaign, which relies on securing a small number of very large gifts first before seeking any gifts at smaller levels. As noted in the passage, Mr. Harvard gave the largest gift, and "*After him, another gave £300; others after them cast in more...*" (This campaign principle is discussed further in Chapter 12).

The reference to the "public hand of the state" is also revealing in its continued applicability. It referred to the General Court of the Massachusetts Bay Colony, which incentivized the establishment of the seminary with a promise of £200 in 1636, followed by another £200 after construction was completed. This feature of the Harvard case also continues to be found in higher education fundraising and campaigns. Public institutions often seek state appropriations for building projects or programs that, if granted, require raising a specific dollar amount in gifts before the appropriation is awarded. Private institutions may also partner with local municipal governments on fundraising projects tied to publicly-owned land or buildings.

On a larger scale, numerous states have also designated public funding to be used as matching funds to incentivize major gifts to state colleges and universities. Efforts in Texas (Branch, 2019) and Florida (Harris, 2017) were so successful that there was a backlog of gifts awaiting the match. And Massachusetts, which operated a successful matching gift program from 1997 to 2007, proposed another focused on strengthening endowments at the state's public universities and community colleges (Voghel, 2019).

USING GIVING HISTORY IN STORYTELLING

Academicians who begin to get more involved in fundraising activities may downplay or intentionally omit altogether references to previous giving to their college or unit. New development staff may do the same. This can be a natural inclination, when embarrassment or apology feels necessary to ask for contributions for funding a specific project, initiative, or program. Henry Rosso (1991), the founder of The Fund Raising School, now part of Indiana University's Lilly Family School of Philanthropy, wrote that giving is a privilege, not a nuisance or a burden:

> There is no reason to apologize for asking for a gift to a worthwhile cause...The solicitation should be so executed as to demonstrate to the prospective contributor that there can be a joy in giving, whether the gift measures up to the asking amount or not. (p. 6)

Donors who give to institutions of higher learning, even those who may be donating for the first time, recognize the longevity of academia in American society. Part of the joy of giving referenced by Rosso may be derived from knowing that a major gift to a long-standing institution will help continue its historic tradition. Gifts to newer institutions may similarly bring joy to donors who believe their gift will provide foundational support for the institution to build upon in the coming decades.

Faculty members and academic leaders alike are able to articulate the historical implications of philanthropy with relative ease, even if they have never done it before. They can do this first by collaborating with their development officer or advancement office representative to practice sharing a compelling story about a past gift. When hearing these stories, potential donors are given a forward-looking opportunity to envision their own giving and the impact that they want to see it have on the institution. These are learning opportunities for donors to gain better insights regarding how philanthropy works, especially in an academic setting where there are specific customs and traditions to be observed.

Another example showing the usefulness of historical stories of philanthropy comes once again from Harvard. It centers on the establishment of the first endowed professorship in this country, which occurred in 1721 and was designated for the study of divinity (Sears, 1922). Donors who have not given in this way may assume they will have a role in determining the faculty member who will be appointed in this role. This was, after all, how Harvard's divinity donor expressed his gift conditions:

> I order and appoint a Professor of Divinity, to read lectures in the Hall of the College unto the students; the said Professor to be nominated and appointed from time to time by the President and Fellows of Harvard College, and that the Treasurer pay to him forty pounds per annum for his service, and that when choice is made of a fitting person, to be recommended to me for my approbation, if I be yet living. (p. 17)

This practice of donor participation and influence in selecting recipients of endowed chairs and professorships is no longer acceptable, as most academic leaders know. By sharing stories about existing endowed chairs at the institution, selection processes, the importance of academic freedom, and the endowed faculty's accomplishments, academic leaders can try to overcome donors' misconceptions early in gift conversations. Academic leaders and development staff alike must embrace serving as forthright advisors, and not only fundraisers, in these cases.

It is a best practice for institutions to use gift acceptance policies, which articulate that donors do not retain the right or authority to approve or disapprove the recipient of an endowed chair or professorship. This also applies to recipients of support funds for graduate and undergraduate students, and other matters such as setting the payout rates of endowed funds. From a historical perspective, a helpful explanation to use when educating potential donors on this issue can be found in *Philanthropy and American Higher Education*, "What college boards and presidents learned over time was that such donor conditions could be at least confining. At worst, they pre-empted institutional prerogative and academic self-determination" (Thelin & Trollinger, 2014, p. 14). In addition, excessive donor control or influence can threaten an institution's legal ability to accept charitable gifts as state and federal courts have consistently demonstrated "...a donor cannot impose restrictions on a gift that inappropriately restrict the duty of care owed by the board of directors over the use of the gift" (Purcell, 2016, p. 491).

Lest one think these situations no longer arise, a 2019 example occurred at the University of Alabama. In that case, the university returned a donor's gift of more than $20 million and removed the donor's name from the law school over what they believed was unwarranted influence in the hiring of an endowed chair (Knox & Jarvis, 2019).

There will always be cases of conflict between donors and colleges. However, there are many more positive examples of donor impact. Countless institutions have intentionally woven stories of philanthropy into their public identities through storytelling and symbolism, tying past support to their current (and future) state of existence. Examples can be found among public and private institutions alike; two stories follow.

Colgate University utilizes the number 13 to link its history to philanthropy while also further building its institutional identity. Colgate's founding was the result of 13 men gathering in the village of Hamilton, New York, to draft an initial constitution with 13 articles. They each gave one dollar, resulting in $13 to establish what began as a Baptist seminary (Leach, n.d.).

Colgate continues to employ their lucky number for many purposes, including Colgate Day, which is scheduled annually on Friday the 13th and serves as a day of celebration through a range of events on campus as well as regionally through dozens of alumni gatherings (Colgate University, n.d.). The school also ties the number into fundraising activities and outcomes, such as in 2013 when an anonymous donor offered $1 million in challenge funds if 1,300 other donors gave during the 24-hour Colgate Day giving initiative (Walden, 2013). In 2015, Colgate celebrated the year's fundraising totals, which increased (quite coincidentally) by 13% over the previous year (Walden, 2015).

At the University of Texas at Austin, the Cockrell School of Engineering uses a tangible relic to symbolize philanthropy. For more than 100 years, students there have honored a small wooden statue of a man enshrined as Alexander Frederick Claire, or "Alec," dubbed to be the Patron Saint of Engineering. The statue was stolen from a local beer garden by a group of engineering students as an April Fools prank in 1908. The school holds a birthday celebration on April 1 every year for Alec, and in 1974 the icon took on the formal identity of the school's annual giving program. Branded as Friends of Alec, the annual campaign regularly raises more than $1 million for the engineering school (Calahan, 2013).

The symbol also retains a strong following as engineering students graduate and become alumni. For example, following the passing of a 1968 engineering alumnus in 2014, the school received a bequest of $35 million designated to create a Friends of Alec endowed scholarship fund (Leahy, 2014). The gift expanded the school's scholarship and fellowship funding by 25 percent and supported 34 students in its first year.

CONCLUSION

Historical forces shape every institution of higher learning in some way. The impact of philanthropy should be one of those forces that is recognized, celebrated, and utilized in ongoing cases for support. If these stories are not readily visible, they are likely awaiting discovery with minimal effort.

For older, established institutions, consulting with the campus archive or library can reveal information about past benefactors, building campaigns, student initiatives, or partnerships with the local community. For example, the University of Pittsburgh regularly recognizes their community partnership in building the Cathedral of Learning, a Gothic tower that was the tallest academic building in the world when it was completed in 1937. The fundraising campaign, begun in 1925, included a drive for local schoolchildren to donate a dime and receive a certificate noting their membership in a "fellowship of builders." More than 97,000 certificates were issued, even though this effort took place during the height of the Great Depression (Fedele, 2007).

Even newer four-year institutions and community colleges likely have some number of benefactors tied to their founding or early formative years. Recognizing them in new ways not only serves as useful and deserved donor recognition, it also raises awareness and prompts new generations of potential donors to reflect on their own philanthropic interests and goals.

ACTIONABLE STRATEGIES

1. Create an inventory of key donors and gifts that have made your unit what it is today. These should include specific funds such as the first endowed professorship and first endowed student scholarship. Confer with longtime and retired faculty as well as development staff who know (or knew) the donors and their motives for giving. Practice telling these stories and use them in your interactions with potential donors to convey the impact and legacy their gifts could have.

2. Retrieve data on giving to your unit as far back as possible and create charts, illustrations, or infographics to visually demonstrate increases in total giving, total donors, endowment, and other measures. Use relevant imagery in gift proposals, annual reports, on your giving

website, and at your events to convey momentum and positive philanthropic trends to inspire confidence in others to give.

References

Branch, D. (2019, February 20). Texas boosted 6 more universities to national research status and we cannot slow down now. *Dallas Morning News*. Retrieved April 2, 2020, from https://www.dallasnews.com/opinion/com mentary/2019/02/20/texas-boosted-6-more-universities-to-national-res earch-status-and-we-cannot-slow-down-now/.

Calahan, R. (2013, April 3). UT engineering's patron saint turns 105. *Alcalde*. Retrieved June 12, 2020, from https://alcalde.texasexes.org/2013/04/ut-engineerings-patron-saint-turns-105/.

Colgate University. (n.d.). *Colgate Day*. Retrieved August 20, 2020, from https://www.colgate.edu/alumni/attend-events/colgate-day.

Cutlip, S. M. (1965 [1990]). *Fund raising in the United States: Its role in America's philanthropy*. New Brunswick, NJ: Transaction Publishers.

Fedele, J. (2007, March 12). *The cathedral of learning: A history*. Retrieved August 21, 2020, from Pitt Chronicle: https://www.chronicle.pitt.edu/story/cathedral-learning-history.

Harris, A. (2017, July 6). Lawsuit demands Florida pay up on $1 billion in donation matches to state schools. *Miami Herald*. Retrieved April 2, 2020, from https://www.miamiherald.com/news/local/education/article16 0007214.html.

Knox, L., & Jarvis, W. (2019, June 11). U. of Alabama's returned gift is a case study in donor relations gone bad. *The Chronicle of Higher Education*. Retrieved April 5, 2020, from https://www.chronicle.com/article/U-of-Ala bama-s-Returned/246473.

Leach, J. (n.d.). *What's in a name? Colgate's origins and evolution*. Retrieved August 20, 2020, from Colgate at 200 Years: https://200.colgate.edu/loo king-back/moments/whats-name-colgates-origins-and-evolution.

Leahy, C. (2014, August 7). *Cockrell school alumnus leaves $35 million for scholarships*. Retrieved June 12, 2020, from UT News: https://news.utexas.edu/2014/08/07/cockrell-school-alumnus-leaves-35-million-for-scholarships/.

New Englands First Fruits. (1643). Retrieved April 2, 2020, from https://arc hive.org/details/NewEnglandsFirstFruitsInRespectFirstOfTheCounversionOf Some/page/n7/mode/2up.

Purcell, P. (2016). The law and fundraising. In E. Tempel, T. Seiler, & D. Burlingame (Eds.), *Achieving excellence in fundraising* (4th ed., pp. 487–500). Hoboken, NJ: Wiley.

Rosso, H. (1991). *Achieving excellence in fund raising*. San Francisco: Jossey-Bass.

Sears, J. (1922). *Philanthropy in the history of American higher education*. Washington, DC: US Government Printing Office.

Thelin, J. R., & Trollinger, R. W. (2014). *Philanthropy and American higher education*. New York: Palgrave Macmillan.

Voghel, J. (2019, November 4). Lawmakers advance endowment match for public colleges. *Daily Hampshire Gazette*. Retrieved April 2, 2020, from https://www.gazettenet.com/EndowmentMatch-hg-110519-30035959.

Walden, M. (2013, December 20). *Colgate raises $5.1 million while celebrating the last Colgate Day in the year of '13*. Retrieved August 20, 2020, from https://www.colgate.edu/news/stories/colgate-raises-51-million-while-celebrating-last-colgate-day-year-13.

Walden, M. (2015, September 10). *Fundraising grows by 13 percent in fiscal year 2015*. Retrieved August 20, 2020, from https://www.colgate.edu/news/stories/fundraising-grows-13-percent-fiscal-year-2015.

CHAPTER 3

Language Matters

Every profession has specific language that is endemic to the people who work in the field every day. For academicians seeking to expand their professional activities into fundraising, there are words and phrases whose adoption and use can facilitate this transition. And there are some that can, at best, demonstrate inexperience and at worst, cause actual harm to the development process.

DEVELOPMENT AND FUNDRAISING ARE NOT THE SAME THING

The most fundamental concept to embrace in this new idiom is that fundraising and development are not synonymous, even though legions of the professoriate and academic administrators alike may believe they are one in the same. This interpretation only reinforces the counterproductive perspective of development work, especially for major gifts, as simply transactional. Academic leaders who rely on philanthropic support for their unit should take the initiative to educate their faculty on the distinction between these terms. Thelin and Trollinger (2014) provide a compelling narrative explaining the difference:

© The Author(s), under exclusive license to Springer Nature
Switzerland AG 2021
A. Conley and G. G. Shaker, *Fundraising Principles for Faculty and Academic Leaders*, Philanthropy and Education,
https://doi.org/10.1007/978-3-030-66429-9_3

Fund-raising is asking for money; it is episodic. Development cultivates and sustains ongoing relationships that often extend over decades, between an educational institution and its constituencies. The distinctions between the two concepts may be subtle, but they are important to the long-term success of people who accept the challenge of raising the funds necessary to advance a college or university toward its goals. (pp. 153–154)

A more systematic distinction is that (1) fundraising is the act of asking for a gift, while (2) development is everything that improves the probability of success when asking. And while "everything" may be considered overly broad and indefinite, so too are the ways in which the vast universe of potential donors may be pulled into an institution's orbit and engaged in ways that lead to giving. (Some institutions use the term "advancement" to recognize the broad functions intended to generate philanthropic support). Using this perspective, development can be illustrated as the centrifugal activity that utilizes an array of formal structures and activities across an institution. Fundraising, as Fig. 3.1 shows, is just one of many ways constituents may become engaged in an institution's development activities.

These functions will be further explored in Chapter 4; however, it is important to note that defining development and fundraising like this

Fig. 3.1   Core functions supporting development

enables academic leaders to better explain the relevance and importance of development activities within their colleges, schools, and units. There are obvious development activities such as a homecoming event, regional alumni gathering, and foundation site visit. There are also many others where deliberate coordination can yield positive development outcomes. Some examples include a parents advisory council meeting, faculty and staff newsletter, distinguished lecture series, new faculty orientation, and student government meeting.

All these activities, and many others, can have a positive effect on development activities and lead to greater fundraising success. Too often however, activities that are organized by other campus units intentionally limit or even prohibit the involvement of development-related staff out of fear that participants will be solicited for gifts. Institutions that are considered high-performing fundraising organizations have moved beyond this antiquated view. The majority of their academic and administrative leaders realize the value of embracing a philanthropic identity and culture, and fully recognize the importance of viewing relevant activities from a development perspective.

Understanding the difference between development and fundraising also necessitates defining philanthropy, which similarly is often associated with the narrow perspective of wealthy people making very large gifts. In Robert Payton's landmark book, he embraces philanthropy as "voluntary action for the public good" (1988).This expansive view makes no mention of money, wealth, or status. It rightly recognizes the value of monetary gifts both large and small, as well as other forms of giving, such as volunteering, and donating services, equipment and materials, or expertise. Other cultural interpretations of philanthropy may vary from this perspective. The term itself comes from the Greek *philanthropos*, or love of humankind.

BANNED WORDS AND PHRASES

In the first article of the *Don't Fear Fund Raising* series at the end of this book, the author describes the feeling of becoming a freshman again upon promotion into an academic leadership role and delving into fundraising for the first time. To overcome this, he took the initiative to read books and articles and attend workshops. But he also noted, "Most of all, I considered myself to be an apprentice to the experienced advancement professionals at our university foundation."

One of the most beneficial outcomes of an apprenticeship is gaining knowledge of a profession's culture, including the language. Longtime fundraising professionals have a mastery of the language they use in their work, as well as language they do not use. As noted already, and to be noted repeatedly again, the process of raising major gifts is not transactional. Donors are not consumers. The amount of their gift is not the equivalent of a price for something they are purchasing.

Despite this, language frequently heard in the for-profit sales arena makes its way into discussions about raising money from wealthy alumni, major corporations, and highly-visible charitable foundations. The following words and phrases discussed by Conley (2019) are listed here along with some common examples of their use.

Hit Up
"We should hit up every former scholarship recipient for a gift to our new scholarship endowment campaign."

Aggressive
"The development staff is not being aggressive enough in closing major gifts."

Low Hanging Fruit
"The Gates Foundation has a history of supporting projects in this area. Clearly they are low hanging fruit."

Money Left on the Table
"We got a gift of only $100,000 from someone who could easily give $1 million? We certainly left money on the table."

Untapped
"Our international alumni are a great, untapped resource for major gifts."

These phrases, and others like them, share the common and painful trait of oversimplifying the process of raising major gifts. When these are used internally among faculty and administrative staff, they advance the misperception of fundraising and development being one in the same. This language also disregards the great variance in time that it may take to cultivate gifts from seemingly similar prospects like two local companies or alumni from the same graduation year. Academic leaders must take the initiative to teach others why this language can be damaging to their unit's efforts to build a stronger culture of philanthropy.

STEWARDSHIP: SAYING "THANK YOU" LIKE YOU MEAN IT

One of the easiest areas for a newly-appointed academic leader to transition into development is through stewardship activities. The act of expressing thanks and appreciation is often overlooked as a critical part of the development process, especially in major gift fundraising, because it is incorrectly viewed as an end point. Borrowing from the field of behavioral economics and the importance of repeat customers, it is far easier to raise a gift from someone who has already given versus someone who has never been a donor.

This sounds easy, but stewarding donors effectively toward a new gift requires thoughtful and strategic effort. In the first edition of *Achieving Excellence in Fundraising*, Henry Rosso (1991) describes stewardship as an exchange that an organization is obligated to provide a donor in response to a gift:

> In accepting the gift, it is incumbent upon the organization to return a value to the donor in a form other than material. Such a value may be social recognition, the satisfaction of supporting a worthy cause, a feeling of importance, a feeling of making a difference in resolving a problem, a sense of belonging or a sense of ownership in a program dedicated to serving the public good. (p. 6)

Where stewardship takes effort lies in determining which of these values resonates most with a donor, and implementing a course of action to demonstrate to the donor that their gift has been impactful in a way that aligns with their values. For example, if social recognition is clearly an important value to a particular donor,they could be offered the opportunity to be profiled on a school's digital channels in a way that can be re-posted to social or professional platforms such as Facebook, LinkedIn, or other regionally-focused outlets.

Similarly, if recognition is not important to the donor but they are moved by the feeling of making a difference or helping resolve a problem,stories about the outcomes of their gift could be shared later through a similar media vehicle, or an annual report. This form of stewardship requires tracking and assessing the impact of specific gifts, and then selecting the most appropriate avenue for reporting how they met a need or addressed a problem. Continuous mentions of gift impact help organizations build their philanthropic identity by constantly reminding internal and external constituencies that donor support is being effectively utilized to advance the mission. (The next chapter includes some specific recommendations on stewardship activities.)

Since this chapter focuses on language, the remainder provides a range of fictional scenarios where opportunities to communicate stewardship messaging arise among various donor constituencies. These could be used in either speaking roles or written in correspondence and publications. Specific data points can also be inserted to incorporate relevant information from a school, department, or program.

To long-time donors:
If you believe the truism of "the only constant is change," then you can understand why we are so appreciative of your generous support. There are so many forces, both positive and negative, impacting how we operate today, and we must be responsive to them all. Your generous gifts over the years, along with others like you, have empowered us to prepare for and embrace the opportunities that change can bring. We simply could not be where we are today, or where we are going tomorrow, without friends and benefactors like you.

To first-time major gift donors:
It's challenging to put into words the depth of our appreciation for your support. While all gifts are important to our department, we know that more than 85% of what we receive in total private gifts in any given year often comes from just a few dozen donors. Without this support, we simply could not provide the educational experience and environment our students and faculty benefit from today.

To a volunteer group, such as an advisory board:
I'm admittedly new to the fundraising and development activities that are part of my role, but I know for a fact that we would not be where we are today without your past involvement and those who served before. It's impossible to put a value on the expertise and enthusiasm you bring, or the impact this has on our students and faculty. We may not say it often enough, but your contributions are truly invaluable to the continued success of our school.

To young alumni:
Last year, our school received a total of 2,571 gifts from all sources including individuals, companies, and foundations. The largest share of gifts came from our alumni, and in particular, those who graduated within the past 10 years. We know that this point in your life brings an endless number of financial challenges as you're establishing your life and career

and moving to new locations, potentially with a spouse and young family in tow. This makes your act of generosity all the more meaningful to us. We are ever grateful as we put your gifts into action to provide an ever greater educational experience to those who are now here in the same classrooms and labs where you were not so long ago.

CONCLUSION

Developing a personal communication style with donors, volunteers and other external audiences takes time, especially when prior experience was limited to engaging largely with students and faculty colleagues. As one develops their own style, it is helpful to remember the key ideas outlined in this chapter, along with one concluding point.

Whether speaking to a group of hundreds or just one person, language should be used in a way that not only reflects one's leadership role or position of authority within an academic unit, but that also elicits an emotional response and sense of connection from the intended audience. For example, scholarships are a continuous need in nearly all institutions, and prospective donors likely know this. Rather than expressing specific needs in terms of the number of new scholarships sought, or a dollar goal for the total scholarship endowment, share an example of a recent graduate for whom a scholarship made a critical difference. There are always remarkable stories of perseverance from those who came from low-income or first-generation households, or overcame learning disabilities, or other seemingly impossible obstacles. Talking about philanthropy in this way shows impact and outcomes on an intimate and personal level and may enable audience members to envision how their own support can have a similarly profound impact on one person's life.

ACTIONABLE STRATEGIES

1. If you have a development officer for your unit, allow them to speak briefly at a faculty meeting to share the definitions of "fundraising" and "development" so your faculty learn how advancement activities lead to successful fundraising. Also ask them to share the banned words and phrases, explaining why these are so damaging.
2. Ask your development office to run a list of consecutive-year donors to your unit. Personally call the top five individuals who have given the most years in a row just to thank them for their

support (Assuming you don't know them already). You will likely be surprised at how enjoyable this experience will be. And some of these conversations may naturally lead to larger gifts!

REFERENCES

Conley, A. (2019, May 12). *Raising major gifts is not easy, but the words we use suggest it is.* Retrieved June 12, 2020, from https://www.linkedin.com/pulse/raising-major-gifts-easy-words-we-use-suggest-aaron-conley-ed-d-.

Payton, R. (1988). *Philanthropy: Voluntary action for the public good.* New York: American Council on Education / Macmillan Publishing Company.

Rosso, H. (1991). *Achieving excellence in fund raising.* San Francisco: Jossey-Bass.

Thelin, J. R., & Trollinger, R. W. (2014). *Philanthropy and American higher education.* New York: Palgrave Macmillan.

CHAPTER 4

Tenets of Operational Effectiveness

As fundraising continues to take on an increasingly critical role across higher education, those institutions that struggle in their advancement activities face a confounding reality. "One of the truisms of American higher education is that the most successful colleges and universities are those that are the most accomplished in fund-raising" (Thelin & Trollinger, 2014, p. 147). It has taken decades, even centuries, for institutions to build strong academic reputations. It equally requires extensive time and effort for these institutions to build highly productive and successful fundraising operations.

In most cases, these institutions share the common characteristic of a highly organized and successful development office or foundation that functions in partnership with academic leaders and senior managers throughout the campus. And conversely, these campus leaders understand and respect the development process and the core operational tenets needed to raise increasing levels of philanthropic support.

While there is a potentially endless list of principles and practices that define a successful higher education development operation, this chapter is limited to just three critical tenets that academic leaders must recognize and embrace to be successful fundraising leaders. These include building and retaining an advancement team, following core policies and procedures, and ethical fundraising. The many other aspects of development

© The Author(s), under exclusive license to Springer Nature
Switzerland AG 2021
A. Conley and G. G. Shaker, *Fundraising Principles for Faculty and Academic Leaders*, Philanthropy and Education,
https://doi.org/10.1007/978-3-030-66429-9_4

operations can be learned along the way, especially with the guidance and counsel of professional development staff, but these three precede all the rest in importance.

BUILDING AND RETAINING AN ADVANCEMENT TEAM

Raising major gifts is an intensely personal process. For this reason, personnel is the first and most important tenet to address. Academic leaders can nearly accomplish the impossible of being in multiple places at once with the right hires for positions in major gifts, alumni and corporate relations, and communications. Nothing is more valuable than passionate advocates who can express their leader's vision, speak in the same voice, and inspire internal and external constituents. The outcomes derived from these various constituencies include financial gifts, as well as volunteer resources, advocacy, and stronger perceptions of leadership and organizational efficiency.

Alternatively, nothing is more counterproductive than having these positions filled by people whose skills, knowledge, and interests do not match the requirements of the roles. Replacing poor performers is a solution, but external constituents who are visited routinely by new staff due to constant turnover may lose confidence in the school's leadership, potentially leading to a loss of interest and support (Shiller, 2016). This highlights the importance of prudent and informed hiring practices and decisions in a job market where turnover is considered particularly problematic and costly.

Academic leaders should have a basic awareness of compensation levels for common development positions. Many command larger average salaries than most faculty and college and university fundraising salaries also tend to be higher than in the nonprofit sector in general, making these positions particularly appealing. The annual compensation study by the College and University Professional Association for Human Resources (CUPA-HR) includes numerous development-related positions. Median salary figures from the study in 2018–2019 include executive-level and other development positions, obtained from more than 1,100 institutions. This is an important resource because academic leaders may find themselves struggling to meet the salary requirements to hire (or keep) their best candidates and may need this data to justify their choices internally.

The structure of development programs within academic units varies greatly depending on a unit's size and nature and available budget resources. In addition, the level of staffing may also depend on an institution's central development office or foundation and what services it provides. Funding models differ, as salaries may be paid entirely by the development office, by the academic unit, or by the two jointly—and hiring and reporting may also vary as a result.

Regardless, academic leaders need to know the roles and responsibilities of each major category of advancement staff (identified in Table 4.1). That knowledge can be used to structure and manage a team (or individual position) in a manner that serves the academic unit's immediate and long-term needs. Figure 3.1 in Chapter 3 illustrated the core functions supporting development. Different types of development staff (with different skills) and a variety of types of activities are required to accomplish the full range of fundraising and programmatic objectives within academic units, which are described in the subsequent sections. Effective planning, goal-setting, and assessment also require information about the categories of development staffing and responsibility.

Alumni Relations

Most institutions provide centralized alumni programs and services through a dedicated office or a formal alumni association. In partnership with these institution-wide units, targeted school or unit alumni activities can increase engagement and provide substantive benefits.

Despite this potential, many schools and departments underutilize their alumni due to lack of effort, misperceptions, and resource limits, individually or in combination. Deans and department chairs may believe they know what their alumni want based on anecdotal evidence or personal bias, but the best approach is to ask them. Periodic surveys and focus groups are valuable tools for gathering feedback on alumni perceptions and interests and can form the basis of selective engagement strategies aligned with the unit type and capacity.

Engagement strategies can vary widely, but at the academic unit level, they should include a combination of regularly-scheduled activities and ad hoc opportunities. Examples of annual activities include distinguished alumni events, summer golf outings, homecoming tailgate receptions, and student-focused activities such as alumni mentoring programs and guest speaker series. Ad hoc opportunities are potentially limitless, can include online events and community building, and are bounded only by available staff and resources.

Table 4.1 Median salaries—Executive & professional roles in development (CUPA-HR, 2020)

Position	Research	Other doctoral	Master's	Baccalaureate
Chief Development/Advancement Officer	$335,351	$222,720	$169,753	$180,000
Deputy Chief Advancement/Development Officer	$189,603	$145,000	$107,420	$126,628
Chief Campus Annual Giving Administrator	$108,981	$88,623	$70,720	$73,296
Chief Campus Corporate/Found. Relations Administrator	$126,175	$93,279	$88,740	$90,750
Chief Campus Planned Giving Administrator	$151,003	$116,085	$96,695	$101,000
Chief Campus Major Gifts Administrator	$170,844	$97,500	$92,381	$104,392
Chief Campus Alumni Affairs Administrator	$153,165	$93,150	$74,033	$79,103
Chief Campus Donor Relations Administrator	$104,560	$80,466	$65,405	$75,000
Chief Campus Advancement Services Administrator	$111,206	$90,275	$81,000	$80,000
Head of Development —College/Division	$102,899	$91,173	$74,495	$85,576
Annual Giving Officer—Entry	$51,250	$49,300	$46,000	$48,000
Annual Giving Officer—Senior	$68,275	$61,080	$61,500	$57,432
Major Gift Officer—Entry	$68,284	*	$62,100	$70,670
Major Gift Officer—Senior	$92,412	$85,480	$83,232	$85,375
Principal Gifts Officer	$92,000	*	$77,770	$92,965
Planned Giving Officer—Entry	*	$77,062	$61,276	$54,883
Planned Giving Officer—Senior	*	*	$81,299	$83,133
Alumni Relations Officer—Entry	$50,367	*	$45,442	$45,838
Alumni Relations Officer—Senior	$64,727	$59,436	$55,050	$58,893

*4 or fewer institutions reported

Whatever the scope of alumni programming, there are two considerations to remember. First, the financial return on investment for alumni engagement activities is most often realized in the long term. Building and maintaining connections between alumni and their school helps develop affinity, loyalty, and identity. As fundraising is defined in this book, these all improve the chances of positive responses when alumni are solicited for gifts. Second, alumni programming should be focused on helping achieve specific development goals for the unit, as articulated in an annual development plan (see Chapter 9 for more).

Communications

The subfield of development (or advancement) communications has grown considerably in recent decades as institutions have recognized it as a strategic tool. Previously, an institution's fundraising efforts may have been partly or entirely serviced in their communications needs through the university's marketing or public relations office. These services commonly include writing, editing, and design for alumni magazines, donor newsletters and brochures, websites, annual fund appeals, and special events invitations and related collateral.

It is now common to find communications staff within a foundation or advancement office comprised of professionals who specialize in communicating with alumni and donors. At major research universities, these staff are also often present within the development offices of larger academic units, such as schools of business, engineering, medicine, and arts and sciences. Although other institutions may still have general communications staff supporting development, "The message of the college and university hiring marketplace increasingly shows that the person managing communications must have fundraising experience" (Mackey, Melichar, & Moran, 2016, p. 27).

Regardless of reporting structure, it is vital for academic leaders to facilitate collaboration and a respectful partnership between development and communications. Each of these functions can dramatically support the other, resulting not only in more donors and funds raised, but also elevating the image and brand of the individual academic units and the institution overall.

Corporate Relations

Like alumni relations, most institutions employ centralized staff who serve in corporate relations roles on behalf of the entire college or university. It is not unusual, however, to also find corporate relations staff within larger academic units.

To be successful in corporate fundraising, especially with major companies, university leaders must realize that companies engage institutions on an "enterprise" basis. This means companies are looking for strategic benefits that may include recruiting future employees, sponsored research opportunities, technology development and licensing, executive education and other employee training, economic development, and joint proposals for federal funding. As noted in a white paper by the Network of Academic Corporate Relations Officers, "Over time, the amount of truly philanthropic support a university receives from a company will depend in part on the number and quality of these non-philanthropic engagements" (NACRO, 2011, p. 1). Corporate relations staff play a vital role in facilitating these engagements for companies among the institution's faculty and staff. Additional insight on engaging corporate donors is provided in Chapter 5.

Donor Relations/Stewardship

Donor relations is "everything that happens between asking for contributions" (Hedrick, 2008, p. 3). As an organization "seeks to be worthy of continued philanthropic support" (Association of Fundraising Professionals, 2003, p. 113), by stewarding gifts and donors, it acknowledges gifts, recognizes donors and honors their intent, and invests and uses funds wisely on behalf of the mission. For a newly-appointed academic leader, stewardship is most familiar through the formal donor recognition societies and events institutions utilize to thank donors, in addition to communication vehicles such as donor newsletters, annual reports, and videos. These tools convey general messages of gratitude on a very broad level.

For donors who specifically designate their giving to a school, department, center or other unit, the leader of that unit is obligated to express thanks and also to ensure the gifts are used effectively for their donor-designated purposes. As Tempel and Seiler explain, "Stewardship is the foundation for holding ourselves accountable. Reporting is the foundation for transparency" (2016, p. 432).

Donors at all levels should be thanked for their support. It is common courtesy, an act of ethical responsibility, and an investment in these donors' continued contributions, possibly at increasing levels over time. Consistent donors are demonstrating brand loyalty. College leaders can help ensure their donors' ongoing support with even minimal investments of time; however, this responsibility is too easily overlooked in the press to move forward with other priorities. Investing in stewardship also impacts organizational fundraising efficiency, as the time and effort required to engage new donors is substantially greater compared with cultivating existing donors to give again (Fundraising Effectiveness Project, 2018).

Foundation Relations

As noted in the VSE study in Chapter 1, foundations provide the largest amount of philanthropic support for higher education. Consequently, most institutions designate staff within their development programs to manage relationships with current and potential foundation funders. At larger institutions, a foundation relations team includes staff members with highly specialized responsibilities for grant proposal writing, compliance and reporting, and financial management. Although faculty members are likely to be more familiar with submitting grant proposals to foundations than they are soliciting major gifts from individuals, both require the same level of institutional coordination. For example, some foundations have a policy of awarding just one grant to an institution in any given year.In these cases, an internal selection process typically determines which proposal will be submitted as the institution's top priority. Foundations with such policies usually provide their processes to campus development offices, and unvetted proposals submitted directly from faculty members can be more than just an administrative inconvenience.

A related area of foundation relations that all academicians should be knowledgeable about is the growth of the donor-advised fund (DAF). Wealthy individuals and their families are increasingly turning to DAFs for their simplicity, rather than establishing family foundations. DAF donors create "giving funds" with charitable sponsors, receive immediate tax deductions for the gift, and then can recommend that grants from the funds be made to other charitable organizations at any time in the future (National Philanthropic Trust, n.d.).

The largest sponsors of DAFs are nonprofit arms of major financial service providers such as Fidelity, Schwab, and Vanguard. Indeed because of DAFs' popularity, Fidelity Charitable is now the largest recipient of donations in the USA (Stiffman & Haynes, 2019). Other sponsors include community foundations, workplace giving platforms, and national charities. Some university foundations are also sponsoring DAFs.

In addition to the immediate tax benefit, donors receive the opportunity for the corpus of the DAF to increase in value with the assistance of professional financial managers and can remain anonymous with potential grantees (Nathan & Lesem, 2016). This last point is especially important, since the DAF custodian is legally recognized as the donor whenever a grant is distributed to a qualifying nonprofit organization and extra administration may be required to associate gifts with individual DAF creators. In 2018, the total amount of grants in the U.S. made from DAFs totaled $23.42 billion. In that same year, contributions into new and existing DAFs totaled $37.12 billion, representing an 86% increase over the previous five years (National Philanthropic Trust, 2019).

Internal Relations

Too often overlooked as a functional area of development, internal relations can be a tremendous catalyst for improving fundraising and engagement activity, especially within academic units. While development staff are not exclusively assigned to internal relations, all staff can actively strengthen this area by engaging colleagues in development activities when appropriate, providing education about philanthropy and fundraising, and remembering that many faculty and staff are donors themselves.

Engaging current faculty, as well as their emeritus peers, is especially important given the inherent connection of philanthropy to academic responsibilities (Shaker, 2015):

> The faculty responsibility to complete some amount of "service" suggest a philanthropic component by its very nomenclature. Philanthropy can be evident in service (the catchall of academic work) as faculty put their knowledge to use for community organizations or sit on university

fundraising committees, for example, but it is also integrated across the spectrum of faculty work. (p. 9)

It is also essential to acknowledge that internal constituents develop their own relationships with external constituents. A senior faculty member engages with the lead scientist in a local company, a student advisor keeps in touch with select alumni, a new assistant professor has personal ties to a local foundation, or a department chair invites a community leader to speak in a class. All of these (and countless other) relationships can be invaluable to the success and growth of development within academic units.

Other Constituents

While the final functional area that supports development activities is broadly termed "other" constituents, these individuals and organizations can be, or can influence, significant potential donors. This population includes parents and family members of students, volunteers, and elected officials. It may also include community leaders, such as the heads of local foundations, civic organizations, or business-advocacy groups like chambers of commerce. For religiously-affiliated schools, this would include the denominational church and ministry.

These people and entities need proper care and active management, but for academic leaders, the greatest fundraising potential lies in those individuals who are actively serving in volunteer roles for their school or unit, or elsewhere within the institution. More attention is given to the role and impact of volunteers in Chapter 10, including substantial evidence of volunteers becoming donors, and giving more, compared to donors who do not volunteer.

Referring again to Fig. 3.1, each of the previous areas is a "Development" function, inclusive of factors that improves the probability of fundraising success. "Fundraising," meanwhile, is defined as the act of asking for a gift. Within fundraising, the three primary categories of higher education donations are annual gifts, major gifts, and planned gifts. Individual fundraising staffing is commonly structured around these areas.

Annual Gifts

At most institutions, this term refers to smaller gifts usually made in response to solicitations that take place on an annual, semi-annual, or other regularly scheduled basis. The primary goal of annual giving efforts is to generate consistent support from alumni and other individuals. Over time, an effective annual giving program will supply an invaluable pipeline of potential major gift donors (Seiler, 2016):

> As donors develop a history of giving they grow more interested and involved with the success of the organization. This base of regular givers becomes the most likely core group of donors for other fundraising programs such as major gifts, capital gifts, and planned gifts. (p. 218)

Annual giving solicitations are often intended to reach large populations of alumni. However, solicitations are also directed at other populations including parents, faculty and staff, members, patrons, and individuals with various connection to the unit or institution.

The delivery method of these solicitations has shifted significantly in recent decades.Annual giving staff previously focused almost entirely on direct mail and telephone solicitations, but today digital delivery methods are also essential. Blackbaud (2020) noted over a five-year period that alumni giving in response to direct mail and phone appeals dropped at public and private institutions, while online giving through email, crowd-funding, websites, and other digital forms increased steadily each year (Table 4.2).

While these figures do not reflect the total amount given through each channel, colleges and universities recognize the increasing importance of digital giving. As a result, a growing proportion of annual giving staff are highly experienced in digital content production and

Table 4.2 Median alumni giving by solicitation method, 2015–2019 (Blackbaud, 2020)

Public institutions				Private institutions			
Year	Digital (%)	Phone (%)	Mail (%)	Year	Digital (%)	Phone (%)	Mail (%)
2019	25.5	20.9	24.6	2019	36.1	11.7	28.3
2018	21.2	21.7	25.2	2018	36.4	12.9	29.7
2017	18.5	26.8	27.7	2017	31.7	16.4	32.8
2016	15.1	27.7	29.5	2016	30.9	16.3	33.0
2015	14.0	30.0	28.6	2015	25.6	19.9	33.1

utilizing data analytics and predictive modeling to better craft their solicitations. Perhaps more than any other area of fundraising, the annual giving program has been transformed through technology so much that it scarcely resembles what it was just a short time ago (Frezza, 2019).

Due to these rapid changes, it is important for newly-appointed academic leaders to be familiar with the multi-channel approach that most institutions utilize in annual giving efforts, and the need for coordination across all campus units. Over-solicitation can occur just as easily at a small, liberal arts college as it can at a major research university, leading to donor fatigue and potentially driving away supporters. In the U.S. Trust study, 28% of the 1,600 high net worth study participants reported that they had stopped giving to an organization they supported the prior year (Bank of America, 2018). The top reason cited, at 41%, was the organization made too many financial requests, or the requests came too close together. The second-highest reason, at 25%, was the donor had a change in their personal philanthropic priorities.

Major Gifts

Institutional approaches to staffing major gift roles vary, but it is common practice to establish these positions based on the depth of existing and potential donors at different giving levels. For example, an institution may have a number of positions focused on securing gifts of up to $25,000 or $50,000. These are commonly held by entry-level staff with limited major gift experience, but other relevant experience such as working in annual giving or alumni relations. Younger institutions with younger alumni populations and institutions just beginning to focus on major gifts would likely dedicate more staff energy at these lower levels.

At older institutions with established fundraising programs, larger numbers of more experienced major gift staff might manage portfolios of individuals with the potential for higher gifts, such as $100,000 and above. Additionally, at many larger institutions, a new category is "principal gifts," in which select staff are assigned to manage relationships with the small but critical population of donors who can make the most substantial gifts. At some institutions, this may be gifts of $1 million and above, while at highly successful fundraising institutions, principal gifts may be demarcated at $10 million and above. As Shiller (2019) notes, the distinction is about more than gift size:

> Principal gifts are not merely major gifts with more zeroes; they are the expression of philanthropic partnership at the highest levels from donors who, together with administrative and board leaders, drive transformational growth in an organization's impact on society. (p. 94)

This is an emerging trend, but reflective of the need for highly strategic and collaborative management of the relationships such donors have with an institution.

As major gift fundraising has become further entrenched as a vital operational activity on college campuses, recent studies have explored the individuals who serve in these roles.In a study of 1,200 major gift officers at 89 colleges (including eight outside the U.S.), five prototypes were created based on key characteristics of gift officers detected in the survey results (Blumenstyk, 2014). The study also asked the participating colleges to rank their gift officers who responded to the survey according to their placement in the top-, middle-, or bottom-third in terms of money raised and goals achieved.

While the study anticipated finding top-performers dominating one of the prototypes, it found high performers across all five. A search for commonalities among these leaders revealed behavioral and linguistic flexibility, intellectual and social curiosity, ability to synthesize information, and a confident and skillful approach to gift solicitation (EAB, 2014). This group, labeled as "curious chameleons," represented just 3.8% of the survey sample but were nearly 50% more likely to be ranked in the top-third at their institution and 78% more likely to have exceeded their goals.

Another study of 500 higher education fundraisers explored demographic characteristics and sought their insights on what made a successful fundraiser (Shaker & Nathan, 2017). The top three personal characteristics found in successful fundraisers were emotional intelligence, a focus on achievement, and ethical grounding. For professional knowledge, ability to manage the fundraising process ranked first. Knowledge of specific giving programs and strategies such as planned giving, corporate and foundation giving, and campaign management was second. And third was maintaining a professional outlook, demonstrated through an understanding of the fundraising profession, legal and tax basics, and institutional knowledge. The study found only 16.7% had learned fundraising through formal educational experiences, suggesting a stronger emphasis on research and knowledge-driven practice.

The chapters in Section II of this book address identifying potential major gift donors and engaging them in ways that take into account their philanthropic motivations, understandings, and decisions. This content will provide the insights needed to facilitate greater partnership with the major gift staff who often serve as the critical link between donors and academicians.

Planned Gifts

Gift commitments, made but not realized by the beneficiary until the donor's death (and potentially that of their spouse or other individuals) constitute a special category of major gifts and, often, require an additional knowledge-base for fundraisers. These types of gifts are referred to as planned, "...for they require thoughtful and focused planning on the part of the donor, oftentimes the donor's family, and the donor's professional financial advisors" (Regenovich, 2016, p. 259).

Most planned gifts are in the form of an estate commitment, typically documented by a donor in their will. However, there are many other types, including charitable gift annuities, charitable trusts, and beneficiary designations, which may include life insurance, retirement accounts, and similar asset-building vehicles where multiple beneficiaries can be designated by the account holder. Given the complexities of this type of giving, most institutions have dedicated planned giving staff within their development teams. These internal experts should always be consulted when working with donors who are considering planned gifts.

The larger issue, however, is for academic leaders to recognize the value of planned gifts and to support development officers' efforts in this area. An all too frequent occurrence is that the urgency of raising funds for current uses guides department chairs, center directors, and deans to the detriment of other considerations. For example, for some donors the only way to fulfill their interests and values is through a planned gift approach.Some of these individuals may have substantial financial capacity and yet could be excluded from the development process out of short-sightedness. Institutions could miss out on future cash support as well as volunteer engagement opportunities and additional benefits associated with this highly desirable donor population. The annual Giving USA (2020) study cited in Chapter 1 reveals that bequests accounted for 10% of all 2019, US charitable gifts, totaling $43.21 billion. In comparison, gifts from corporations were half this amount, totaling $21.09 billion.

Development as a Profession

This section on development staff closes with an important discussion on this growing profession. These individuals and the processes they facilitate must be viewed as more than a means to an end. Development staff do indeed serve to engage various constituencies to support the institution. However, current and aspiring academic leaders can aid in the development function by learning about fundraising and viewing it as a worthy and skilled profession.

But taking this learning approach can be difficult if a faculty member rises through the ranks holding a negative or indifferent perspective, as Worth (2002) observes:

> Although development officers have become almost universally a part of college and university administrations, there continues to be a perceived cultural gap between them and members of the academic community, particularly faculty. Faculty are sometimes suspicious of development professionals, viewing them as apart from the academic world and lacking in institutional commitment. (p. 28)

Admittedly, many of the hallmarks that define an established profession have been largely absent from fundraising, until recently. Bloland and Tempel (2004) noted considerable progress using a list of common characteristics defining a profession. These characteristics include a body of applicable expert knowledge with a theoretical base acquired through a lengthy period of training (preferably in a university), a demonstrated devotion to service, an active professional association, a code of ethics, and a high level of control over credentialing and application of the work.

One of these in particular, the body of expert knowledge, has been strengthened greatly by the proliferation of academic degrees, certificates, and other coursework in the fields of philanthropic studies and nonprofit management. This growth has led some to acknowledge nonprofit studies to be approaching a tipping point of becoming an autonomous field of study (Mendel, 2014). Researchers at Seton Hall University (n.d.), led by Roseanne Mirabella, maintain a census of the more than 300 colleges and universities in the U.S. that offer academic degrees and certificates, as well as non-credit and continuing education courses, in this field. A similar census previously maintained by CASE noted a total of just 65 in 1997 (Murphy, 1997).

In addition, professional credentialing has grown through CFRE International, which offers the Certified Fund Raising Executive program. Two formerly separate organizations merged in 1997 to form CFRE, which offers the world's only certification for philanthropic fundraising professionals accredited by the American National Standards Institute (CFRE, n.d.).

CFRE also conducts research on the profession through a global study every five years measuring factors including the tasks fundraisers perform in their work and the knowledge used to perform these tasks. Past results of this study confirm that fundraising is a global occupation and that fundraising professionals perform the same tasks no matter their geographic area (Aldrich, 2016).

Opportunities to join professional associations also abound today. The largest and most comprehensive is the Council for Advancement and Support of Education, widely known as CASE. Membership is open to anyone working in any area of educational external relations including fundraising, marketing and communications, and alumni relations. CASE was established in 1974 and is global in scope, with more than 90,000 members in 82 countries (Council for Advancement and Support of Education, n.d.a).

In addition to CASE, there are countless specialty associations for subfields within academic advancement, such as corporate relations, planned giving, and donor research, as well as organizations devoted to fundraising within specific academic disciplines and purposes including libraries and athletics.

The subject of ethics is covered later in this chapter as a critical tenet of effective fundraising operations. Fortunately, there is considerable guidance available today in the form of accepted principles and codes of ethical fundraising embraced by major professional societies, as well as extensive scholarly writing on the subject.

In closing, recognition and appreciation for the development profession may also contribute to greater staff retention and longevity, which is especially critical for major gift fundraising positions. Individuals seeking advancement into roles with greater responsibilities, and the increased salary that typically comes with them, will always be difficult to retain. However, positive attitudes toward development expressed by academic leaders as well as the unit faculty and staff can help reduce the premature departures of strong performers. Some activities found to be effective across the nonprofit sector include providing thorough orientation and ongoing training, greater autonomy to carry out responsibilities, accessibility to top leaders within the organization, collegiality and a team-focused culture, and recognition not just by fundraising supervisors, but also by the organization's senior administrative leadership (Lindsay, 2015; Sandoval, 2017).

CORE POLICIES AND PROCEDURES

As noted earlier, there are myriad practices and principles that define a high performing fundraising program. Of the related and extensive policies and practices, it is most important for academic leaders to know and observe those that address prospect management, gift proposals, and gift acceptance. These are often interrelated, but will be addressed separately to ensure clarity on the importance of each.

Prospect Management

Coordinating a potential or existing donor's engagement is a core function of what is commonly referred to as "prospect management." This topic is addressed first since it is often the least understood among faculty members and others beginning academic leadership roles. It can also be one of the most contentious internal issues between leaders of academic units and other parts of campus, including the president's office, library, athletics, student affairs, and other major administrative units.

The chief development officer is responsible for managing this process, which is carried out by designated staff who facilitate data collection and reporting. This information is maintained in a database containing thousands of donor files. These files can also include the outcomes of research about individuals' interests, career background, and financial capacity, conducted using a wide range of public information sources. (Databases also include records for companies and foundations.) In addition, "Vital is information about regular meetings with institutional leaders to discuss the benefactor, his or her deepening involvement in the nonprofit, a realistic potential gift amount, and details of any projects of great potential interest" (Hodge, 2016, p. 238).

Individuals who are already major gift donors, or have that potential, are commonly assigned to a development officer who functions as the prospect manager. Major gift staff are expected to actively manage a portfolio of individuals ranging in size from several dozen to 100 or more.

Again, information gathering is a key function of prospect management, and gift officers are expected to work collaboratively with fellow development staff as well as across the institution with faculty and others in areas of interest to their assigned donors. As Hodge (2016) also notes:

> All encounters, engagements, and experiences with the benefactor should be appropriately documented, for these relationships are a result of the alignment of the institution and the donor, and they do not belong solely to development officers who manage the relationships. (p. 238)

Newly-appointed academic leaders may well be interested in meeting with potential major gift donors to share their vision and priorities. Prospect management exists to facilitate this type of engagement, as well as to prevent it. Some donors have highly specific interests, which are known to gift officers or others on campus. Some potential donors are also already engaged with units on campus. This information, if recorded appropriately in the database, helps to assure that the donor's interest and preferences are observed and respected.

Institutional credibility can take years to develop with major gift donors, and it can be lost in a moment by an unwanted call, email, or meeting attempt perceived as discordant with other institutional relationships or the donor's interests. Adherence to policies for interacting with external constituents is a hallmark of a high performing fundraising program, and everyone across the institution shares this responsibility. Many colleges and universities make their prospect management policies available online, and academic leaders should take the initiative to ensure their faculty and staff are aware of their institution's polices. For examples, see Carnegie Mellon University (n.d.), University of Georgia (2017), and University of San Francisco (n.d.).

Gift Proposals

Most institutions also have clearance policies and procedures guiding written and verbal gift solicitations. These policies may apply only to gifts above a certain dollar amount, as well as for specific purposes, such as facilities, equipment, or new academic initiatives. For examples, see Guilford College (n.d.), University of Kansas (n.d.), and Southern Methodist University (n.d.).

Gift proposal policies protect relationships with donors and ensure that fundraising efforts are strategic and well-conceived. An example relates to memorial fundraising efforts launched upon the passing of a long-serving and highly popular professor. It is easy to assume that such a beloved figure would inspire an outpouring of gifts in support of naming a new scholarship, endowed chair, or physical space.These well-intentioned "mini-campaign" efforts, however, should not be undertaken without a significant amount of due diligence to assure that the goal will be met. When they fall short—and many do—the school is left in an awkward position with the deceased's family.

For any multi-donor initiative like this, most institutions' gift solicitation policy requires a detailed plan and approval before a launch and public announcement. To the faculty, this may come across as administrative overreach; however, it is a necessary procedure to follow. In addition to the aforementioned issue with family members, repeated failed fundraising efforts are damaging to the development program's reputation internally among the faculty and staff, as well as externally among alumni and other potential donor constituencies.

Gift Acceptance

The governing boards of most colleges and universities set policy on the types of gifts that can and cannot be accepted. In some cases, policy may also address acceptable sources of gifts, which can mean declining contributions from specific industries or organizations with incongruent political, religious, or social viewpoints. Policies also stipulate conditions in which the institution would consider returning a gift and/or removing a naming due to an act on the donor's part that reflects negatively on the institution. For examples of all these policies, see Loyola University Chicago (n.d.), University of Texas System (n.d.), and Wellesley College (n.d.).

Recently, gifts have drawn the attention of students and others who question the ethical and moral standing of the donors and the means they employed to build their wealth. Individual and corporate benefactorsfrom industries including energy, financial, and pharmaceutical, are frequent recipients of attention. These critics and concerns have been present throughout the history of higher education, but the reach of social media and current sentiments about the influence and power of big donors have broadened discussions about which gifts are acceptable.

Consequently, some institutions have revisited their gift acceptance policies to emphasize a stronger donor vetting process before any proposal or gift discussions take place (Diep, 2019).

ETHICAL FUNDRAISING

The previous two tenets on building and retaining an advancement team and understanding core policies and procedures are directly dependent on the final tenet, ethical fundraising.Ethical standards of practice are a central feature of any established profession and educational fundraising has several sources, which most fundraising staff will recognize.

The first is the Donor Bill of Rights (Council for Support and Advancement of Education, n.d.b). This ten-point document was collectively established in 1993 among four major professional fundraising societies. It is commonly found on the institutional advancement websites of many colleges and universities to assure donors of their commitment to honor these rights which include confidentiality, transparency, responsiveness, and utilization of gifts as the donor intended.

In addition, CASE also provides a Statement of Ethics (2020a) as well as Principles of Practice (2020b) for educational fundraisers to observe in the course of their work. These resources are valuable guides for advancement staff to consult when confronted with a situation they perceive as a potential ethical conflict. A similar Code of Ethical Standards exists for fundraisers throughout the nonprofit sector, provided by the global Association of Fundraising Professionals (1964). Ethical lapses are often preventable if academic leaders, faculty members, and development staff alike follow established protocols related to fundraising in their organizations, typically developed based on these professional standards.

The intent of this section is not to provide a comprehensive treatment of ethics in fundraising, which includes appropriate consideration of donors, beneficiaries, and institutional missions and responsibilities. Others do this exceptionally well, including Anderson (1996), Beyel (1997), O'Neill (1997), Fischer (2000), and Tempel (2016). Instead, ethics is addressed with consideration of unit and institutional fundraising professionals who collaborate with academic leaders. Understanding where development staff turn to for guidance and direction on ethical fundraising practice will help academic leaders navigate ethical situations in partnership as they arise.

CONCLUSION

As the concluding chapter of this first section, it is important to note that the content thus far is an introduction to understanding higher education fundraising and the development structures that enable the successful solicitation of philanthropic support. Chapter 1 identified key sources of data and research insights, while specifically illustrating alumni giving participation. Chapter 2 provided a brief introduction of some historical aspects of philanthropy and emphasized the importance of continuously acknowledging the impact of past giving using storytelling techniques. Chapter 3 provided a focus on language, with definitions and an acknowledgment of words and phrases that reinforce negative or inaccurate perceptions of fundraising.

Grounding these opening chapters in the research and literature will hopefully inspire readers to further explore other resources in this field. The first substantive effort to survey the research on advancement was the seminal book, *The Campus Green* (Brittingham & Pezzullo, 1990). A follow-up study, *Institutional Advancement: What We Know* (Proper & Caboni, 2014) reviewed the literature from 1991 to 2013. Looking further back into history, *Philanthropy and American Higher Education* (Thelin & Trollinger, 2014) provides an exhaustive examination of the origins and influences of giving in this sector, along with contemporary treatments on endowments, government influence on educational philanthropy, and the professionalization of fundraising.

Another critical early study of this field can be found in the book, *New Strategies for Educational Fundraising*, edited by Michael Worth (2002). This was followed by a substantive edited volume of 80 new and previously-published works assembled in *Philanthropy, Volunteerism & Fundraising in Higher Education* (Walton & Gasman, 2008). More recently, Noah Drezner contributed *Philanthropy and Fundraising in American Higher Education* (2011) and, with co-author Frances Huehls, provided *Fundraising and Institutional Advancement* (2015). Drezner also edited *Expanding the Donor Base in Higher Education: Engaging Non-Traditional Donors* (2013), and is the founding editor of a journal dedicated to this field, *Philanthropy & Education*, published by Indiana University Press.

Lastly, a research-focused look across advancement is available in the edited collection, *Facilitating Higher Education Growth through Fundraising and Philanthropy* (2016), and *Advancing Higher Education* (Worth & Lambert, 2019) provides a collection of 20 chapters on contemporary issues in academic philanthropy and fundraising authored primarily by accomplished fundraising practitioners. All of these works are positive contributions to the growing body of literature in higher education philanthropy and provide substantive context for academicians seeking to strengthen their understanding of academic fundraising.

ACTIONABLE STRATEGIES

1. Review how much time you spend with your development director, and if applicable, the larger advancement team in your unit and how you respond to their requests. High attrition rates for these positions directly impacts fundraising success, especially for major gifts. A minor investment of time with your development staff will generate a substantial return of goodwill, loyalty, and confidence that their roles are taken seriously.

2. Establish a dollar amount for what you consider a major gift to your unit. Then establish an amount for a principal gift, with the understanding that gifts of this size may only be realized occasionally. Work with your development director to segment potential principal gift donors (who may be individuals, companies, or foundations) from the rest of your potential donor universe and determine your role in engaging with each of them. The value of this exercise will be reinforced again in Chapter 8.

3. If you are completely new to fundraising, arrange to meet with your institution's chief development officer. Ask them about how they have navigated ethically-questionable situations they have experienced during their career. These examples will help you be more aware of how to identify and respond to situations that may arise within your own academic unit.

REFERENCES

Aldrich, E. (2016). Fundraising as a profession. In E. Tempel, T. Seiler, & D. Burlingame (Eds.), *Achieving excellence in fundraising* (4th ed., pp. 503–516). Hoboken, NJ: Wiley.

Alphin, H., Jr., Jennie, L., Stark, S., & Hocker, A. (Eds.). (2016). *Facilitating higher education growth through fundraising and philanthropy.* Hershey, PA: IGI Global.

Anderson, A. (1996). *Ethics for fundraisers*. Bloomington: Indiana University Press.

Association of Fundraising Professionals. (1964). *AFP code of ethical principles*. Retrieved June 5, 2020, from https://afpglobal.org/ethicsmain/code-ethical-standards.

Association of Fundraising Professionals. (2003). *AFP fundraising dictionary*. Retrieved August 21, 2020, from https://afpglobal.org/sites/default/files/attachments/2018-11/AFPFundraisingDictionary.pdf.

Bank of America. (2018). *The 2018 U.S. Trust study of high net worth philanthropy*. Retrieved May 14, 2020, from https://scholarworks.iupui.edu/handle/1805/17667.

Beyel, J. (1997). Ethics and major gifts. In D. Burlingame & J. Hodge (Eds.), *New Directions for Philanthropic Fundraising, Major Gifts* (16), 49–59.

Blackbaud. (2020). *2019 donorCentrics annual report on higher education alumni giving*. Retrieved August 21, 2020, from https://institute.blackbaud.com/asset/2019-donorcentrics-report-on-higher-education-alumni-giving/.

Bloland, H., & Tempel, E. (2004). Measuring professionalism. In L. Wagner & J. P. Ryan (Eds.), *New Directions for Philanthropic Fundraising* (43), 5–20.

Blumenstyk, G. (2014, September 23). Building a better major-gifts officer. *The Chronicle of Higher Education*. Retrieved August 22, 2020, from https://www.chronicle.com/article/building-a-better-major-gifts-officer/.

Brittingham, B., & Pezzullo, T. (1990). *The campus green: Fund raising in higher education* (Vols. ASHE-ERIC Higher Education Report No. 1). Washington, DC: School of Education and Human Development, The George Washington University.

Carnegie Mellon University. (n.d.). *University policies, administrative and governance, prospect management*. Retrieved June 4, 2020, from https://www.cmu.edu/policies/administrative-and-governance/prospect-management.html.

CFRE. (n.d.). *About CFRE*. Retrieved June 12, 2020, from https://www.cfre.org/about/.

Council for Advancement and Support of Education. (n.d.a). *About CASE*. Retrieved June 11, 2020, from https://www.case.org/about-case.

Council for Advancement and Support of Education. (2020b, March 12). *Principles of practice for fundraising professionals at educational institutions*. Retrieved June 4, 2020, from https://www.case.org/resources/principles-practice-fundraising-professionals-educational-institutions.

Council for Support and Advancement of Education. (n.d.b). *Donor Bill of Rights*. Retrieved June 4, 2020, from https://www.case.org/resources/donor-bill-rights.

Council for Support and Advancement of Education. (2020a, March 12). *CASE statement of ethics*. Retrieved June 5, 2020, from https://www.case.org/res ources/case-statement-ethics.

CUPA-HR. (2020, May 29). *2018-19 employees in higher education surveys*. Retrieved from https://www.higheredjobs.com/salary/.

Diep, F. (2019, October 30). Universities are facing criticism for taking dirty money. do their donor policies protect them? *The Chronicle of Higher Education*. Retrieved June 4, 2020, from https://www.chronicle.com/article/Uni versities-Are-Facing/247454.

Drezner, N. D. (2011). *Philanthropy and fundraising in American higher education*. San Francisco: Jossey-Bass.

Drezner, N. D. (Ed.). (2013). *Expanding the donor base in higher education: Engaging non-traditional donors*. New York: Routledge.

Drezner, N. D., & Huehls, F. (2015). *Fundraising and institutional advancement: Theory, practice, and new paradigms*. New York: Routledge.

EAB. (2014, September 10). *Inside the mind of a curious chameleon*. Retrieved August 22, 2020, from https://eab.com/insights/infographic/adv ancement/inside-the-mind-of-a-curious-chameleon/.

Fischer, M. (2000). *Ethical decision making in fund raising*. New York: Wiley.

Frezza, D. (2019). Annual giving. In M. Worth & L. Matthew (Eds.), *Advancing higher education; New strategies for fundraising, philanthropy, and engagement* (pp. 71–82). Lanham, MD: Rowman & Littlefield.

Fundraising Effectiveness Project. (2018, April 12). *2018 fundraising effectiveness survey report*. Retrieved August 21, 2020, from http://afpfep.org/wp-con tent/uploads/2018/04/2018-Fundraising-Effectiveness-Survey-Report.pdf.

Giving USA. (2020, June 16). *Giving USA 2020: Charitable giving showed solid growth, climbing to $449.64 billion in 2019, one of the highest years for giving on record*. Retrieved August 20, 2020, from https://givingusa.org/giving usa-2020-charitable-giving-showed-solid-growth-climbing-to-449-64-billio nin-2019-one-of-the-highest-years-for-giving-on-record/.

Guilford College. (n.d.). *Fundraising [by those outside advancement office]*. Retrieved June 4, 2020, from https://www.guilford.edu/fundraising-those-outside-advancement-office.

Hedrick, J. L. (2008). *Effective donor relations*. Hoboken, NJ: Wiley.

Hodge, J. M. (2016). Major gifts. In E. R. Tempel, T. L. Seiler, & D. F. Burlingame (Eds.), *Achieving excellence in fundraising* (4th ed., pp. 225–242). Hoboken, NJ: Wiley.

Lindsay, D. (2015, July 7). Case study: Keeping fundraiser poachers at bay. *The Chronicle of Philanthropy*. Retrieved August 23, 2020, from https://www.phi lanthropy.com/article/Case-Study-Keeping-Fundraiser/231393.

Loyola University Chicago. (n.d.). *University policies, gift acceptance policy.* Retrieved June 4, 2020, from https://www.luc.edu/policy/gift_acceptance.shtml.

Mackey, C., Melichar, C., & Moran, M. (2016). Communication impact: Building a powerful development and communications relationship. *Journal of Education Advancement & Marketing, 1*(1), 26–34.

Mendel, S. C. (2014, Winter). A field of its own: After many years of operating on others' academic turf, nonprofit studies is ready to claim new ground. *Stanford Social Innovation Review*, pp. 61–62.

Murphy, M. K. (Ed.). (1997). *The advancement president and the academy: Profiles in institutional leadership.* Phoenix, AZ: The American Council of Education and Oryx Press.

NACRO. (2011). *Five essential elements of a successful twenty-first century university corporate relations program.* Retrieved May 29, 2020, from https://nacrocon.org/resources.

Nathan, S. K., & Lesem, E. (2016). Foundation fundraising. In E. R. Tempel, T. L. Seiler, & D. F. Burlingame (Eds.), *Achieving excellence in fundraising* (4th ed., pp. 101–112). Hoboken, NJ: Wiley.

National Philanthropic Trust. (2019). *2019 donor-advised fund report.* Retrieved May 28, 2020, from http://www.nptrust.org/reports/daf-report.

National Philanthropic Trust. (n.d.). *What is a Donor Advised Fund (DAF)?* Retrieved August 21, 2020, from https://www.nptrust.org/what-is-a-donor-advised-fund/.

O'Neill, M. (1997). The ethical dimensions of fund raising. In D. Burlingame (Ed.), *Critical issues in fund raising* (pp. 58–64). New York: Wiley.

Proper, E., & Caboni, T. C. (2014). *Institutional advancement: What we know.* New York: Palgrave Macmillan.

Regenovich, D. (2016). Establishing a planned giving program. In E. Tempel, T. Seiler, & D. Burlingame (Eds.), *Achieving excellence in fundraising* (4th ed., pp. 259–289). Hoboken, NJ: Wiley.

Sandoval, T. (2017, May 1). Keys to low staff turnover: One nonprofit's advice. *The Chronicle of Philanthropy.* Retrieved August 23, 2020, from https://www.philanthropy.com/article/Keys-to-Low-Staff-Turnover-/239957.

Seiler, T. (2016). The total development plan built on the annual giving program. In E. Tempel, T. Seiler, & D. Burlingame (Eds.), *Achieving excellence in fundraising* (4th ed., pp. 215–223). Hoboken, NJ: Wiley.

Seton Hall University. (n.d.). *Nonprofit management education: Current offerings in university-based programs.* Retrieved April 10, 2020, from http://academic.shu.edu/npo/.

Shaker, G. G. (Ed.). (2015). *Faculty work and the public good: Philanthropy, engagement, and academic professionalism.* New York: Teachers College Press, Columbia University.

Shaker, G. G., & Nathan, S. K. (2017). Understanding higher education fundraisers in the United States. *International Journal of Nonprofit and Voluntary Sector Marketing, 22,* e1604.

Shiller, R. J. (2016). *Belief and confidence: Donors talk about successful philanthropic partnership.* Washington, DC: CASE.

Shiller, R. J. (2019). Major and principal gifts. In M. J. Worth & M. T. Lambert (Eds.), *Advancing higher education: New strategies for fundraising, philanthropy, and engagement* (pp. 83–98). Lanham, MD: Rowman & Littlefield.

Southern Methodist University. (n.d.). *University policy manual, solicitation of gifts and pledges.* Retrieved June 4, 2020, from https://www.smu.edu/Policy/5-Development-and-External-Affairs/5-2-Solicitation-of-Gifts-and-Pledges.

Stiffman, E., & Haynes, E. (2019, November 5). Can the boom times last? *The Chronicle of Philanthropy.* Retrieved August 21, 2020, from https://www.philanthropy.com/interactives/20191101-Charitable-Giving-2018.

Tempel, E. (2016). Ethics and accountability. In E. Tempel, T. Seiler, & D. Burlingame (Eds.), *Achieveing excellence in fundraising* (4th ed., pp. 467–485). Hoboken, NJ: Wiley.

Tempel, E., & Seiler, T. (2016). Stewardship and accountability. In E. Tempel, T. Seiler, & D. Burlingame (Eds.), *Achieving excellence in fundraising* (4th ed., pp. 431–438). Hoboken, NJ: Wiley.

Thelin, J. R., & Trollinger, R. W. (2014). *Philanthropy and American higher education.* New York: Palgrave Macmillan.

University of Georgia. (2017, June 20). *Office of prospect management policies and procedures.* Retrieved June 4, 2020, from http://dar.uga.edu/GAIL/wp-content/uploads/2017/06/Combo_Prospect-Management-Guide-as-of-6.20.17.pdf.

University of Kansas. (n.d.). *Office of the chancellor policy, university fundraising.* Retrieved June 4, 2020, from http://policy.ku.edu/chancellor/university-fundraising.

University of San Francisco. (n.d.). *Prospect research and management policy.* Retrieved June 4, 2020, from https://myusf.usfca.edu/prospect-research-management/Policy.

University of Texas System. (n.d.). *UT system policy library, UTS 138 gift acceptance procedures.* Retrieved June 4, 2020, from https://www.utsystem.edu/sites/policy-library/policies/uts-138-gift-acceptance-procedures.

Walton, A., & Gasman, M. (Eds.). (2008). *Philanthropy, volunteerism & fundraising in higher education.* Boston: Pearson Custom Publishing.

Wellesley College. (n.d.). *Wellesely College gift acceptance policy.* Retrieved June 4, 2020, from https://www.wellesley.edu/alumnae/give/giftacceptance.

Worth, M. (Ed.). (2002). *New strategies for educational fund raising*. Westport, CT: American Council on Education and Praeger Publishers.

Worth, M. J., & Lambert, M. T. (Eds.). (2019). *Advancing higher education: New strategies for fundraising, philanthropy, and engagement*. Lanham, MD: Rowman & Littlefield.

PART II

Research Insights to Drive Fundraising

CHAPTER 5

Understanding Donor Motivation

For non-fundraisers, one of the great mysteries of this field is how to inspire transformational gifts in support of the academic mission. These headline-grabbing gifts occur across the higher education landscape frequently enough to imply that there are ample donors who want to name a school, or are compelled to fund grand construction projects, new academic programs, or scholarships for generations of future students. But what leads donors to make these decisions?

This unknown confronts not just newly appointed department chairs, deans, provosts, and presidents, but also the development professionals supporting them. As this chapter explains, successful major gift fundraising is much less about "making the ask," and far more dependent on discovering what donors care about. The countless hours development teams commit to identifying, researching, and engaging with potential donors are necessary to learn their interests and values. This process applies not just to individuals, but also to corporations and foundations. Gaining first-hand knowledge of interests and values informs the engagement of potential donors in ways that facilitate gift discussions and solicitation. The development of engagement strategies includes determining how and when to best utilize academic leaders, faculty members, and other individuals in the process.

A. Conley and G. G. Shaker, *Fundraising Principles for Faculty and Academic Leaders*, Philanthropy and Education,
https://doi.org/10.1007/978-3-030-66429-9_5

GIVING MOTIVES BY SOURCE: INDIVIDUALS, CORPORATIONS, FOUNDATIONS

The act of successfully raising a major gift is frequently described as an art. This portrayal has endured in part because of an absence of science. Over the past three decades, however, there has been an unprecedented expansion in research about why people give. This body of knowledge continues to grow and there is still much to learn but reviewing some of the findings to date is beneficial for novice faculty members and seasoned fundraising executives alike. Those who seek major gifts may certainly apply their own "art" in engaging someone, but they can be much more effective by grounding it in the science about philanthropic motivation.

As noted in Chapter 1, the annual VSE report tracks charitable giving to higher education and differentiates the contributions with the categories of individuals (alumni, non-alumni) and organizations (foundations, corporations, and other organizations). This review examines key concepts and studies on giving motives using this structure.

Individuals

As a starting point for understanding why people give—including alumni and non-alumni alike—donor motives can be segmented along a spectrum bounded by two categories. As defined by Burlingame (1993), the first is altruism, which is an unselfish action for the welfare of others. The other is egoism, which is an action in regard to one's own interest. Donor motives most often fall somewhere within this spectrum, "Both motives come together in the human condition to form a cooperative venture to achieve nearly all ends in society" (p. 1). This is further acknowledged by Frank (1996), who contends "...any theory of charitable giving based exclusively on one type of motive or the other will inevitably fail to capture an essential aspect of reality" (p. 137).

Drezner (2011) applies this perspective to giving for higher education as mutual benefit, where altruism is present, but also includes "the donor's or volunteer's receiving some level of intrinsic or extrinsic gain from the action to assist others" (p. 48). Intrinsic benefits can vary widely and may include a greater sense of self-worth, feelings of loyalty or doing one's duty, and even assuaging guilt. Extrinsic benefits are similarly broad and could include recognition in a donor honor roll, access to special events, receipt of exclusive stewardship items such as plaques or lapel pins, and qualifying for a tax deduction on the gift.

Another valuable resource in understanding why people give is a literature review of more than 500 research articles conducted by Bekkers and Wiepking (2011). While the oldest study dates to 1899, the timeframe does not pick up again until the 1960s, where 10 studies were found. As a reflection of the recent emergence of philanthropy as a field of academic study, the majority of the reviewed works come from the 1990s and 2000s.

Their review was structured around the central question of why people donate money to charitable organizations and revealed eight mechanisms that drive giving. These included:

1. Awareness of Need: Potential donors must be informed or aware of a need in order to respond.
2. Solicitation: Philanthropy most often occurs in response to a solicitation from an organization, or by someone on its behalf.
3. Costs and Benefits: Philanthropy is enhanced when it can be done at a lower cost to the donor, and when it yields more benefit.
4. Altruism: Gifts made purely out of concern for the well-being of the recipient, or the creation of a public good or service.
5. Reputation: Philanthropy that gains or builds a positive social impression from others.
6. Psychological Benefits: A private, internal benefit to the donor often called the "warm glow."
7. Values: Acts of giving that reflect the personal beliefs of the donor, which may include religious, political, or altruistic values.
8. Efficacy: Giving made in response to the belief that a contribution will be effective and impactful.

In alignment with Burlingame (1993) and Frank (1996), this model finds that individuals are motivated by a mix of these mechanisms, with different motives taking precedence for different donors in relation to different gifts. This structure is a valuable starting point for exploring giving motives and can be used to "unpack" the complexities of individual decision-making. It is notable that these mechanisms apply to individual giving generally, and are not limited to major gifts or wealthy individuals. This is especially important for the solicitation mechanism. As noted later in this chapter from the 2018 U.S. Trust study, "the ask" may not be as compelling as one would expect.

Visualizing donor types based on a predominant motivator can provide a different approach to the relationship-building process. The landmark book, *The Seven Faces of Philanthropy*, provides a useful taxonomy of affluent prospective donors. The book emerged from research by Prince and File (1994) based on 200 high net worth donors and resulted in seven categories including:

> The Communitarian: Giving because it makes good sense to help our community.
> The Devout: Giving to support nonprofits for religious reasons.
> The Investor: Giving for the cause and for any personal tax and estate benefit.
> The Socialite: Giving to make a better world while having a good time doing it.
> The Altruist: Giving as the selfless donor purely out of generosity and empathy.
> The Repayer: Giving out of loyalty or obligation for benefits received.
> The Dynast: Giving as a family-driven tradition.

By understanding an individual's dominant "face," the authors contended fundraisers can take informed approaches in their engagement with prospective donors. Like other researchers, they too recognized additional layers of motivation: "The Seven Faces form of segmentation is revealing because one set of motivations tends to dominate people's decisions, even though close questioning will reveal that any individual donor will also feel additional motivations" (p. 13).

The donors in *The Seven Faces* were not ethnically diverse and this is a historical shortcoming of research in the field, which also signals a shortcoming of advancement practice. As Drezner (2013) reminds readers in *Expanding the Donor Base in Higher Education*: "There is an increased importance to engage all populations in advancement strategies…advancement offices must engage in culturally sensitive fundraising practices that honor prospective donors' different social identities" (pp. 1, 9). Academic leaders need to be informed about different perspectives of giving and to be inclusive in their approach to fundraising. More research is available than ever—about the giving motives and concerns of female donors, donors who are people of color, LGBTQ donors, and donors of different faith traditions—but research and practice still have work to do.

The literature on donor motives is far more extensive than summarized here; the illumination of select research findings is meant to validate that the art of securing major gifts can be substantively improved with awareness and application of the science. The next chapter is dedicated to one giving model and its application to alumni. For further inquiry, higher education fundraising-specific examples are available in Cascione (2003), Drezner and Huehls (2015), and Proper and Caboni (2014). For research on giving across the nonprofit sector, see Herzog and Price (2016), Rooney and Osili (2016), Schervish (1997b), and Tempel and Burlingame (2000).

Corporations

As noted in Chapter 4, companies today are likely to engage colleges and universities on an enterprise basis, seeking strategic benefits across a spectrum beyond just recruiting or sponsored research. And the benefits being sought are likely tied to specific motives and purposes. Companies, just like individuals, each have distinct purposes for giving. Learning as much as possible about the corporate values and priorities underlying the motives can significantly improve the chances of securing corporate philanthropic support.

In a major study of industry partnerships, NACRO (2019) noted that motives vary by industry sector. Supporting basic and applied research was found to be a higher priority among healthcare, pharmaceuticals/biotech, software, and computer/electronics companies. Campus recruitment was highest among financial and business services and energy companies. Manufacturing, which was the largest sector represented in the study, ranked building brand awareness as the highest goal of academic engagement.

It is also noteworthy that 42% of the NACRO study participants indicated that their company maintained ongoing relationships with more than 25 universities. Another 24% indicated between 11 and 25 university partnerships. Three-fourths of the companies had revenues of $1 billion or more. The takeaway from this study is the need for absolute focus on creating gift solicitations that stand out in a competitive environment and bring value to the company.

Seeking guidance on how charitable giving decisions are made within a company can be particularly valuable. This may be obtained directly from the company, or with the assistance of corporate relations staff in the development office. As these insights are gathered, consider the four models developed by Young and Burlingame (1996) for discerning a company's giving motives.

The first model is corporate productivity, where giving is directed in ways that will help the company increase profits and return more value to shareholders. Second is the ethical or altruistic model, where giving is viewed as the right thing to do and will help the community. The third is a political model in two variants. The external version suggests giving helps build or protect corporate power and influence, and the internal focuses on awareness of who makes or influences giving decisions beyond just the corporate giving officer. Fourth, the stakeholder model broadly acknowledges that giving helps address the interests of many including shareholders, suppliers, customers, employees, community groups, and government officials. As noted in the summary of individual giving motives, one or two motives may predominate, and identifying which one/s can greatly inform the strategy for a successful solicitation.

Finally, before engaging the corporate sector, recognize that beginning in the early 1980s, corporations shifted from giving for the sake of being good corporate citizens to giving to build alliances (Burlingame & Dunlavy, 2016). The most common forms of giving in support of this strategic objective are cause-related marketing and sponsorships. While these giving vehicles may serve corporate interests effectively, the challenge for the beneficiary organizations is realizing that any positive effects are likely to be short lived. These forms also may not be effective in building donor loyalty over time.

Foundations

Recognizing foundations' giving motives and requirements begins with understanding the four primary foundation types; independent, corporate, community, and operating. Each type has specific objectives, and recent trends indicate that foundations are more clearly defining their interests and expectations of recipient organizations, especially in evaluating their grants' outcomes (Nathan & Lesem, 2016).

Independent foundations are the most common type, constituting more than 90% of the 86,000 foundations in the U.S. and 70% of the total dollars granted to nonprofits (Foundation Center, 2015). These organizations typically define specific areas of interest and may limit grants to particular geographic regions. Family foundations fall within this category. By law, independent foundations are required to distribute a minimum of 5% of their endowment value annually.

Corporate foundations are actually another type of independent foundation; however, they are different in that they usually derive their assets from an associated for-profit company (Nathan & Lesem, 2016). These foundations often follow grant-making strategies driven by their company's business interests, but typically are governed by separate boards that may include current and former employees as well as select community leaders with a history of company engagement.

Community foundations have existed for more than a century in the US with the first, the Cleveland Foundation, established in 1914. However, it wasn't until the 1990s that this segment rapidly expanded. These foundations receive assets from a large pool of donors and fund a wide range of community needs (Nathan & Lesem, 2016). Most community foundations make grants from three asset groups: unrestricted funds, donor-designated funds, and donor-advised funds.

Although community foundations only represent about 1% of all foundations, they trail only independent foundations in the amount of total dollars granted, accounting for nearly $7 billion (Foundation Center, 2015). Community foundations are exempt from the 5% distribution requirement.

Community foundations are also increasingly important to higher education, as local institutions may be eligible for grants from programmatic, donor-designated, or unrestricted funds. As noted in Chapter 4, community foundations are also experiencing considerable growth in donor-advised funds.

Operating foundations differ from other foundations because they fund their own programs and do not make grants to other nonprofit organizations. Consequently, the IRS requires operating foundations to expend 85% of their income on their programs. Other nonprofits' operating foundations may support a purpose that overlaps with university or faculty interests (such as a museum foundation's focus on arts preservation) and serve as conveners or collaborators for those in related fields.

The first step in knowing a foundation's giving purposes is to review their guidelines, usually available online, which will articulate what they will, and will not, support. Also, explore the foundation's leadership as there may be personal or professional relationships between the board or senior staff and the college's leaders or major donors. Engaging these individuals can yield valuable insights into decision-making processes not evident in the foundation's published guidelines.

Most importantly, academic leaders need to partner with the development office. Even small liberal arts colleges likely employ a specialist in foundation fundraising. Larger institutions are usually staffed with several of these professionals. They can assist with researching foundations that fund particular areas, reviewing foundation grant-making histories, speaking with program officers, and assuring that campus protocols are followed in making contacts. Foundation relations staff can be particularly supportive of faculty members who are composing grant proposals and arranging site visits. They should also be involved in reporting and compliance activity, as well as stewardship, when grants are awarded (Schneider, 2000).

Other Organizations

The catch-all designation of "other organizations" can represent a notable source of philanthropic support for colleges and universities. As noted in the VSE report, more than $6 billion came from this segment of donors in 2018–2019.

This category is diverse, making the motivations for giving difficult to specify. Some examples of organization types are provided as a reminder that these potential donors could be hiding in plain sight and may simply need initial philanthropic engagement.

Many cities, large and small, are home to membership organizations that raise money from members and activities to redistribute to the community for specific charities and causes. These include formal service organizations like Rotary, Kiwanis, and Lions Clubs. Other groups are formed around well-defined membership criteria, such as young professionals' societies, women's groups, and neighborhood associations. Another area to focus on is retiree groups. Most colleges and universities have a faculty and staff retiree association, with a mission component of providing some form of service to their institution. Large corporations also similarly have retiree associations that include a service component through charitable gifts, volunteering, or both.

This category also includes churches and other religiously-affiliated entities, which may provide support to denominational colleges, as well as nonprofits like the United Fund (also known as the UNCF or United Negro College Fund).

While there are potentially limitless types of organizations that support higher education, the process of engaging them is not unlike individuals, corporations, or foundations. By attempting to identify their giving motives either through the mission statement, giving criteria, or personal conversations with individual officers or members, one can begin the process of linking organizational needs with donor interests and values.

THE IMPERATIVE OF EMPATHY

Recognizing the giving motives of an individual, corporation, or foundation first requires gaining perspective on their own needs and priorities. This is easier said than done, as it is institutional needs and priorities that drive the urgency of most fundraising activity. The co-author of a study about the giving motives and habits of ultra-high net worth individuals in northern California noted this regarding the study's recommendations:

> I think what the nonprofit leaders can do is really be thoughtful about listening and empathizing with the philanthropist. I know that sounds crazy, because most nonprofit leaders are like, "You have all the money. You have all the wealth. I need some of it." (O'Neil, 2018, para. 9)

It is unfair and erroneous to characterize a person simply by their wealth or lack thereof, as master fundraiser and best-selling author Lynne Twist adroitly tells her readers, and doing so holds people back in life and fundraising (Twist & Barker, 2003). Academic leaders who are successful in building relationships with donors have a strong command of empathy, which allows them to put themselves in donors' shoes, intellectually and/or emotionally. Rather than viewing fundraising activity as about institutional needs only, they recognize that donors have needs too and work to discern and intuit those needs and purposes. Indeed, one study of university fundraisers' written reports of their contacts with major gift donors found a connection between the inclusion of empathy and the donors' cumulative giving (Bout, 2020).

Skillful fundraising leaders also recognize that philanthropic gift-making is based on a values exchange in which the organization returns a value to the donor that is beyond the material (Rosso, 2016). This can be providing a sense of satisfaction, feeling of making a difference, and/or sense of belonging, among others. A part of this is also recognizing that giving is a joyful act and institutions and their representatives offer something(s) powerful to donors, just as donors provide something(s) important to institutions and those they serve (Konrath, 2016).

To conclude this section on the importance of empathy, consider the findings in Table 5.1. Taken from the 2018 U.S. Trust study, the data reveal factors high net worth individuals acknowledge as most influential in gift-related decision-making. It should not be unexpected to see personal values as the top consideration and interest in the issue area as the second. It should be revealing that the ask itself is the least important factor. Other institutional factors lie in the middle with varying levels of emphasis. This is a reminder of the necessity of making a match between donor and institutional interests. Once this is done, the actual request for support becomes a respectful reflection of something the donor cares deeply about.

Subsequent chapters attend further to the dynamics of engaging potential donors; it is critical to remember that donor decisions are driven by personal motives and feelings. And the core purpose of engagement activities is to discover these and find alignments. Alumni may be unsuccessfully

Table 5.1 Factors that led, or would lead in the future, to decisions about contributing to a particular cause or organization (Bank of America, 2018)

Factors	% (Among all respondents)
Personal values	74
Interest in the issue area	57
First- or second-hand experience benefitting from the organization	54
Recognizable or reputable nonprofit	50
Perceived need of the organization or issue area	49
Association with another institution	26
Nonprofit report rankings	18
Endorsement, recommendation or pressure from a friend/social circle	10
Compelling pitch (in-person or collateral)	9

solicited for major gifts even following extensive personal interaction. The shortcoming in such cases is often a failure of the interactions to reveal the prospective donor's true cares and concerns before the solicitation for an institutional need.

The Dangers of Thinking for the Donor

Those who engage in fundraising face the risk of making inaccurate assumptions about what donors want to support. As noted throughout this chapter, major gift donors are driven by values and interests. Discovery of the primary motivations for their giving can help inform how to articulate needs in ways that align with how they think and feel. But the time and effort necessary for this discovery is too often discarded in favor of moving expediently into a solicitation for pressing priorities. As one dean advises:

> It is important to listen to the donors rather than drive too hard with your own notion of an end result. We have some gifts that are great for the school that we otherwise would not have received if we had pushed hard for gifts that were of less interest to the donor. (Weidner, 2008, pp. 397–398)

One area of major gifts in which experienced fundraisers and academic leaders alike often substitute their own thoughts is in donors' preferences to support specific, or restricted, purposes rather than to give unrestricted gifts. Indeed, the data here do indicate a preponderance of gifts designated for restricted purposes.

A study of 30 years of higher education giving based on a longitudinal sample from the VSE survey (about 400 institutions, majority four-year) found a rising proportion of gifts for restricted purposes and a concomitant decline in unrestricted giving at the institutional level (Shaker & Borden, 2020). This was the case for both public and private institutions, though unrestricted giving totals were always notably lower in public institutions. Individuals (and alumni more so than non-alumni) consistently gave more unrestricted than organizations, but they too focused more on restricted giving by the end of the study period in 2018. It is worth noting that support whose only restriction was for use by a particular academic unit was more consistent over time. Giving rose in general during the time period so that means that the unrestricted and restricted dollars received increased, but proportionally more went to restricted use as time passed.

While unrestricted gifts—especially large ones—are admittedly far fewer in number than restricted gifts, there are enough to challenge the conventional wisdom that drives many solicitation strategies. In a review of million-dollar gifts in 2017, *The Chronicle of Philanthropy* identified 15 unrestricted gifts of $1 million or more, including eight above $10 million (Daniels, 2018). These included a $140 million unrestricted gift to MIT and $150 million to the University of Illinois at Urbana-Champaign.

While the study of this question will likely, and hopefully, continue to proceed, one should not automatically assume a prospective donor wants to support a specific purpose. This is especially the case for high net worth individuals as evidenced by the 2016 U.S. Trust study. More than 1,600 participants were asked if their largest gift the previous year was restricted or unrestricted. As a surprise to many, 73.6% indicated unrestricted. In a follow-up question, the donors were asked whether they generally preferred to give to restricted or unrestricted purposes. Only 20.1% indicated restricted. The remainder indicated either unrestricted (29.4%) or no preference (50.5%). (Bank of America, 2016, pp. 20–21).

It is also limiting to assume that higher education major donors always prefer restricted endowment giving, such as scholarships, professorships, and chairs, over unrestricted endowment funding. As a challenge to this assumption, Conley (2017) conducted a ten-year case study of an unrestricted endowment initiative in the Swanson School of Engineering at the University of Pittsburgh. Between 2006 and 2015, 114 unrestricted funds were established. Also, there were 127 individual gift agreements on file, indicating numerous donors signed new gift agreements to add to their funds later.

The cumulative value of the funds committed through all the gift agreements was more than $5.5 million. The book value (or cash received) of all the funds in 2015 was $3.24 million and market value was $3.77 million. Donors were initially given options to designate endowments to the school or to one of the school's six academic departments. The school later expanded these options and donors responded with unrestricted endowments for diversity programs, study abroad, and a student organization to be utilized for any purpose at the discretion of each unit's administrative leader.

The two largest funds resulted from gift commitments of $1.5 million each. One was a bequest designated to the school, and the other was a cash gift designated to the Department of Bioengineering. But most of the funds established were less than $25,000. While these are relatively small endowments, they did represent a significant jump in the particular donors' giving levels. This population had a history of giving, with a median of 24 gifts to the university prior to establishing their unrestricted endowment. But the gifts were relatively small, with median lifetime giving of just over $4,400 and a median largest gift of $1,000.

This same unrestricted endowment model was later replicated in 2010 at another institution and expanded to allow donors to establish funds for any unit or program across the university. By 2020, donors there had established more than 150 funds designated for each of the academic schools, as well as for athletics, the library, and numerous research centers (University of Texas at Dallas, n.d.).

The findings presented here on unrestricted giving are not intended to imply that all donors will give for unrestricted purposes if asked. The purpose is to serve as a reminder that donor preferences should be revealed by the donor, and not through personal biases or assumptions held by those seeking their support. A donor's deep care about one academic unit or one portion of that unit and their desire to be most helpful may translate as easily into an unrestricted gift for that unit as into a more narrowly focused gift within that unit. Donors and academic leaders themselves may carry biases about unrestricted funds' lack of structure or impact that masks how valuable they can be. This perception should be routinely challenged, as noted by a foundation president: "An organization can faithfully carry out the activities funded with restricted money and still not have much impact. The attempt to achieve tight control and close observation can miss the impact forest for the operational trees" (Starr, 2011, para. 7).

Conclusion

This chapter emphasizes the benefits of understanding that donors' values, interests, and perceptions drive their giving, much more so than what they are asked to support. As the gift request increases, so too does the donor's level of personal scrutiny and self-reflection. If there is no alignment between their beliefs and the gift's purpose, there is little chance of securing the gift. Or alternatively, the donor may still give out of consideration for the cause or respect for the person asking, but it will not be what Hodge (2016) refers to as a "gift of significance," where there is clear overlap between the core values of the institutional mission and the core values of the donor's life mission.

Drawing on this understanding of motives, the remaining two chapters in this section apply a fundraising model specifically to engaging and soliciting alumni and provide strategies that can help start gift discussions. Goals of the section include illuminating how major gifts are raised, and providing academicians with information about how development teams apply this knowledge every day in their pursuit of philanthropic support.

ACTIONABLE STRATEGIES

1. List the top five prospective major gift donors to your unit. These can be individuals who have been donors, but not yet at the level you believe they are capable of giving. Ask yourself (and your development officer, if applicable) the following questions:

   – Who has the strongest relationship with them?
      Has this person asked them what they really care about, not just at our institution?
      Do we know if they are fully confident in our institution's senior leadership?

2. Using the categories from *The Seven Faces of Philanthropy* as a guide, can you identify which "face" most closely matches each of the five prospective donors outlined in strategy #1?

SECTION II CASE STUDY: ONE DONOR, TWO NAMING GIFTS: THE MOTIVES FOR GIVING

Prominent naming gifts are a staple of contemporary fundraising efforts on the American college campus. Names of benefactors can be found on schools, centers, academic and residential buildings, athletic venues, and large public spaces. The stories of these gifts provide insights into donor motivation, aligning with the research and countering assumptions and stereotypes of wealthy donors. Reading naming announcements closely, along with other public information, can reveal donors' interests and beliefs. These models can aid fundraisers and academic leaders by illuminating what to listen for and attend to in interactions with their potential donors.

A useful example can be found in Lois and Sidney Eskenazi, an alumni couple of Indiana University. Both earned undergraduate degrees from the Bloomington campus in the early 1950s, and he also earned a law degree in 1953. They married the following year (Simic & Bate, 2019).

The Eskenazis' most recent and largest gift to IU came in 2019 with a $20 million gift resulting in the naming of the Eskenazi School of Art, Architecture + Design. The gift supports scholarships, faculty development, academic programs, research initiatives and facilities (Indiana University, 2019). The gift announcement specifically noted the creation of an endowed scholarship in Mrs. Eskenazi's name for first-year students interested in painting.

This gift was preceded by a $15 million commitment in 2016 for the university's art museum, which was also named in honor of the donors. This served as the lead gift for a complete renovation of the museum, which was designed by I.M. Pei and built in 1982. The gift also included a donation of the Eskenazis' personal collection of nearly 100 works of art (Indiana University, 2016).

The 2016 announcement also noted their previous giving in support of arts education at the Indianapolis campus, IUPUI, where the building housing the Herron School of Art and Design is named Eskenazi Hall. A second facility there, the Eskenazi Fine Arts Center, houses sculpture and ceramics programs, classrooms, and a large fabrication space.

Additional public sources provide insightful background information. Mr. Eskenazi was born and raised in Indianapolis, which is also home to the commercial real estate development company he established in 1963 (Indiana University, n.d.). They endowed their first scholarship at IU in 1970 to benefit law students at both the Bloomington and Indianapolis campuses. And they endowed other scholarships for Indianapolis students in the IU School of Medicine and the Herron School of Art and Design.

Their most visible gift that was not directly designated to IU was made in 2011. The couple gave $40 million for the construction of a new public hospital in Indianapolis to replace the aging and outdated facility located on the IUPUI campus. This facility historically served as the teaching hospital for the IU School of Medicine, and this relationship continues with the new facility, which opened in 2013 as the Sidney and Lois Eskenazi Hospital.

A video interview following the hospital's completion reveals compelling insights and motives that propelled this gift, and possibly others, based on Mr. Eskenazi's childhood during the Great Depression,

"I didn't have anything when I was young. But I can still remember there was always a little something that my father, when he was alive, and my uncle afterwards, would give to charity. And they had very little, but there was still something that they could give to help other people" (Eskenazi Health Foundation, n.d.).

A clearer perspective of likely donor motives can be formulated using frameworks cited in Chapter 5. Applying *The Seven Faces of Philanthropy* (Prince & File, 1994),the most dominant motive behind the hospital gift may be "The Communitarian," where the donor gives because it makes good sense to support the community. Growing up poor but witnessing generosity by his father and uncle to help others in their community clearly left a lasting impression. Experiences from one's youth is also one of the key components of the Identification Model noted in Chapter 6 (Schervish, 1997a).

The gifts to IU may have been driven by another *Seven Faces* motive. "The Repayer" is recognized for giving out of loyalty or obligation for benefits received. Interestingly, the largest gifts to IU have not been for business or law, but for art. So while elements of the repayer are likely present, they are secondary to the couple's shared interest and passion for art. The power of these factors is clearly evident in Table 5.1, where personal values and interest in the issue area are the top two factors driving high net worth individuals' decisions to give.

One final public source yields perhaps the most insightful motive regarding the donors' prominent attachment of the family name to their gifts. Mr. Eskenazi in particular was affected by other philanthropists who believed gifts made in anonymity missed the opportunity to influence others with similar wealth. "If you lend your name to a project, it encourages others to say, 'Well, if he can do something like that perhaps I can do something too.' By linking our names to initiatives or letting our names be put on a building, for example, Lois and I hope that others may find inspiration to take action for similar good" (Simic & Bate, 2019, p. 46).

Key Lessons

- **Don't assume the degree or major drives giving.** Neither of the Eskanzis majored in art, but that's where the bulk of their philanthropy to IU has been directed.

- **Pay attention to personal history.** Stories of childhood and family are often revealed early in the cultivation phase. Witnessing philanthropic gestures while poor, as Mr. Eskanazi did in his childhood, leaves a lasting impression and may influence how a donor views their present-day giving.
- **Don't lead with the name.** It can be natural to assume donors who often attach their name to prominent gifts want the recognition. However, it is always better to first understand why they give, and then learn whether they believe using their name brings additional value to the gift.

REFERENCES

Bank of America. (2016). *The 2016 U.S. Trust study of high net worth philanthropy.* Retrieved June 19, 2020, from https://scholarworks.iupui.edu/handle/1805/11234.

Bank of America. (2018). *The 2018 U.S. Trust study of high net worth philanthropy.* Retrieved May 14, 2020, from https://scholarworks.iupui.edu/handle/1805/17667.

Bekkers, R., & Wiepking, P. (2011). A literature review of empirical studies of philanthropy: Eight mechanisms that drive charitable giving. *Nonprofit and Voluntary Sector Quarterly, 40*(5), 924–973.

Bout, M. (2020, January 1). Motivation and inspiration: All aboard the empathy express. *Advancing Philanthropy.* Association of Fundraising Professionals.

Burlingame, D. F. (1993). Altruism and philanthropy: Definitional issues. *Essays on Philanthropy, No. 10.* Indiana University Center on Philanthropy. Retrieved June 16, 2020, from http://ulib.iupuidigital.org/cdm/ref/collection/PRO/id/32036.

Burlingame, D. F., & Dunlavy, S. (2016). Corporate giving and fundraising. In E. R. Tempel, T. L. Seiler, & D. F. Burlingame (Eds.), *Achieving excellence in fundraising* (4th ed., pp. 85–99). Hoboken, NJ: Wiley.

Cascione, G. L. (2003). *Philanthropists in higher education: Institutional, biographical, and religious motivations for giving.* New York: Routledge.

Conley, A. (2017). Securing donor support for unrestricted endowments: A case study in higher education. *Philanthropy & Education, 1*(1), 48–63.

Daniels, A. (2018, February 7). No strings attached: Advice from groups that landed big unrestricted gifts. *The Chronicle of Philanthropy.* Retrieved August 27, 2020, from https://www.philanthropy.com/article/How-to-Land-Big-Unrestricted/242456.

Drezner, N. D. (2011). *Philanthropy and fundraising in American higher education.* San Francisco: Jossey-Bass.

Drezner, N. D. (Ed.). (2013). *Expanding the donor base in higher education: Engaging non-traditional donors.* New York: Routledge.

Drezner, N. D., & Huehls, F. (2015). *Fundraising and institutional advancement: Theory, practice, and new paradigms.* New York: Routledge.

Eskenazi Health Foundation. (n.d.). *Eskenzi video.* Retrieved August 17, 2020, from http://eskenazihealthfoundation.org/donor-video/.

Foundation Center. (2015). *Foundation stats.* Retrieved June 18, 2020, from http://data.foundationcenter.org/.

Frank, R. (1996). Motivation, cognition, and charitable giving. In J. Schneewind (Ed.), *Giving: Western ideas of philanthropy* (pp. 130–152). Bloomington: Indiana University Press.

Herzog, P. S., & Price, H. E. (2016). *American generosity: Who gives and why.* New York: Oxford University Press.

Hodge, J. M. (2016). Major gifts. In E. R. Tempel, T. L. Seiler, & D. F. Burlingame (Eds.), *Achieving excellence in fundraising* (4th ed., pp. 225–242). Hoboken, NJ: Wiley.

Indiana University. (2016, May 11). *IU Art Museum receives $15 million gift from Sidney and Lois Eskenazi.* Retrieved August 17, 2020, from https://archive.news.indiana.edu/releases/iu/2016/05/art-museum-gift.shtml.

Indiana University. (2019, April 10). *IU School of Art, Architecture + Design Renamed for Sidney and Lois Eskenazi.* Retrieved August 10, 2020, from https://news.iu.edu/stories/2019/04/iu/releases/10-soaad-eskenazi-naming.html.

Indiana University. (n.d.). *University honors & awards.* Retrieved August 17, 2020, from https://honorsandawards.iu.edu/search-awards/honoree.shtml?honoreeID=6153.

Konrath, S. (2016). The joy of giving. In E. R. Tempel, T. L. Seiler, & D. F. Burlingame (Eds.), *Achieving excellence in fundraising* (4th ed., pp. 11–25). Hoboken, NJ: Wiley.

NACRO. (2019). *Industry perspectives on academic corporate relations: Results, opportunities and best practices from a NACRO survey.* Retrieved June 16, 2020, from https://nacrocon.org/resources.

Nathan, S. K., & Lesem, E. (2016). Foundation fundraising. In E. R. Tempel, T. L. Seiler, & D. F. Burlingame (Eds.), *Achieving excellence in fundraising* (4th ed., pp. 101–112). Hoboken, NJ: Wiley.

O'Neil, M. (2018, January 16). Ultra-rich face insecurities about giving, report finds. Here's how charities can help. *The Chronicle of Philanthropy.* Retrieved June 19, 2020, from https://www.philanthropy.com/article/Ultra-Rich-Face-Insecurities/242242.

Prince, R. A., & File, K. M. (1994). *The seven faces of philanthropy*. San Francisco: Jossey-Bass.

Proper, E., & Caboni, T. C. (2014). *Institutional advancement: What we know*. New York: Palgrave Macmillan.

Rooney, P., & Osili, U. (2016). Understanding high net worth donors. In E. R. Tempel, T. L. Seiler, & D. F. Burlingame (Eds.), *Achieving excellence in fundraising* (4th ed., pp. 185–199). Hoboken, NJ: Wiley.

Rosso, H. A. (2016). A philosophy of fundraising. In E. R. Tempel, T. L. Seiler, & D. F. Burlingame (Eds.), *Achieving excellence in fundraising* (4th ed., pp. 3–10). Hoboken, NJ: Wiley.

Schervish, P. G. (1997a). Inclination, obligation, and association: What we know and what we need to learn about donor motivation. In D. F. Burlingame (Ed.), *Critical issues in fundraising* (pp. 110–138). New York: Wiley.

Schervish, P. G. (1997b, Summer). Major donors, major motives: The people and purposes behind major gifts. *New Directions for Philanthropic Fundraising, Developing Major Gifts* (16), 85–112.

Schneider, J. C. (2000, Summer). Universities and foundation support: Working with faculty and administrators. In S. A. Glass (Ed.), *New Directions for Philanthropic Fundraising: Approaching Foundations, 28*, 97–110.

Shaker, G. G., & Borden, V. M. (2020). How donors give to higher education: Thirty years of supporting U.S. college and university missions (Research Dialogue, No. 158). TIAA Institute. Retrieved August 27, 2020, from https://www.tiaainstitute.org/publication/how-donors-give-higher-edu cation.

Simic, C. R., & Bate, S. (2019). Sidney & Lois Eskenazi: Lessons in philanthropy. In *The spirit of generosity: Shaping IU through philanthropy* (pp. 43–50). Bloomington: Indiana University Press. Retrieved August 17, 2020, from https://publish.iupress.indiana.edu/projects/the-spirit-of-generosity.

Starr, K. (2011, August 3). Just give 'em the money: The power and pleasure of unrestricted funding. *Stanford Social Innovation Review*. Retrieved June 20, 2020, from https://ssir.org/articles/entry/power_and_pleasure_of_unrestric ted_funding.

Tempel, E. R., & Burlingame, D. F. (Eds.). (2000, Fall). Understanding the needs of donors: The supply side of charitable giving. *New Directions for Philanthropic Fundraising, 29*.

Twist, L., & Barker, T. (2003). *The soul of money: Transforming your relationship with money and life*. New York: Norton.

University of Texas at Dallas. (n.d.). *Endowments/opportunity funds*. Retrieved June 11, 2020, from https://www.utdallas.edu/development/endowments/ opportunity-funds/.

Weidner, D. J. (2008, Winter). Fundraising tips for deans with intermediate development programs. *The University of Toledo Law Review, 39*, 393–398.

86 A. CONLEY AND G. G. SHAKER

Young, D. R., & Burlingame, D. F. (1996). Paradigm lost: Research toward a new understanding of corporate philanthropy. In D. F. Burlingame & D. R. Young (Eds.), *Corporate philanthropy at the crossroads* (pp. 158–176). Bloomington: Indiana University Press.

CHAPTER 6

Applying the Identification Model

One day, a development officer in the engineering school at a large research university informed their dean about a recent phone call from a colleague. The call came from a development officer from the medical school and was related to an engineering alumnus and donor. The donor was a longtime supporter who had given several major gifts to the engineering school, including a sizeable estate commitment in their will. The engineering gift officer was assigned as the donor's prospect manager in the university's development database and, like the dean, had a long-standing relationship with the donor.

The medical school development officer was calling to inquire about the possibility of meeting with the donor and to seek the engineering school's approval. Due to privacy policies, the medical school gift officer could not provide details regarding the school's connection with the donor, but they did indicate that one of the physicians wanted to contact the donor under the auspices of the hospital's grateful patient program.

This donor was a highly visible figure in the community due to their success in business and their support of many local nonprofit organizations. The individual was also a past recipient of the engineering school's distinguished alumni award, an active member of the engineering school's advisory council, and played in the school's alumni golf outing every summer.

A. Conley and G. G. Shaker, *Fundraising Principles for Faculty and Academic Leaders*, Philanthropy and Education, https://doi.org/10.1007/978-3-030-66429-9_6

The engineering gift officer expressed no objection to the medical school's request because engineering had no immediate plans to seek another major gift and was focused on stewarding the donor's gifts and the relationship itself. The dean, on the other hand, protested that the individual was their alumnus and donor, and that the medical school should have ample other prospects to pursue, a very different reaction hinging on the school's perspective rather than the donor's.

An instinct to "protect" the donor, like the dean's, is often apparent on college campuses, much to the detriment of the institution, the development program, and most importantly, to donors. It is a natural reaction to view as intrusive any engagement attempts similar to the one illustrated in this case. But this one-dimensional perspective focuses only on the donor's formal connection as an alumnus. In this scenario, this connection is evident through the donor's membership on the dean's advisory council, receipt of the distinguished alumni award, and participation in regular events. The weight of these associations, from the dean's perspective, paled in comparison with any connection to the medical school.

However, what if the physician saved this person's life, or the life of one of their family members? Could the engineering school morally justify refusing the medical school's request for a conversation with the donor? Even if the medical treatment did not address a life-threatening condition, both gift officers' behavior represents donor-centric best practices and an institutional perspective driven by mission. One showed courtesy and respect by following prospect management protocols, recognizing a long-standing relationship, and first seeking permission for a meeting. The other embraced the possibility of enabling a valued benefactor to become engaged on an even deeper level with the university.

To further explain this story and the evidence about donor motivations shared in Chapter 5, this chapter focuses on a model of donor motivations that is exceptional for navigating major gift fundraising from alumni. Utilizing this particular model can help academic leaders and development staff to be highly empathetic by focusing more on the donor's needs and less on assumptions of alumni status.

EXPLAINING THE IDENTIFICATION MODEL

Paul Schervish, professor emeritus of sociology at Boston College, is an authority on the subject of philanthropy and donor motivation. Specifically, he developed an identification model (1997) which emerged from earlier research with colleagues Andrew Herman and John Havens studying millionaires and the influences on their giving decisions. The model includes the following eight variables and is an effective conceptual framework for understanding giving.

1. *Communities of participation*: Groups and organizations in which one participates.
2. *Frameworks of consciousness*: Beliefs, goals, and orientations that shape the values and priorities that determine people's activities.
3. *Direct requests*: Invitations by persons or organizations to directly participate in philanthropy.
4. *Discretionary resources*: The quantitative and psychological where-withal of time and money that can be mobilized for philanthropic purposes.
5. *Models and experiences from one's youth*: The people or experiences from one's youth that serve as positive exemplars for one's adult engagements.
6. *Urgency and effectiveness*: A sense of how necessary and/or useful charitable assistance will be in the face of the onset of an unanticipated or previously unrecognized family, community, national, or international crisis.
7. *Demographic characteristics*: The geographic, organizational, and individual circumstances of one's self, family, and community that affect one's philanthropic commitment.
8. *Intrinsic and extrinsic rewards*: The array of positive experiences and outcomes of one's current engagement that draws one deeper into a philanthropic identity. (pp. 112–113)

This model provides another perspective on the motives and factors that influence giving cited in Chapter 5, however, the first two points are especially relevant for understanding alumni and their giving to higher education. Schervish provides additional insight and explanation of these factors as they apply to giving across the charitable spectrum.

Communities of participation are the networks of formal and informal relationships with which people are associated. Communities of participation may be formal organizations such as schools, soup kitchens, or weekend soccer leagues. Communities of participation may also be quite informal, such as extended family visiting and caring for an elderly grandparent or neighbors rallying to help a family burned out of its home. Some communities of participation (such as a political party) require little voluntary activity while others (such as a cooperative nursery school) require participation as a condition of membership. Some communities of participation are entered only out of choice, such as a volunteer fire department or volunteer counseling at a shelter for battered women. Others are entered as a result of circumstances; for example, parents with school-age children are automatically put into contact with numerous school, extracurricular, and sports programs that offer opportunities to volunteer time and to contribute money. As I indicated, many communities of participation directly request and sometimes require time and money from their participants. But the important point is that being connected to an array of such life-settings is the basis for people becoming aware of needs and choosing to respond. (1997, pp. 113–114)

From a higher education perspective, alumni may be engaged with their alma mater through a wide range of communities of participation. Following their highest affiliation with the institution, alumni also identify with their school or major area of study. Development activities at these levels, such as school magazines and newsletters, social media presence, homecoming and other campus-based events, and regional outreach through alumni networking events, all focus on sustaining the identification of alumni with the institution and their home unit.

As Schervish notes, activities such as these are also the basis for making community members (like alumni) aware of needs and providing opportunities to respond. At the annual giving level, solicitations through postal mail, digital methods, or by phone are routinely organized by academic units to build on alumni status as forming a community of participation. And at the major gift level, most deans and their development officer(s) expend the bulk of their fundraising efforts on alumni of their programs.

While the identification model effectively presents alumni status (and engagement) as a community of participation, another aspect of the model demonstrates the complexity of alumni-institutional associations as motives for giving. The alumni-institutional interface also leads to giving when it is in alignment with the individual's values and interests, a concept reflected in the frameworks of consciousness variable. As noted in Chapter 5, emotional factors like values and interests are a critical dimension of giving decisions.

Frameworks of consciousness are ways of thinking and feeling that are rooted deeply enough in one's awareness to induce a commitment to a cause based on political ideology, religious beliefs, social concerns, or other values. An awareness of the redemptive value of Alcoholics Anonymous' twelve-step program in one's own or a family member's life is one example. Equally common are the deeply felt convictions about political prisoners that lead concerned citizens to join Amnesty International, about home-less people or battered women that lead volunteers to work at shelters, about community violence that lead parents to patrol the streets as part of a neighborhood watch, about the value of religious faith that lead church members to work in a food bank or a program for racial justice. The list of motivating concerns is as long as the list of deeply cherished beliefs. Just as there are different types of organizations in which one may partic-ipate, there are different types of beliefs. Some mobilizing beliefs are in fact better described as general values, other beliefs are really fundamental orientations, while still other beliefs concern causes to which one is dedi-cated. Again, there are no impermeable boundaries separating these kinds of beliefs any more than there is a sharp demarcation between what one does because of heartfelt feelings, on the one hand, and communities of participation, on the other. Communities of participation and frameworks of consciousness almost always work together. (1997, p. 114)

As Schervish suggests, emotional and engagement drivers almost always work together. In a higher education context, this helps explain why a business school graduate may choose to make most, or all, of their gifts to another part of the institution rather than the business school. If they developed a passion for the arts later in life, they may give exclusively to the university art museum. Or if one of their children died of cancer, they may give for research purposes to the medical school or patient care in the university hospital.

For those who are newer to fundraising, it can be especially helpful to think first about a prospective donor's emotional drivers rather than their points of engagement. For example, discovering that a successful entrepreneur is also a graduate of a particular school and expecting them to give because of that connection is a mistake. Next, an equally—if not more—important discovery about the entrepreneur is needed—what are the emotional forces that influence their giving decisions? Sometimes these frameworks can be discerned through research. It is most effec-tive, however, to determine these through conversation and personal interaction.

In most cases, initial visits by development staff aim to validate if interest and capacity to give are present. Recognizing how this preliminary process works can make academic leaders far more effective fundraising partners with development teams. It can also provide academic leaders with confidence to initiate this process when conducting an initial conversation on their own. The following exercise is designed to help illustrate the application of this model in this context.

Applying the Identification Model

To begin thinking about prospective alumni donors using the identification model, consider the following hypothetical couple. Both are alumni, but graduated with different degrees (Table 6.1).

From an engagement perspective (i.e., communities of participation) he served as a volunteer on the dean's advisory board for the School of Arts and Sciences. The school also honored him with their distinguished alumni award. For her, there is no evidence of direct engagement with the education school; however, the couple are life members of the university's alumni association, season ticket holders for basketball, and regular annual donors but not at a major level. They also have a daughter who attended the institution.

To complete this visioning exercise, think about what types of questions should be asked during a first visit. These questions should help elucidate the couple's emotional connections or influences based on knowledge of their communities of participation within their alma mater.

Table 6.1 Summary of a prospective donor couple

His engagement points	*Her engagement points*
B.S., Chemistry, 1971 Dean's Advisory Board, 2008–2014 Distinguished Alumni Award, 2005	B.S., Elementary Education, 1972

Joint engagement points
Alumni association, life members 15-year men's basketball season ticket holders 17-year consecutive donors to the university (Largest gift = $1,000) Daughter also attended. B.S., Marketing, 1993, and varsity athlete (volleyball)

The key benefit of this exercise is practicing empathetic interest. Rather than talking about what each school needs from the donors, focus on asking questions based on genuine interest in the couple's institutional engagement and their priorities. And be prepared to respond with institutional information that is applicable to their responses. Questions could include:

- *What are your favorite memories from your campus days?*
- *Did the two of you meet while you were students? If so, how did you meet?*
- *Do you keep in touch with any classmates?*
- *Did you have any professors who influenced your lives?*
- *Did you encourage your daughter to attend too, or was it her decision?*
- *Did your daughter have a good experience in her school? What about her volleyball experience?*
- *How involved have you been in the alumni association, beyond just your life membership?*
- *What aspects of the university are you most interested in now?*
- *What prompted you to buy your basketball season tickets all those years ago?*

Specific questions should also be directed individually to help determine each person's own emotional drivers. For example, she earned a degree in elementary education but little else is known so questions around her degree could yield valuable insight. Did she go into teaching after graduation? If so, did she enjoy it? Were there any faculty or staff who inspired her? For him, it is known that he volunteered on the advisory board and received the distinguished alumni award. Questions can explore those experiences and related personal relationships with faculty members or others.

As this discussion proceeds, other aspects of the identification model will likely emerge. These points can also be invaluable in better understanding their giving decisions. For example, they may mention something or someone from childhood that influenced their thinking as adults. Also, if they reveal other organizations that they support, they may also share details on giving decisions, providing insight on intrinsic or extrinsic rewards they receive through their relationship with those causes.

DISCOVERING HIDDEN NETWORKS

One specific aspect of the identification model requires particular attention as an additional feature of its applicability to fundraising from alumni. As noted in the communities of participation summary, networks of engagement can be formal and informal. The formal engagements are relatively easy to discover between alumni and institution. Beyond the obvious connecting point of the academic degree, alumni may serve on an advisory board, hold season tickets for the performing arts or athletics, be active in racial/ethnic-affinity alumni programs, volunteer for the class reunion committee, or participate in a stewardship society event, among other activities.

Informal networks also justify attention. Discovering them can be an extremely valuable asset in the cultivation process and may reduce the amount of time needed to initiate a gift discussion. Consider this scenario to better understand informal communities of participation and why they can be so useful.

A development officer for a pharmacy school at an urban private university has a routine stewardship meeting with a longtime donor. This alumna graduated in 1980 and remained in the city where the university is located for her entire career. She's a model alumna and donor, giving annually and establishing an endowed scholarship ten years prior. She regularly speaks in classes, attends alumni events, and recruits pharmacy interns and graduates on behalf of the pharmaceutical company where she is a senior executive.

During lunch, the alumna asks the development officer if she's ever mentioned her "holiday lunch group." Noting that she has not, the development officer listens in awe as the donor explains that she gets together every year around the holidays with a group of fellow pharmacy graduates. They have kept in touch since college days and have held this lunch gathering at the same restaurant for more than three decades. As a further surprise, she invites the development officer to join their upcoming gathering.

At the event, the alumna personally introduces her guest and notes how helpful they've been keeping her connected to the school, especially in making arrangements to speak in classes and meet with her scholarship recipients. Two of the dozen alumni attending this gathering are major gift prospects, These individuals are in the gift officer's portfolio, but the officer has not met them. The event goes so well, the group asks if the dean would consider attending next year.

The power of this informal community of participation is evident on multiple levels as it relates to major gift fundraising from alumni. From a stewardship perspective, the alumna who invited the gift officer was recognized for her scholarship and its impact on current students. The two new prospective major gift donors also have been engaged, and the gift officer has advanced the effort to develop a personalized cultivation strategy. And the rest of the group, many of whom were not donors, got to hear personally from their school rather than through the alumni magazine, annual fund solicitations, and other impersonal communication vehicles received by all alumni.

Examples such as this one often center on alumni of the same school or major, but there are other types of informal networks. Former student-athletes from the same sport may gather to attend the current team's games or other sporting events. Also, members of student organizations may hold reunions on campus without notifying the institution.

Informal associations can even evolve from shared living experiences. An article in the alumni magazine of Purdue University (2018) recounted how a group of several dozen men and women from the same section of a large residence hall complex have held a summer reunion on their own initiative annually for 45 consecutive years. Labeled as "Summer Party," the group rotated the meeting between pilgrimages to campus and ventures to other parts of the country. At first, it was just alumni, but in the 1980s, spouses and children began to join. The strength of this group reflects important insights about frameworks of consciousness among these graduates, as well as their communities of participation. This has become especially noticeable as the group has aged and began to lose members. One of them noted:

> What started as just a group of guys drinking together has evolved into a deep connection with one another's lives. It's more than just a group of grads getting together. We've relied on these friendships to get us through the lowest points in our lives. (p. 33)

Conclusion

The information in this chapter is further reinforced in the next chapter, in which cultivation strategy and activity leading to gift discussions are discussed. Before moving into this next stage, it is critical to recognize that alumni do not give primarily because they are alumni. The identification model provides a structural context to overcome the natural inclination to initiate engagement with alumni based on assumptions and fundraising priorities.

A concluding point to this chapter draws from the relevant experience most faculty possess from their years immersed in research and the advancement of knowledge. The outcomes of experimentation and exploration in every academic field are based on completing and disseminating rigorous study. Discoveries made through these efforts advance the field. The same principle applies in engaging alumni through personal visits and other development activities.

When development staff meet with alumni, especially those who may become major donors, vital information is collected. This deepens an institution's knowledge of these individuals' experiences, interests, motives, and passions. Collectively, this information greatly benefits an institution for years and decades to come, but only if it is recorded in the donor database. If a gift officer fails to do this, it is not just an oversight. It is potentially adding months and years onto the cultivation timeline of a major gift prospect since new staff must re-discover all these critical factors. Mistakes may also be made that can severely damage donors' impressions of the institution, its leadership, and the development team.

It follows that deans and academic leaders must be equally diligent in communicating about and participating in record-keeping related to development activities. These records assure that insights, experiences, and feelings shared by alumni with academic leaders, and that articulate their frameworks of consciousness, are not lost in times of transition. This information is needed at decision points, such as in navigating a potential donor's various communities of participation. Positive, collaborative relationships with the development staff can assure that knowledge about alumni can benefit the institution in perpetuity (and can be used to create the most satisfying and meaningful experience for the donor).

Actionable Strategies

1. Think about the most generous donor to your unit. Identify all of their communities of participation (Engagement Drivers) within your unit as well as your institution. Ask your development officer to do the same and then compare your lists. Major donors are often connected in more ways than we realize across an entire college

or university. What new insights do you have about the donor's interactions and preferences?

2. Also considering your most generous donor, try to identify the frameworks of consciousness (Emotional Drivers) associated with their giving to your unit and other units. What evidence can you point to that affirms the Emotional Drivers behind their giving? In addition to overarching personal values and beliefs, there may be other influential institutionally-specific factors such as gratitude for a positive student experience, admiration or respect toward you or other leaders, or preserving the legacy and traditions for future generations to experience.

3. Can you identify any informal communities of participation through your unit? For example, are there members of your advisory board who meet as a smaller group on their own initiative, perhaps because they work in the same industry? Or do you know a group of alumni who regularly gather for football tailgates or other university-related events? If you are aware of any such groups, does your development officer know as well? There may be creative ways to engage with these communities. Moreover, evidence of relationships between alumni or other individuals should be recorded in those database files for future reference.

References

Schervish, P. G. (1997). Inclination, obligation, and association: What we know and what we need to learn about donor motivation. In D. F. Burlingame (Ed.), *Critical issues in fundraising* (pp. 110–138). New York: Wiley.

Summer Party Rages On: Cary A Unit Friends Celebrate 45th Annual Reunion. (2018, Fall). *Purdue Alumnus*, pp. 32–33.

CHAPTER 7

Engaging Potential Donors

This chapter builds upon the data, research findings, and donor scenarios presented thus far as foundational to direct engagement with prospective major gift donors. As such, this chapter transitions from much of the "science" of fundraising, and into the "art."

Each person is unique, and how academic leaders and fundraisers engage with potential donors is just as varied as the ways donors respond when solicited for gifts. To navigate this uncertainty, this chapter offers a framework for engaging individuals in fundraising that emphasizes the importance of asking questions. Posing well-conceived questions can yield significant triggers that help donors progress toward positions of readiness to consider giving.

In light of this section's focus on raising major gifts, it is notable that institutions apply their own standards in defining the size of a major gift. It is equally important to remember that this is simply an internal metric. A major gift will most certainly be considered differently by every individual being solicited. An individual with a substantially high net worth, but who is a new philanthropist or has a number of other significant financial commitments, may consider $10,000 to be a major gift. Conversely, a frequent donor who also has considerable wealth may not consider anything less than $1 million as a major gift.

© The Author(s), under exclusive license to Springer Nature
Switzerland AG 2021
A. Conley and G. G. Shaker, *Fundraising Principles for Faculty and Academic Leaders*, Philanthropy and Education,
https://doi.org/10.1007/978-3-030-66429-9_7

For an academic leader, knowing what range of gift request is appropriate requires partnering with development staff. By working together and drawing on information collected during the donor engagement process, academic leaders can approach conversations with confidence knowing that the gift range is realistic and considers the prospective donor's financial capacity and circumstances. As cultivation activity progresses, the range can often be narrowed. There is great variation in the amount of time and cultivation effort needed to make this determination. Navigating this requires sensitivity and adaptation—and can sometimes lead to uncertainty and frustration.

To ease uncertainties, this chapter begins with a review of the stages of the major gift fundraising process. While there is no definitive timeframe for these stages, the discussion and illustrations provide insight into the time investment that may be needed for each stage. Subsequently, the discussion turns to key concepts and strategies for efficient and productive cultivation, leading toward donor readiness for gift solicitation.

THE MAJOR GIFT PROCESS

The process of raising a major gift can be metaphorically described as a journey. There is a starting point and an endpoint with a variety of memorable moments in between. While the endpoint can easily be envisioned with the signing of a gift agreement, the starting point is often less well-defined. The beginning stage can be particularly hard for those who are not directly involved from the start, such as faculty, academic leaders, and even current development staff. Figure 7.1 illustrates a commonly accepted perspective of the formal aspects of this cycle from the development perspective. (The roots of a gift, for the donor, however, may have formed much earlier, as described in the prior chapter.)

A major goal for development programs is the ongoing search for new prospective major gift donors, thus development staff typically manage the identification, research, and qualification stages. These early functions are largely invisible to the rest of the academic enterprise, except when certain faculty, staff, or other individuals outside of development directly assist. For example, a dean's advisory council volunteer may share information regarding a successful business colleague with an interest in a particular school program. In this case, the dean and development officer would coordinate with the volunteer to determine who should engage the colleague and by what method.

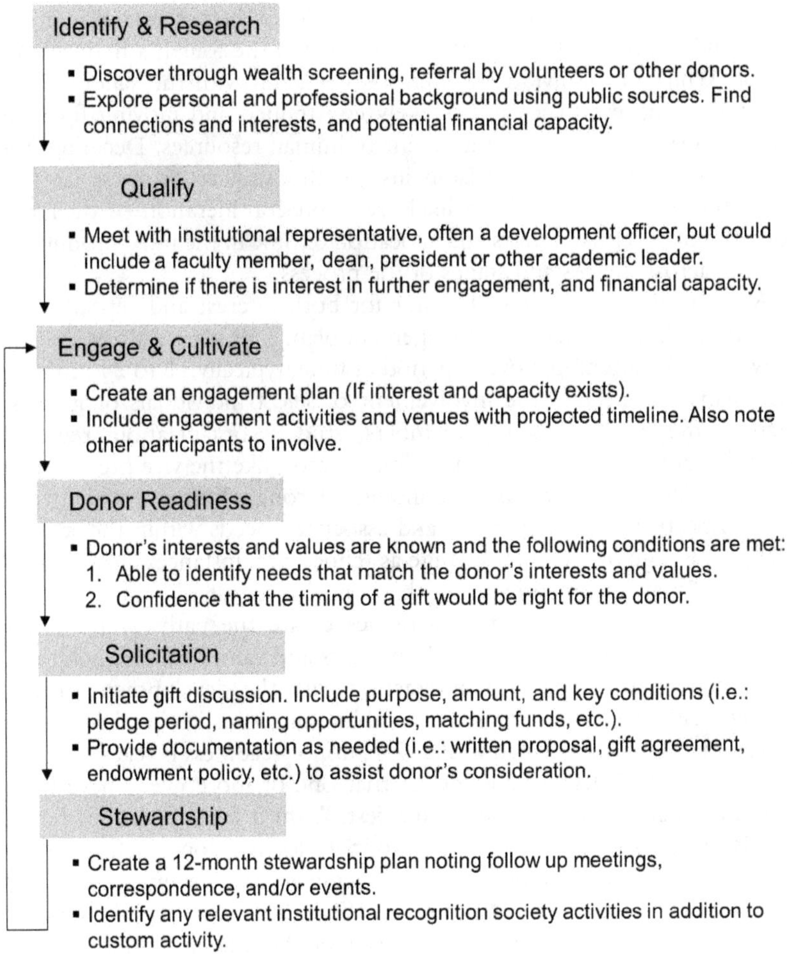

Identify & Research

- Discover through wealth screening, referral by volunteers or other donors.
- Explore personal and professional background using public sources. Find connections and interests, and potential financial capacity.

Qualify

- Meet with institutional representative, often a development officer, but could include a faculty member, dean, president or other academic leader.
- Determine if there is interest in further engagement, and financial capacity.

Engage & Cultivate

- Create an engagement plan (If interest and capacity exists).
- Include engagement activities and venues with projected timeline. Also note other participants to involve.

Donor Readiness

- Donor's interests and values are known and the following conditions are met:
  1. Able to identify needs that match the donor's interests and values.
  2. Confidence that the timing of a gift would be right for the donor.

Solicitation

- Initiate gift discussion. Include purpose, amount, and key conditions (i.e.: pledge period, naming opportunities, matching funds, etc.).
- Provide documentation as needed (i.e.: written proposal, gift agreement, endowment policy, etc.) to assist donor's consideration.

Stewardship

- Create a 12-month stewardship plan noting follow up meetings, correspondence, and/or events.
- Identify any relevant institutional recognition society activities in addition to custom activity.

Fig. 7.1 Stages of prospective donor engagement

It is also important to note that the process of qualifying potential donors for their interest and financial capacity can often result in "disqualifying." Using the previous scenario, the development officer and volunteer could meet with the prospective donor but discover this person is leading a new start-up company and investing most of their personal assets in the endeavor. In addition, they may learn the potential donor has four children, three of whom are in college and the fourth a high school senior. While this individual's interests may align with the school, their capacity to make a major gift is likely constrained and moving forward may not make sense as a commitment of human resources. Deciding not to proceed is a strategic decision just as choosing to progress is. The development officer's decision likely rests on consideration of their full portfolio of potential donors and allocation of time in the most productive manner across donors and stages of the process.

After qualifying a potential donor for both interest and capacity, the gift officer should develop an engagement plan. This plan outlines specific activities to be attempted over a period of time, typically 12 to 24 months. The plan also specifies the involvement of select individuals or groups, such as the dean or faculty members, student organization, regional alumni chapter, or senior campus administrator, like the vice president of research. All activities focus on building a stronger connection between the prospective donor's interests and associated needs within the school. The plan is a guide that may change as school circumstances change or as a result of new information about the donor's interests.

Engagement and cultivation activities create the pathway to donor readiness. At this point the donor's interests and values are clearly known as a result of direct personal interaction with the development officer, faculty, academic leaders, or some combination of institutional representatives. In addition, as noted in Fig. 7.1, donor readiness is reached when there is a high degree of confidence that one or more needs have been identified that match the donor's interest. A third factor in donor readiness is recognizing the timing is appropriate for the donor. This is often overlooked as the pressing needs of a college and its units can easily inhibit practicing empathy at this stage. While there are some dimensions of donor readiness that are certainly out of the academic unit's hands, such as donors' personal financial cycles, academic leaders can progress by using information and systematic approaches in areas they can influence.

First, during initial meetings and subsequent interactions, it is helpful to look for evidence of emotional drivers discussed in Chapter 6. Values and interests are often reflected in conversational statements but these are too often missed. Consider the following sample statements by alumni and the emotions they may be signaling (Table 7.1).

By recognizing that an individual is providing clues about their feelings toward a college, the cultivation process can be considerably advanced.

Table 7.1 Common conversational statements and emotional drivers

Statement	Emotion
"*Professor Smith was so tough on us, but I learned why later. I was so much better prepared in my first job than my colleagues.*"	Gratitude
"*I wasn't a very strong student back then, and I doubt if I'd even get admitted into the school today.*"	Pride
"*I owe so much to this university. I wouldn't be where I am today without my education.*"	Obligation
"*College was the best years of my life.*"	Nostalgia

A deeper discussion can then provide even more insight into how these sentiments may pair up with a particular need. For example, a follow-up to the statement that reveals a sense of obligation might be, "*What is the most rewarding aspect of your professional career?*" The initial comment already reflected positive sentiments about the university, and this kind of follow-up question would likely provide evidence of values and circumstances of importance in their life.

Development officers who are successful relationship-builders may appear to be natural at this type of structured and deliberate conversation, always knowing when to say the right thing or ask the right question. But for many, it is a skill acquired over years of experience. Faculty and academic leaders can become just as effective with practice and intentionality, even if engaging with high net worth individuals is an unnatural occurrence.

To begin, visualize a puzzle in preparation for any development meeting. Most of the pieces contain known facts about the prospective donor. These may include their graduation year and major, giving history, occupation, home address, and family details. But there are always blank pieces, even after multiple meetings and dutiful documentation of those conversations. The key is to think about the necessary information for continued progress toward donor readiness, and then to craft at least three questions that may yield the missing information and continue filling in the pieces.

But asking questions is difficult for many. Brooks and John (2018) acknowledge numerous reasons for this. Some people are egocentric and eager to impress others by talking rather than questioning. Apathy is another reason; some simply don't care to ask. Overconfidence causes others to believe they already know the answer to a question. And fear may hold back people who don't wish to be viewed as either rude or incompetent. But the most common reason "is that most people just don't understand how beneficial good questioning can be. If they did, they would end far fewer sentences with a period–and more with a question mark" (p. 61).

Additionally, studies cited by Huang et al. (2017) note verbal behaviors that focus on the other person, such as mirroring their mannerisms, affirming their statements, and seeking additional information, have been shown to increase likeability. Active listening and achieving likeability helps build rapport and trust, which can enable information-gathering well beyond the initial objectives and expectations.

Developing skills in these areas requires academic leaders to be self-aware and to reflect on their own communicative tendencies. These tendencies can both help and hamper philanthropic conversations, which proceed best when following these principles of quality communication in relationships: affiliation/support, social relaxation, empathy, behavior flexibility/adaptation, and interaction management (Ragsdale citing Wiemann, 1995). To become better development communicators, academic leaders may also draw on research skills, such as qualitative interviewing, which requires a certain set of behaviors and strategies to ascertain meaningful responses leading toward a particular purpose, while also assuring the well-being of the interviewee. Academic administrators can also use their leadership skills, which include creating and navigating strategic conversations to move toward particular goals.

Conversational or behavioral information that helps advance from engagement to cultivation and closer to donor readiness serves as cultivation triggers. Many statements by and observations of donors can provide critical guidance in formulating potential gift solicitations and should always be documented for future reference. For example, a couple might mention that their donation to their young daughter's prep school campaign resulted in their naming of the gymnasium. This trigger reveals not only their financial capacity and generosity, but also a willingness to support large capital projects and amenability to recognition through a prominent naming.

Triggers can also reveal beliefs or preferences that help eliminate potential options from future solicitations. For example, the same couple in the previous scenario may confide that they don't fully understand how endowments work. After some explanation, they question why such a small percentage of the fund is expended annually. They also make some disparaging remarks about multi-billion dollar endowments at elite private universities and public flagship institutions, and the crippling debt most students leave college with today. While this conversation does not preclude the possibility of seeking an endowed gift at some point, these triggers suggest a solicitation for their first major gift be for current use.

When donor readiness is achieved and solicitation is planned, the development office should always be involved. Even if the individual or organization was discovered and cultivated by a lone faculty member without a development officer, there are potentially serious donor issues that can result from a solicitation that lacks institutional review and clearance. This is a standard process, as noted in Chapter 4, as most institutions have formal gift acceptance policies approved by their governing boards.

Institutional development professionals can also provide counsel on asking for the gift. Insightful coaching from a development officer and role-playing are common preparations undertaken by even the most experienced fundraising deans and presidents. This advance work and visualization of how a solicitation may unfold enable preparation for the donor's questions and potential responses.

The act of asking for a major gift epitomizes the art of fundraising on the highest order. Academicians new to fundraising may benefit from applying a familiar science tool to envision how a typical solicitation unfolds. Figure 7.2 illustrates the solicitation bell curve. As this visual suggests, the least amount of time is spent during the opening and

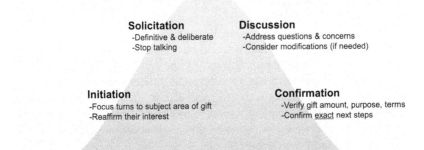

Fig. 7.2 The solicitation bell curve

closing. Initiation serves to focus the conversation on the gift's subject area while also reaffirming that the donor is indeed interested in a deeper discussion on the related institutional need. The solicitation takes place at that point with a definitive delivery of a proposed gift amount for that specific purpose. This is often not the most difficult part of the solicitation. That distinction goes to the duty of the solicitor who must stop talking and allow the donor to respond.

The apex of the bell curve is where the joy of philanthropy often presents itself for both the donor and the solicitor. Some donors may agree without hesitation. Others will respond positively, but with some questions or desire for clarification. There is rarely outright rejection, and if there is, it is most often because of circumstances that could not have been discovered in advance despite the best cultivation and engagement efforts. If there is a rejection, the response is usually not an outright no, rather a "not right now," leaving the door open for revisiting at a later date.

To conclude a successful solicitation, always practice confirmation by verifying central or complex gift terms, along with devising the exact next steps. For example, if a gift officer is with a dean on a solicitation, the dean should verify that the development officer will prepare a gift agreement for the donor's review by a specific date.

Soliciting major gifts can be disconcerting initially, but like all things, experience helps inform how to navigate future instances. Confidence and optimism are a fundraiser's greatest ally, coupled with a constant focus on the donor, as Shaker (2016) observes, "Fundraising requires self-assurance and a certainty of purpose, made strong by the knowledge that donors want to share their resources for worthy causes..." (p. 373).

A solicitation technique that can be especially well-suited for academic leaders is to first ask permission to solicit (Hiles, 2010). This is carried out over two meetings or interactions. At the first, an idea is shared with the donor to determine if they are interested in learning more about how to support it. If the response is affirmative, a specific dollar amount and purpose would be discussed at a second meeting. Between the meetings, a written proposal or other forms of documentation might be provided for their review and consideration.

This technique is especially effective for projects or needs with extended timeframes. For example, a dean who has received board approval for a building renovation could begin speaking immediately with top potential donors possibly interested in supporting the project.

But rather than asking for a naming gift for a prominent space in the facility, the first meeting would be solely to provide information about the board's approval and project timeline, beginning with bids for the architect and construction contractor. Next, the dean and development team would determine the types of spaces available for naming. If the donor had expressed interest in seeing the building plans in the first conversation, permission to ask has been granted and the eventual second meeting creates the opportunity to discuss a specific gift amount and purpose.

The Virtue of Patience

Major gift donors give when the timing is right for them. No matter how compelling the need, or who is soliciting the gift, little can be done to alter this reality. Even for those who are vastly wealthy, there are still times when they may feel uneasy about their finances. This may be during economic downturns or particularly challenging times for their industry or source of wealth. This reality reinforces the dangers of relying on only a few donors and the importance of a healthy pipeline of potential major donors. This subject is addressed in greater detail in the next chapter.

While patience is a virtue in raising major gifts, it should be noted that the impetus for moving a gift forward still rests on the development staff and the academic leader, whether this means engaging in more cultivation activities or following up with a donor at a predetermined time for a solicitation. A study of donors to Northwestern University showed enormous diversity in the investments of time and effort in major donor relationships and variation in time-to-gift by the type of donor (alumni versus nonalumni) and the nature of the gift (outright or estate) (Lindahl & Winship, 1994).

It is not unprecedented for a prospective donor to express interest in a gift during a first meeting. Or they may indicate that the school is in their will for a substantial sum. Or an estate gift may come to an institution with little or no warning. Instances like this are the exception, not the norm. Some donors may be willing to discuss a commitment rather quickly and make their gift within a few months. But, for others, a major gift commitment or multiple commitments may come across a period of decades.

It is better to ground oneself in the reality that donors are not predictable. Following the guidance offered in this or any other book on fundraising does not assure a commitment of a major gift for every solicitation. This includes situations where the alignment of certain donor characteristics is believed to be optimal for fundraising success. Kelly (1998) recognizes this as the magic button theory, which holds that "there is a causal linkage between giving and donor demographics, cogni-tions, and attitudes, if just the right combination can be found" (p. 352). As she notes, this theory is limited in the assumption that potential donors are passive participants in the philanthropic exchange, and that donor characteristics determine behavior.

This maxim of donor unpredictability is based on not just modern experience, but throughout the history of higher education fundraising. An apt example was penned more than a century ago by Booker T. Washington (1900) in his autobiography, *Up from Slavery*. He dedicated an entire chapter to his fundraising experiences in support of the Tuskegee Institute (now Tuskegee University) where he served as founding president. His chronicle of the countless trips to court wealthy benefactors throughout the mid-Atlantic and Northeast includes a particular anec-dote that reinforces unpredictability and the importance of patience in the pursuit of major gifts. While in Connecticut, Washington was informed of an individual living outside Stamford who might be interested in supporting the school:

> On an unusually cold and stormy day I walked the two miles to see him. After some difficulty I succeeded in securing an interview with him. He listened with some degree of interest to what I had to say, but did not give me anything. I could not help having the feeling that, in a measure, the three hours that I had spent in seeing him had been thrown away. Still, I had followed my usual rule of doing my duty. If I had not seen him, I should have felt unhappy over neglect of duty.
>
> Two years after this visit a letter came to Tuskegee from this man, which read like this: "Enclosed I send you a New York draft for ten thousand dollars, to be used in furtherance of your work. I had placed this sum in my will for your school, but deem it wiser to give it to you while I live. I recall with pleasure your visit to me two years ago." (pp. 186–187)

This gift, which would be valued around $300,000 in present dollars, was surely celebrated for its impact on the fledgling institution. But for Washington, it was completely unexpected. The key to this story is fundraising activity must be embraced, as he notes, as "doing my duty." It is unrealistic to expect to secure a gift from every potential donor who meets with a development officer, dean, or institutional representative.

But it is also a certainty that few gifts will ever be raised without the investment of time, effort, and enthusiasm for the cause of advancing knowledge.

CONCLUSION

Engaging potential donors for major gifts can be a mysterious, tiresome, and lonely endeavor. It is also one of the few administrative functions of academic leadership that can bring joy, excitement, and momentum to an academic unit or entire institution. It is possible for raising money to begin as an academic leader's most unfamiliar, intimidating, and dreaded task and to end as among the most satisfying and invigorating of their assignments.

The three chapters of this section provide a base for understanding the giving motives of high net worth individuals and the purposes of foundations' and corporations' giving. Empathy was also emphasized in the context of discerning and attending to donors' cares and concerns rather than making assumptions and soliciting based only on school needs and conditions. These sections showed how information, research, and models from best practice can be used to elevate solicitation approaches into strategic efforts.

The information about the diversity of donor motivations, behaviors, and related fundraising journeys is foundational for the next section and application of operational strategies and tactics to a universe of existing and potential donors. Within this, the focus is on three of the most critical applications for an academic leader: managing a portfolio, creating an annual development plan, and utilizing partners in the development process. Time is possibly the most valuable resource for anyone charged with managing an academic unit. The knowledge and tools in this book will help maximize the impact of time invested in development activities leading to both short- and long-term returns.

ACTIONABLE STRATEGIES

1. Review the giving histories of your unit's five largest donors, even if their earliest gifts occurred before your arrival. Were there a number of small gifts that preceded their first major gift? What was the period of time between their first gift of any amount and their

first major gift? Did they give to multiple units across the institution or just yours? If you can, read the reports of their interactions, including solicitation meetings, and consider how what you read aligns with the models presented in this chapter.

2. Ask some of your institution's most experienced fundraisers how they know when to initiate a gift discussion with a prospective major donor. Have they recognized cultivation triggers and donor readiness in their dealings with major gift donors?

3. Role play or simulate a gift discussion you envision having with a potential major donor to your unit. Partner with someone who knows the individual equally well. Take turns, first as yourself soliciting the gift, and then switching roles. Experiencing the solicitation as the donor may provide insights you were not expecting.

REFERENCES

Brooks, A. W., & John, L. K. (2018, May–June). The surprising power of questions. *Harvard Business Review*, pp. 60–67. Retrieved July 1, 2020, from https://hbr.org/2018/05/the-surprising-power-of-questions.

Hiles, T. S. (2010). Determining the success of fundraising programs. *New Directions for Higher Education; Perspectives on Fundraising, 2010*(149), 51–56.

Huang, K., Yeomans, M., Brooks, A. W., Minson, J., & Gino, F. (2017). It doesn't hurt to ask: Question-asking increases liking. *Journal of Personality and Social Psychology, 113*(3), 430–452.

Kelly, K. S. (1998). *Effective fund-raising management*. New York: Routledge.

Lindahl, W. E., & Winship, C. (1994). A logit model with interactions for predicting major gift donors. *Research in Higher Education, 35*(6), 729–743.

Ragsdale, J. D. (1995). Quality communication in achieving fundraising excellence. In D. A. Brehmer (Ed.), *New Directions for Philanthropic Fundraising, 1995*(10), 17–31.

Shaker, G. G. (2016). Personal solicitation. In E. R. Tempel, T. L. Seiler, & D. F. Burlingame (Eds.), *Achieving excellence in fundraising* (4th ed., pp. 363–374). Hoboken, NJ: Wiley.

Washington, B. T. (1900). *Up from slavery: An autobiography*. Garden City, NY: Doubleday & Company, Inc. Retrieved June 12, 2020, from https://docsouth.unc.edu/fpn/washington/washing.html.

PART III

Operational Strategies and Tactics for the Academic Unit

CHAPTER 8

Narrow Your Universe

This section addresses the strategic areas that are essential for academic leaders' success in development. It applies the information from the book's first two sections in this larger context. The need to master these areas, as explained in the four parts of this chapter, is inescapable regardless of one's leadership role on campus. As one Harvard dean observed, "Fundraising will always be the leitmotif of academic life. Rich or poor, public or private, college or university – there is never enough money to go around" (Rosovsky, 1990, p. 255). Mastering the content of the next three chapters will help make development an enabler for the successful operation of a school, department, or research center.

To begin, development must be viewed from the perspective of time, not dollars. Experienced development professionals know that in raising major gifts, time is their most valuable asset and their scarcest resource. The amount of development time, wisely invested by academic leaders, is often directly proportional to fundraising outcomes. As the famous logging aphorism notes, time spent sharpening an axe may well be spared swinging it. In one survey, public comprehensive university presidents reported spending an average of nearly seven days per month on fundraising duties (Jackson, 2013). Although this may be more than academic leaders at lower levels, the quality of the time always matters just as the quantity does. Thus, academic leaders need to make intentional

© The Author(s), under exclusive license to Springer Nature   113
Switzerland AG 2021
A. Conley and G. G. Shaker, *Fundraising Principles for Faculty and Academic Leaders*, Philanthropy and Education,
https://doi.org/10.1007/978-3-030-66429-9_8

choices to assure that their dedication of precious hours has the desired results. The following sections provide information on allocating development time in a manner that ensures interactions with major donors and other alumni are impactful and lead to continuously stronger fundraising returns.

Finding More Needles in the Haystack

Whether just beginning or advancing deeply into academic leadership experience, it is vital to attend closely to top donors while also expanding the base of potential donors. The improvement of data technologies has made this notably less of a Sisyphean task than previously.

Wealth screening, data mining, predictive modeling, and other informational analyses are now ubiquitous research tools for development offices. A database of hundreds of thousands of alumni and non-alumni individuals can be dissected against an array of variables and indicators that suggest probabilities of giving as well as likely gift amounts. These findings are never infallible and can require complementary qualitative knowledge. However, the insights are valuable enough that most development programs screen their records annually and complete even more frequent analyses for specific projects, initiatives, and campaigns.

Deans and department chairs do not need technical knowledge about these tools. It is critical, however, to recognize the basic premise of these fundraising tools. The outcome of a wealth screening exercise is often organized in a hierarchy or matrix to illustrate which individuals show the most promise. Two criteria are used to make this determination. One is financial capacity or indications of wealth. The other is inclination or affiliation, suggesting the likelihood that a gift will be made.

There are a number of ways to discern wealth and affiliation. Wealth might be discovered through public sources such as home property values and zip codes, filings of stock holdings in publicly-traded companies, political contributions, and published accounts of gifts to other nonprofit organizations (Filla & Brown, 2013). Affinity can be determined using an institution's records. Evidence of past giving is the first and most obvious clue, and there may be additional data including attendance at alumni functions, musical and theater performances, and sporting events. Service on an academic advisory board, regional alumni chapter, or other volunteer involvements can also be telling.

Again, reports from wealth screenings and similar data analyses provide no guarantee of a gift, or even a meeting with a newly-discovered prospective donor. Instead, they organize substantial numbers of donor records into a workable dataset that can be further investigated and parsed out to specific development staff to make contact. Academic leaders will then meet with the most promising prospective donors and help discover alignment between donor interests and academic priorities.

A chart based on the capacity and inclination matrix is offered in the next section for those leaders without development staff to organize the efforts. The matrix may also be helpful as a discussion tool with development staff or for mapping the allocation of an academic leader's time and assuring a focus on top potential donors.

Another tool for academic leaders is the application of research about high net worth individuals; development officers can use this information to help prioritize academic leaders' involvement in fundraising. As noted, the science of philanthropy is advancing rapidly and utilizing research findings for managing portfolios of donors can generate substantial returns. The proliferation of academic degree programs in philanthropic studies and nonprofit management is also preparing fundraisers who are versed in the science of fundraising just as much as the art of the craft, and who are prepared to use and test that knowledge.

For example, academic leaders often disregard planned giving out of concern for their school or program's immediate needs. But what if chances of securing planned gifts in large numbers, and bigger dollar amounts, could be improved through a narrowed focus on a smaller segment of potential donors?

In a case study of several US universities, the Indiana University Lilly Family School of Philanthropy (2016) reviewed donor data from approximately 9,700 planned gifts. About 73% of the donors were alumni of the case study institutions. One of the most important findings was the differing sizes of gifts from donors with children versus those without. Evidence came from two institutions with a substantial number of planned gifts (264 donors with children and 268 donors without children). Planned gift donors with children gave a median amount of $580,844 and average of $114,159. Donors without children gave a median of $1,242,120 and average of $313,578.

Research like this suggests that although donors with and without children both make planned gifts, academic leaders (and development staff) may want to be especially mindful when discovering alumni couples in their 50s or 60s, or older, who do not have children. In addition, they may also want to think creatively with their development teams to explore strategies for blended gifts, whereby a donor combines an immediate gift with a planned gift—aiding academic units with short- and long-term priorities.

Applied research findings are also awaiting discovery within most institutions' own donor populations. High-performing fundraising programs regularly research their own donors' patterns, characteristics, and behaviors to better inform deployment of development resources. This practice can also help inform how, when, and where to utilize academic leaders for individual-focused activities, as well as with particular constituent groups.

Building and Managing a Portfolio

Development staff or teams guide academic leaders' time prioritization for planning activities and donor relationship building. Prioritizing those who show the most promise for major giving can be challenging for long-serving leaders who have interacted with a large universe of alumni and other supporters. Newly appointed leaders can face similar time management issues, but for different reasons; knowing where to begin a development agenda within the alumni universe can be daunting.

These instances can be addressed with a donor management matrix. Illustrated in Fig. 8.1, this visual tool is often used to organize the

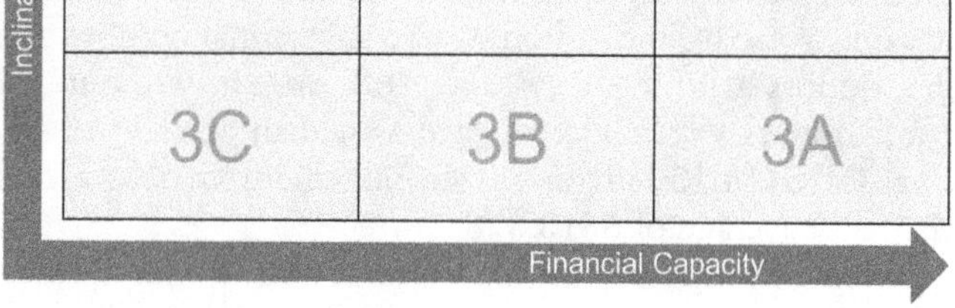

Fig. 8.1 Donor management matrix

outcomes and recommendations of wealth screenings. But it can also help organize an academic unit's top 25–50 (or more) potential donors who require cultivation effort to progress toward donor readiness.

To construct and manage an individual portfolio or a unit's most promising gift constituency using this tool, start by entering the names in the 1A box of the biggest existing donors. Then exclude any donors who are not expected to make any future major gifts (Removing them from this matrix does not exclude them from proper stewardship and donor recognition, just from this management tool.). Next, include any wealthy non-donors who have been qualified by development staff as having interest in the school along with the evidence of their wealth. Without firsthand knowledge of affinity or interest, place them in 2A or 3A. Through these simple acts the matrix has already become a management tool. It is a visual reminder to develop strategies for building affinity that will enable individuals to be resorted into the 1A box as the relationships grow stronger. Although the tool itself is simple, it also should be remembered that the individuals themselves are complex and multifaceted, making matrix "assignments" a qualitative and sensitive process.

To use the matrix in another way, recall the fictional alumni couple that illustrated the identification model in Chapter 6. The information about them included some indication of financial capacity through consistent, but relatively small, annual gifts. With no other information, they would be considered a "C" on the matrix for low financial capacity. But their affinity could arguably be rated as a "1" given his volunteer service and distinguished alumni award, in addition to their alumni association life membership, longtime basketball season tickets, and daughter's alumni status.

Research or engagement activity with this couple should then focus on discovering evidence of financial capacity to warrant moving them into 1B or 1A. If evidence is ascertained, then greater attention from a dean, other unit leaders, or specific faculty members could be justified.

This alumni donor couple also raises a common portfolio management dilemma regarding the many wonderfully passionate alumni gift officers and academic leaders encounter. Assigning people who are delightful in their devoted love of alma mater to 1C and 2C is easy. But if they truly have no near-term potential for a major gift or planned gift, then time spent can come at the expense of time needed with 3A and 2A potential donors with much greater financial capacity. This is not to imply that these constituents are unimportant. But they need to be engaged in ways that do not monopolize an institution's most senior academic leaders and gift officers. Events, volunteer activities, and individual engagement with junior development and alumni staff can provide effective alternatives.

While this discussion may seem superfluous, this type of imbalance occurs frequently and is revealed through wealth screenings or careful discussion of a matrix/portfolio of donors. All too often, development officer activity shows far greater activity with low-gift potential, but highly involved alumni, and incredibly, little to no activity with substantial numbers of the highest-rated potential donors.

Deans and department chairs can be equally prone to over-engaging with friendly and well-known faces, even though portfolio management responsibilities differ from gift officers. This also happens in the context of longtime donors with great wealth who have become opinionated, acerbic, or prone to criticizing a president, trustee, athletic director, or other institutional figure. Taking this path of least resistance can come as a relief personally, but avoiding difficult donors may also come at a substantial cost professionally.

Strategies for Meaningful Engagement

It is one thing to commit to diligently focusing on the most promising major gift prospects. It is quite another to focus the necessary effort to design potential strategies to initiate, and then build, successive steps that will potentially lead to donor readiness.

Building engagement strategies around the donor matrix is good practice, but only if it is applied consistently. Setting a designated period, such as every several months, to add and remove names as well as shift names to different boxes based on new information or insights will provide structure and discipline to realize the value of the tool. It is all too easy for six weeks to turn into six months of inactivity with promising donors. If even greater time passes, donors can interpret inattention as disinterest, increasing the risk of losing them to another organization or cause. The 2018 U.S. Trust study noted that high net worth donors gave annually to an average of seven organizations (Bank of America, 2018), so this risk is very real.

After committing to using the matrix or some tool to prioritize development time, next comes the creative process of thinking through the complexities of each individual and how to act on their motives for giving.

The fictional alumni couple again provides a useful scenario to consider that reinforces the importance of developing meaningful engagement strategies driven by more than institutional needs.

At a recent event for basketball season ticket holders, the couple spent time speaking with an athletics development officer who they met at a recent game. She made a point of asking about their daughter, who she had not met but knew was a 1993 alumna and volleyball team captain. They boasted as proud parents that her marketing agency, which she started less than five years ago, just hired their 100th employee and landed another Fortune 500 client. They also shared disappointment that visits home are relatively rare because of her career demands and the company's location on the other coast.

The athletics gift officer spoke the next day with her counterpart in the business school. The daughter had earned her degree in marketing, and there were several contact reports in her record noting attempts by the business school to meet with her, all with no success. The gift officers collaborated on an initial engagement strategy. They asked the parents if they would convey a request to their daughter to meet with the two development officers on an upcoming trip to the coast. The plan worked.

The meeting was a great success. The alumna had simply been overwhelmed building her business, traveling the world, and raising a young family to meet previously or to return to campus for athletics or business alumni events. She shared wonderful memories of her volleyball teammates and coaches, and pointed to a marketing professor who was directly responsible for inspiring her career path. She acknowledged being ready to get involved in some volunteer activities, and her alma mater was among her key interests.

This scenario aptly illustrates the importance of the process of engagement strategy for potential major gift donors. The effort opened the door to build an institutional relationship with the alumna, but to also deepen the relationship with her parents. And recall that the parents' high level of affinity for the school was known but their capacity for a gift was unknown. Engaging their daughter could provide new insight as well.

As noted in the previous chapter, qualification activities like this are largely invisible to most faculty and academic administrators. However, the qualifying visit with the daughter confirmed both affinity and gift capacity. Thus, this 1A potential donor will come to the attention of many at alma mater including marketing faculty members and the department chair, the business school dean, and athletics personnel. This scenario, which will continue in Chapter 10, starts in this way to illuminate the major gift process (as depicted in Fig. 7.1) and reinforce to academicians that donors are often discovered through a combination of gift officer initiative and collaboration. The next stages focus on the involvement of partners in the development process, such as deans and professors, students, advisory board members, and others. These individuals can be vital in executing engagement activities built on the emotional elements of the identification model.

Reaching an Alumni Population at Large

This chapter closes with a brief treatment on engaging an alumni population, especially at the school and department level. This topic, like many others in this book, justifies far greater attention than can be provided here. A significant number of research studies explore the various levels of alumni institutional engagement and its outcomes on their philanthropy (Proper & Caboni, 2014). For this chapter's purposes, the focus remains on maximizing academic leaders' time and effort to achieve the greatest philanthropic potential.

To reinforce again, the sustained decline in alumni giving participation should eliminate any expectation that all—or most—alumni will give. One dean even advocates viewing alumni relations entirely separate from fundraising. "Good alumni relations should be an end in itself, and not just because you hope it will bring in money" (Perlmutter, 2020).

This perspective should also be coupled with awareness that not all alumni want to engage, reconnect, or utilize any university service or activity. For those who are new to alumni relations, consider this constituency along a spectrum of three core identities.

The most favorable identity is held by those alumni who are emotionally bonded with their alma mater, regardless of active engagement or even setting foot on campus since graduation. They have an endearing love and affection, strengthened by the passage of time and will likely respond positively to potentially any form of request for alumni service.

The second identity is held by alumni who are passively disconnected. For them, college was an experience, neither overly good nor bad. They may engage sporadically as volunteers or donors (or both) if presented with the right opportunities at the right times.

The third alumni identity is held by those who are intentionally disengaged. Their college experience may have been financially or personally burdensome, or just unfulfilling. Experiences later in life may have also contributed to a cynical or hostile reaction to notions of "giving back" to alma mater, or charitable organizations in general.

The focus for an academic unit's alumni engagement activities should be, logically, on those alumni in the first and second groups. Alumni in the first include the greatest current and future donors, as well as volunteers, advocates, and influencers. And it is with this group that an academic leader should invest the majority of the available development time. For example, while traveling to an academic conference in a city with a number of involved alumni, consider arranging an informal gathering. It could be an intimate networking reception with just 10 to 15 alumni. The development office can help create a list of potential invitees by searching area alumni by job title, annual giving participation, alumni association membership, and other positive indicators. While this is not a fundraising activity per se, it will likely be remembered the next time these alumni receive a solicitation for an annual gift. And it can serve as an effective discovery tool for alumni with major gift potential.

The second group of alumni shows signs of interest through modest or occasional giving participation, event attendance, and a willingness to meet or volunteer. Selective activities directed toward this group over time will result in a pipeline of alumni who elevate into the first group. However, the amount of time the academic leader commits to this group should be limited. Development and alumni staff are responsible for the bulk of the contacts, and an institution's alumni association or central alumni office creates most of the engagement opportunities rather than the academic unit.

For the disengaged alumni in the third group, time may be selectively allocated, perhaps through simple inclusion in alumni invitations and communications. Significant and specialized efforts should be reserved for the first and second groups, in that order, where the returns will be far greater.

Annual giving activities directed at alumni as a whole can also take on a nearly infinite variety of approaches. However, it is advisable to consider offering at least some targeted giving options that align with the identification model and appeal to an emotional connection or type of personal interest. For example, giving opportunities can be provided to support particular departments, scholarships for various types of students, and special initiatives. When donors support specific efforts even with small gifts they provide information about what they care about, which is invaluable if the relationship deepens.

One particularly effective model for building on alumni interests and welcoming various giving capacities is the use of giving circles. As the name implies, this fundraising effort is built either around individual identities (i.e., giving circles for female, LGBTQ, or African American alumni) or around focused causes. In both cases the circles can be supported by donors who share an interconnected sense of urgency for that purpose or set of experiences. Efforts at Alma College, a private liberal arts college in central Michigan, provide an illustrative example of this alumni giving strategy.

Alumni, parents, and friends of Alma with interests in particular areas have banded together over the last few years to support specific causes and programs and meet fundraising goals. Projects have included enhancing the Model United Nations program, aiding musical groups including choir and the band and percussion ensemble, and renovating an athletics facility (Alma College, n.d.). Each effort hinges on a giving circle with a volunteer leadership structure including a chair or co-chairs and a small steering committee of alumni donors. Donors to the circles then receive votes, proportional to their contributions, regarding the specific distribution of the funds. These efforts have generated hundreds of thousands of dollars for the college and for areas which may not have otherwise received the support necessary for making significant changes in a short amount of time (Alma College, 2018). The circles have engaged new donors and existing donors in new ways, and have helped Alma's annual giving program set fundraising records. Such efforts could be undertaken at the unit level as well as institutionally.

In closing, stewardship of alumni donors who make small gifts to academic units is often viewed as a task best delegated to development teams or institutional stewardship structures. This is appropriate but a minimal and directed investment in time by a dean or department chair could generate consistently higher levels of giving and identify potential first-time major gift donors.

Annual giving programs commonly use gifts of $1,000 and above as a benchmark for tracking. The number of alumni donors who give at this level for the first time, as well as those who upgrade their giving to this threshold, is important to follow as evidence suggests this alumni donor population is diverging from the larger trend of declining participation.

Table 8.1 Retention rates of alumni donors (Blackbaud, 2018)

	> $1,000 donors (%)	< $1,000 donors (%)	First-time donors (%)
Private institutions			
2018	79.6	64.1	25.8
2017	80.5	66.1	28.1
2016	80.7	65.9	27.5
2015	81.4	66.0	27.6
2014	81.6	67.2	27.0
Public institutions			
2018	74.4	55.9	23.0
2017	75.4	56.0	24.0
2016	74.5	55.9	23.3
2015	75.0	55.9	24.2
2014	75.2	55.9	23.4

In their study of alumni giving, Blackbaud (2018) noted that public and private institutions experienced a five-year high in the median percentage of alumni donors giving $1,000 or more. The figure at privates grew from 12.3% in 2014 to 14% in 2018, and publics increased from 8.4 to 10.6%. In addition, the study also documented the retention rate of these donors compared to those who gave less than $1,000 as well as those who were first-time donors at any level (see Table 8.1).

Remarkably, 75 to 80% of alumni at the institutions gave at least $1,000 again the next year. This compares to about half to two-thirds of alumni who gave less than this amount, and roughly a quarter of alumni who gave for the first time. These figures suggest that careful stewardship by a dean or department chair for alumni donors supporting their unit at $1,000 and above is a worthwhile investment likely to be recognized in continued giving. Simple gestures like a brief email, personal notecard, or phone call take little time but could be welcomed by a donor. These could also be a cultivation trigger that helps lead to a deeper discussion about supporting the school in a larger way.

Conclusion

One of the greatest challenges and joys of development is building a pipeline of supporters at levels significant enough to confidently plan for the future. Private support is increasingly the deciding factor in whether schools and colleges innovate and thrive, or simply survive with the status quo. Building and managing this pipeline is a process that was once relegated exclusively to gift officers, but with the proper tools and discipline, any academic leader can become a partner and savvy development manager, to the benefit of their unit and their institution.

Some benefits of these partnerships can be immediate through securing more support to meet current needs. The greater benefit, however, is in strengthening and standardizing an academic unit's development process. Fundraising's importance and potential are directly affirmed when academic leaders attend to and track relationship-building activities with top donors and prospective donors. This motivates development staff and leads to fundraising successes—which in turn generate more activity and more positive outcomes.

Prioritizing activities that narrow the focus to the most promising supporters must also be part of the academic leader's management charge. The examples provided here are a starting point and impetus to draw on the creativity and expertise of professional staff in alumni relations, stewardship, communications, prospect research, and others to help translate the leader's vision and priorities into actionable tactics.

ACTIONABLE STRATEGIES

1. If you are newly-appointed in your role, determine the 25 largest donors to your unit. Draft a letter to this group thanking them for their support, and indicating you will be contacting them in the coming months to visit by phone or in person. Use the 25-5-1 Rule to complete this task by contacting all 25 over the course of 5 weeks, which equals just 1 contact per day.

2. Ask your development office to conduct a wealth screening of your unit or to provide findings from the most recent screening. Many of the names in the top category will be known to you; however, there are nearly always new discoveries of highly promising prospects. Using the donor management matrix, prioritize these new individuals in the grid with specific outreach strategies for all those in the 1A category. Do the same for 1B and 2A. Work with your development staff to determine who should make the first contact.

3. Review a list of alumni of your school or department who have been donors (at any level) for the past three consecutive years. These gifts may be designated to any program at your institution. Organize the

list by zip code to identify the one city/region beyond your institutional home that has the largest concentration of these alumni donors. Work with development staff and your faculty leaders to strategize engagement with these alumni. Remember to collaborate with your institution's alumni office if any specific plans are developed.

REFERENCES

Alma College. (2018, September 4). *2017–18: A top 3 year for private support*. Retrieved August 29, 2020, from https://www.alma.edu/live/news/1798-2017-18-a-top-3-year-for-private-support.

Alma College. (n.d.). *Giving circles*. Retrieved July 12, 2020, from https://www.alma.edu/giving/ways-to-give/giving-circles/.

Bank of America. (2018). *The 2018 U.S. Trust study of high net worth philanthropy*. Retrieved May 14, 2020, from https://scholarworks.iupui.edu/han dle/1805/17667.

Blackbaud. (2018). *2017 donorCentics annual report on higher education giving*. Retrieved June 23 2020, from https://www.blackbaud.com/industry-ins ights/resources?&pager=5.

Filla, J. J., & Brown, H. E. (2013). *Prospect research for fundraisers: The essential handbook*. Hoboken, NJ: Wiley.

Indiana University Lilly Family School of Philanthropy. (2016). *The 2016 planned giving study*. Retrieved May 29, 2020, from https://scholarworks.iupui.edu/handle/1805/11006.

Jackson, R. L. (2013). The prioritization of and time spent on fundraising duties by public comprehensive university presidents. *International Journal of Leadership and Change, 1*(1), 47–51.

Perlmutter, D. D. (2020, February 7). Admin 101: What to know about alumni relations. *The Chronicle of Higher Education*. Retrieved August 29, 2020, from https://community.chronicle.com/news/2303-admin-101-what-to-know-about-alumni-relations.

Proper, E., & Caboni, T. C. (2014). *Institutional advancement: What we know*. New York: Palgrave Macmillan.

Rosovsky, H. (1990). *The university: An owner's manual*. New York: W. W. Norton.

CHAPTER 9

The Annual Development Plan

Faculty members serving as department chairs, deans, or other leadership positions have likely experienced a variety of academic planning exercises and activities. These may range from providing input on departmental teaching requirements to participating in extensive strategic planning for an entire school or university.

Shifting into an academic leadership role brings into focus the importance of planning in order to manage an academic unit. The complexities often include planning for budgets, enrollment, faculty hires, and facilities. They also include development, but too often this is excluded from planning processes.

Effective planning for development is not limited to simply reviewing how much was raised last year and then setting a goal of raising a fixed percentage more next year. The total dollars raised by a school, center, or unit in a given year is typically dependent on a very small number of large gifts. These gifts also usually come from those top potential donors who have been qualified, are actively managed, and have documented engagement plans that are followed and modified as needed. The absence of these well-developed individual plans and coordinated activities makes the creation of an effective and accurate annual development plan extremely challenging.

© The Author(s), under exclusive license to Springer Nature   127
Switzerland AG 2021
A. Conley and G. G. Shaker, *Fundraising Principles for Faculty and Academic Leaders*, Philanthropy and Education,
https://doi.org/10.1007/978-3-030-66429-9_9

Attention to these "plans within the plan" is but one factor that shows that development planning is a qualitative effort as well as a quantitative one. Joyaux (2011) notes some of the most critical elements of a plan are not about money but about achieving three broader goals. These include professionalizing the process of fundraising within the institution, assuring quality information to support strategic conversations and decision-making, and improving board support for fund development activity.

This chapter provides general guidance and does not identify a single annual plan format as an industry standard or best practice. Institutions approach annual planning and goal-setting processes differently, making a one-size-fits-all approach impractical. Gaining a better understanding of the core elements of a sound development plan, however, can facilitate more productive coordination between academic leaders and development teams, fostering the partnership necessary for long-term fundraising success.

Setting Priorities

Every academic leader has a list of unit needs, which is often reinforced by faculty, students, and staff. In addition, a set of strategic priorities has likely been identified over a longer term. Some of these priorities may substantially enhance aspects of the unit, while others may be completely transformational. Regardless of the scope of possible impact, considering immediate needs and long-term priorities is the first consideration in building an effective annual development plan to address both domains.

Once priorities are identified and connected with fundraising, the planning process can be used to create a formal linkage between an academic leader's agenda and the activities of development staff. This applies whether there is a dedicated unit development team or central development staff supporting the academic program. In either case, choices must be made about the dedication of time, energy, and resources. Making these decisions in a strategic and aligned manner can lead to better outcomes and more confidence as development staff plan their own activities.

Frontline fundraisers, those who interact directly with donors, are evaluated using a range of metrics often based on face-to-face visits with potential donors, proposals submitted, and an overall dollar goal. Wherever possible, these metrics should reflect activity dedicated to supporting the fundraising efforts of core priorities, and not just basic numbers to achieve by year-end. Greater collaboration in the planning process between development and academic leadership can help give needed meaning and context to fundraiser expectations.

In those cases where there is a strategic plan, fundraising priorities should always be associated with the plan's objectives. In the absence of a strategic plan, the same principle applies–focus fundraising activities on those major priorities that require outside funding. And it is important to remember that major priorities are achieved through major gifts, not through annual gift mailings, day of giving exercises, or the latest crowdfunding vehicle. Gifts from these sources are indeed important, but setting goals for them as part of the planning process is secondary to the effort needed for projecting potential major gifts and the specific actions needed to raise them. Annual giving-focused efforts require close attention, but this is typically the purview of the development staff. The academic leader can reserve their time for the more foundational elements of the planning process.

CORE COMPONENTS OF THE PLAN

After implementing any type of plan, the outcomes may accurately align with what was envisioned or may not be as predicted due to unforeseen events, poor execution, or countless other variables. This is especially true in major gift fundraising. Individuals change their minds, companies have unexpected downturns, and foundations can take new directions.

The true value of a plan, then, may rest in the process of conceiving it rather than the actual plan itself. As General Dwight D. Eisenhower observed from his Army experience, "Plans are worthless, but planning is everything" (Dwight D. Eisenhower Presidential Library, n.d.). It is, therefore, valuable for academic leaders to be involved with planning and, to a lesser degree, implementation, except in their own activities. They also need to attend to evaluation and adaptation. Keeping with the focus on brevity and high-level planning, three critical components are central to the creation of an annual development plan.

Data Review

Just as a school or department would not make significant structural changes to a degree program without reviewing enrollment and other data, plans guiding development should be informed by financial and donor data. In cooperation with the central development office or foundation, academic leaders should have access to current and historic data about the amount of private support the unit receives and the purposes and sources of that support.

Informed projections of future outcomes can be made using the historical giving data. Adaptations can be made to recognize investments of additional effort in selected areas. For example, a newly appointed dean of a law school in a large urban setting learns of the lack of giving from area law firms and considers directing more development efforts in this area. Before reassigning gift officers away from their existing portfolios or creating a new corporate relations position, the dean should first review past giving data. This data should include not just total giving by local law firms, but also gift ranges, recency, and frequency of giving. In addition, the school should assess how many of their alumni work in the major firms, and at what levels—with particular attention on senior partners. This information is essential for determining whether the development plan should prioritize this donor group.

Giving data can also be parsed in several ways for planning purposes. It is beneficial, for example to understand the number and dollar totals of gifts made by alumni in comparison with others such as parents, faculty and staff, and community members. Reviewing the total number and dollar amounts of contributions across different dollar thresholds or "bands" is helpful as well. Some units lacking a significant giving tradition may simply look at major gifts below and above one amount, such as $10,000 or $25,000. Those with a more established donor base and fundraising program may segment gifts received into five or more specific bands ranging at the low end from $25,000 to $50,000 and at the high end between $1 million and $5 million.

Utilizing giving data can significantly help in setting challenging, but realistic goals. For example, a unit receiving only two gifts of $1 million over the past five years would be (very) ambitious in intending to meet a dollar goal of $10 million for the coming year. Such a goal would likely require not only one or more gifts of $1 million or above, but also a considerable number of gifts in other bands, such as $500,000 to $999,999 and $100,000 to $499,999. It would be realistic to set such a goal only if aligned with close assessment of the readiness of specific donors and in consideration of the donor matrix discussed in Chapter 8. Moreover, such a goal would likely require evaluating more than enough donors as being ready to give in the proposed time period, since unforeseen events will almost always prevent some gifts from coming to fruition.

A data-driven approach should be employed in goal-setting for gifts at smaller levels as well. For example, if the law school dean noted earlier is seeking $75,000 in annual unrestricted gifts to the Dean's Excellence Fund in order to enhance ongoing efforts to support pro bono services for small nonprofit organizations, past giving data can be used to determine feasibility. Ideally, a review of the past 10 years of gifts to this fund would allow for the calculation of compound annual growth rates in total donors and total dollars raised. This data would then support the construction of specific strategies and tactics to consider what an appropriate funding goal is within the school's development plan. Notably, if $75,000 is deemed an unfeasible one-year goal, perhaps it can become a multi-year goal with increased attention and incremental measures.

Priority Horizon

The second component in the development plan is referred to as a priority horizon, since it lists immediate priorities and identifies anticipated emphases for the near-future. Even though an annual development plan focuses on a 12-month period, it is helpful to also document priorities that are expected or that span multiple years. These are most readily identified by the unit's leader, however, an inclusive process that engages faculty and staff—including development—creates broader ownership of a plan and more vested participants in its success.

There are several reasons that a priority horizon is useful. First, a unit's strategic plan is likely to span years and may be phased in its implementation. It is useful to keep these nuances at the forefront in annual development planning by allowing space for a horizon that attends to a longer time period. Second, as noted in the prior section, some fundraising priority areas or goals may not be achievable or attainable within a single year, but may be extremely important to build toward. Third, a review of a unit's donor matrix or portfolio may show important potential donors to engage in the coming year, but who are unlikely to make a major gift because the timing is not conducive to their personal or professional circumstances. Identifying ongoing giving priorities or new ones that may come along within 18 to 24 months helps gift officers maintain interest and engagement to continue moving toward donor readiness. This approach also can ensure a steady volume of major gift proposals and closures over extended periods of time. Continuity of major gift activity is among the most defining characteristics of a high-performing development program.

Priority Prospects

The third and most important component of the planning process is documenting the top prospective donors who are expected to reach donor readiness in the coming year, meaning substantive gift discussions will take place. These can be individuals, corporations, and foundations, and are nearly always well known, qualified prospective donors with a history of recent engagement. There is always the possibility of unexpected windfalls from bequests or newly-discovered donors who are engaged quickly and make major gifts within a single year. But a sound plan is not overly reliant on large numbers of these unanticipated gifts.

Plans should take care to document activities and efforts that are needed from academic leaders and others. Gift officers do not (and should not) work entirely in isolation, and there are moments where the involvement of a specific academician or senior administrator is essential. This creates shared accountability in achieving the plan and when assessing performance at the end of the year, but attention to this is all too often omitted from annual development planning processes and the plans themselves. Attending to academic leaders' roles in some detail will also effectively counter any perception that academic leaders are primarily "closers." Priority prospects represent the very top donors an academic unit is depending on to support their greatest needs and opportunities. Reaching donor readiness is highly unrealistic without some ongoing interaction with the academic leader.

Lastly, the projected gifts from this exclusive donor population should represent a substantial proportion of the overall total dollar goal for the unit, as stated in the final development plan. There is no established industry standard or best practice given the vast variation in gift capacity from one academic unit to the next. For some it may be more than 50%, while others could see priority prospects provide 75% or more of all gifts in a given year. A unit could determine this historical percentage based on past years of giving and then benchmark to inform future predictions.

Other Considerations

Many other components could be included in a development plan—such as detailed calendars for the year including communications activities. Some components may be formally incorporated within the plan while others should at least be discussed as part of the process. This section concludes with two of the most important for consideration.

The first is acknowledgment of the mechanisms for assessing the plan along the way. A plan that is set aside until the end of the year is a wasted effort. Since the academic leader and development staff are accountable for specific plan actions, ongoing assessment of the status of key priorities is imperative as is the ability to make related adjustments. These reviews could be completed monthly or quarterly as part of a standing meeting, or even more frequently and informally. Some deans and development directors use time while traveling together to share important updates and do additional planning. The important point here is talk about the plan rather than waiting until the end of the year to make a summative assessment of the plan's success or failure.

The second component to consider including is an accounting of the development activities at the unit level that are planned for the year. As noted in the definition of development in Chapter 1, the programs and activities directed by development offices, alumni associations, and other external-facing units are not all conducted explicitly for fundraising purposes, but they can help influence a potential donor's thinking when they are solicited for a gift. Those activities to highlight in a plan could include dates of advisory council meetings or other key volunteer activities in which priority donors may participate. Also, standing events like homecoming and class reunions, a distinguished alumni award ceremony, special guest lectures, end-of-year celebrations, and regional alumni events are appropriate to identify because of their influence on the plan's deployment. A caveat is that such listings can become unwieldly and should be limited to those with true potential value and impact on the unit's development program.

Celebrating Success, Learning from Mistakes

Just as a plan that is relegated to the shelf is a useless plan, one that is successful but not celebrated is a missed opportunity. Unit level fundraising can be aided considerably over time if accomplishments are regularly recognized and celebrated. This is particularly helpful to build a stronger internal culture of philanthropy (Worth, 2015). Evidence that donors believe in the mission and are giving to support it can lead to feelings of momentum and pride among faculty and staff, as well as externally among donors and other constituents. Knowing that philanthropy is truly assisting in accomplishing core objectives and goals can be both an inspiration and a confidence-builder.

There are almost always positive outcomes of development activities that should be celebrated, even in cases where the total dollar goal for the year was not met. This is one reason it is recommended to incorporate more than just a dollar goal in an annual plan. Signs of positive progress can include growth in the total number of gifts, or the number of gifts specifically from alumni or faculty and staff. Increases in donor retention may suggest positive results from new stewardship activities implemented a year or two prior. And a record number of new endowed scholarships may reveal an opportunity to leverage this momentum with a future scholarship campaign. Raising major gifts is challenging work that does not often yield immediate gratification. Academic leaders should closely review a diverse set of giving data at year-end and acknowledge all areas of success in order to continue building further momentum.

Year-end assessments are also opportunities to review where results fell short of the goal. Science has greatly informed the art of fundraising, but it is far from an exact science and certainly never will be. Missteps and mistakes happen and efforts that seemed destined to succeed sometimes fall short. Development staff and teams that are fearful of ever making mistakes will likely generate nothing more than consistent but modest returns.

Conversely, those who work with academic leaders who value creativity, innovation, and risk-taking are empowered to pursue new ideas and opportunities that may generate exponential returns. The conditions for this environment can also be supported by the senior development managers who supervise gift officers. Organizational behavior studies extol the virtues of workplace environments that embrace the value of learning from mistakes (Harteis, Bauer, & Gruber, 2008; Weinzimmer & Esken, 2017). These environments require senior managers who can view a mistake or misjudgment as a learning opportunity. Referred to as failure-tolerant leaders, they are defined as those who, "through their words and actions, help people overcome their fear of failure and, in the process, create a culture of intelligent risk taking that leads to sustained innovation" (Farson & Keyes, 2002, para. 5).

Accountability, of course, must still exist in the management of the academic enterprise. But leaders who use their annual development plan to try new ideas and objectively evaluate their impact will be rewarded through the creativity and commitment of development staff who feel more empowered and inspired to succeed.

CONCLUSION

Strategically engaging potential major gift donors and recognizing the importance of infusing development planning with consideration of those strategies are integrated efforts—and important ones for academic leaders of all experience levels. This and the prior chapter addressed these topics in relation to a relatively short-term time horizon, but the lasting impact of the work can be truly transformational for an academic unit in the longer term.

In the near term, maintaining the status quo may be relatively easy for those schools, departments, and units that feel financially secure and have not attempted a formal and structured approach to development. It is indeed difficult to miss what one has never had. However, this perspective ignores the ongoing trend of fundraising becoming an increasingly greater priority for deans and other academic unit leaders (Masterson, 2011; Mercer, 1997). It also ignores the current environment for higher education that suggests a sustained and thoughtful fundraising program (and the formation or growth of philanthropic assets) may be more important than ever (Lambert, 2019).

Taking the initiative to get serious about fundraising can start by embracing the process outlined in this chapter for creating a development plan. As one newly appointed dean revealed what they wished they knew prior to the appointment: "Training in how to create a development plan would expose future deans to the fund-raising process as well as help to generate early cooperative energy among chairs, deans, institutional-advancement staff members, and foundations" (Scriven, 2019, para. 18). This observation accurately reflects the integrated nature of development across an entire campus, and the momentum that can be generated by the cooperative energy of all the partners.

ACTIONABLE STRATEGIES

1. If you have a development director, review the core components of an annual plan advocated in this chapter. Discuss how your planning process is similar to or different from this model. What can be adopted, adapted, or considered for your unit and constituency based on this model?
2. If you don't have a development director, take stock of all of your resources related to development, review your overall priorities for the unit, and map out a plan that prioritizes engaging those key current and potential donors identified in the matrix tool provided in the previous chapter.
3. Determine which of the development plan metrics your unit is not tracking. Coordinate with your institutional advancement office to retrieve the data for these metrics for at least the past three years (but preferably five years). Continue deliberately tracking these figures annually moving forward. If you are a dean, consider replicating these metrics and adapting the figures for your academic departments. This tool can be used to help your department chairs better understand the impact of these measures on dollars raised and set their own goals.

REFERENCES

Dwight D. Eisenhower Presidential Library. (n.d.). *The Eisenhowers/Quotes.* Retrieved July 17, 2020, from https://www.eisenhowerlibrary.gov/eisenh owers/quotes#Leadership.

Farson, R., & Keyes, R. (2002, August). The failure-tolerant leader. *Harvard Business Review.* Retrieved July 16, 2020, from https://hbr.org/2002/08/the-failure-tolerant-leader.

Harteis, C., Bauer, J., & Gruber, H. (2008). The culture of learning from mistakes: How employees handle mistakes in everyday work. *International Journal of Educational Research, 47*(4), 223–231. Retrieved July 18, 2020, from https://doi.org/https://doi.org/10.1016/j.ijer.2008.07.003.

Joyaux, S. P. (2011). *Strategic fund development* (3rd ed.). Hoboken, NJ: Wiley.

Lambert, M. T. (2019). The present and future of higher education. In M. J. Worth & M. T. Lambert (Eds.), *Advancing higher education: New strategies for fundraising, philanthropy, and engagement* (pp. 3–11). Lanham, MD: Rowman & Littlefield.

Masterson, K. (2011, March 6). Off campus is now the place to be for deans. *The Chronicle of Higher Education*. Retrieved July 19, 2020, from https://www.chronicle.com/article/For-Deans-Off-Campus-Is-Now/126607.

Mercer, J. (1997, July 18). Fund raising has become a job requirement for many deans. *The Chronicle of Higher Education*. Retrieved July 19, 2020, from https://www.chronicle.com/article/Fund-Raising-Has-Become-a-Job/74549.

Scriven, D. (2019, January 27). 8 deans share: What I wish I had known. *The Chronicle of Higher Education*. Retrieved July 19, 2020, from https://www.chronicle.com/article/8-Deans-Share-What-I-Wish-I/245551.

Weinzimmer, L. G., & Esken, C. A. (2017). Learning from mistakes: How mistake tolerance positively affects organizational learning and performance. *Journal of Applied Behavioral Science, 53*(3), 322–348. Retrieved July 18, 2020, from https://doi.org/https://doi.org/10.1177/0021886316688658.

Worth, M. J. (2015). *Fundraising: Principles and practice*. Thousand Oaks, CA: Sage.

CHAPTER 10

Engaging Partners

The closing chapter of this section on operational strategies identifies the role of partners in development and fundraising activities. Engaging a broad scope of individuals who are invested in the unit's mission and are willing to advocate for others' support and involvement is vital for building and maintaining a high-performing development program.

Identifying potential partners is the first, and easier step, in this process. The greater challenge is to actively manage their involvement and expectations. Partners must feel needed and valued. There is no greater disappointment for a volunteer or advocate who answers the call for help, and then is underutilized. This is a frequent occurrence since philanthropy is often promoted as the giving of time, talent, and treasure, but the focus is far too often on gaining the treasure, or financial assets (Walton & Gasman, 2008). It must be remembered that a contribution of skills or expertise, and the time given to share it, can be just as impactful.

Negative experiences with poorly managed volunteer efforts can be particularly harmful to future fundraising when high net worth individuals walk away with these feelings. The same risk applies when campus colleagues are asked or offer to help, and their voluntary contributions are squandered or mismanaged. This chapter explores internal partnerships with faculty, students, and the institution's chief administrative and academic officers. It also examines external partnerships with governing

© The Author(s), under exclusive license to Springer Nature Switzerland AG 2021
A. Conley and G. G. Shaker, *Fundraising Principles for Faculty and Academic Leaders*, Philanthropy and Education, https://doi.org/10.1007/978-3-030-66429-9_10

board members, alumni, and friends of the institution. Examples and research evidence show the positive effects of these collaborations when partners are properly oriented, engaged, and stewarded.

COLLABORATING WITH FACULTY

Faculty members can be the most effective fundraisers on a college campus without even realizing it. Many of their existing skills in teaching, critical thinking, and research design are directly transferrable to the process of major gift fundraising. But this transfer is too frequently curtailed out of a fear of asking for money. This is the primary reason this book includes the seven articles of the *Don't Fear Fund Raising* series from *The Chronicle of Higher Education*. This series is authored by a dean and reinforces faculty members' pivotal role in fundraising, which does not always require asking for money.

Faculty also make effective partners because many of them are donors themselves (Shaker, 2013). Although most will not be among their institution's top donors, it is wise to refrain from making assumptions about the limited financial capacity of colleagues. After all, headlines and data show that some do make transformational gifts resulting from a research discovery, successful business enterprise, inherited wealth, or simply years of wise investing. Recent examples include a $50 million gift to the College of Natural Resources at the University of California Berkeley from a former dean (Manke, 2020), and a $7.5 million gift from an Ohio State University emerita professor to the College of Education and Human Ecology (Ohio State University, 2020). Ultimately, a number of faculty and staff are donors at some level, which adds a special dimension to their rapport with prospective donors.

Faculty members are effective partners in engaging many types of donors, but the most natural and obvious constituency is alumni. Reflecting on the identification model in Chapter 6, alumni are members of a particular community of participation formed between an institution and its graduates. But many feel an even closer bond stemming from experiences with and memories of the school from which they earned their degree. And for many, the identification is strongest with their academic program, department, or professors.

As noted in the identification model, "Communities of participation and frameworks of consciousness almost always work together" (Schervish, 1997, p. 114), meaning that a physics major from a big state university who became uber-wealthy is not going to give to the university or even the physics department on the basis of that connection alone. Any hope for reaching donor readiness with this alumnus must focus on determining their frameworks of consciousness. A physics faculty member or department chair is a valuable ally in the process of discovering interests, values, and aspirations.

Development work is not usually among faculty members' assigned responsibilities, but it can align with their deeper commitments to education in society and to furthering intellectual topics and institutional goals to which they are personally committed (Shaker, 2015). Development staff should collaborate with faculty and make sure their time is well utilized, effective, and in alignment with overall major gift strategies. The following scenario, using the same hypothetical alumni family from Chapters 6 and 8, shows how faculty can make multiple kinds of contributions to donor engagement and cultivation.

In Chapter 8, the business school and athletics development officers had completed a fruitful qualification visit with the alumna at her marketing firm. Details of the meeting were shared with the business school dean and marketing department chair, as well as the athletic director and volleyball coach. These briefings were an initial step in plans for a day on campus planned for a few months later.

The final plan thoughtfully included business and athletics, areas the alumna identified as personally important. The agenda also included specific moments with the goal of yielding additional, deeper insights about her personal interests. Respective development officers briefed each institutional participant in-person about their role and specific questions to pose if the opportunity arose.

The experience began with a lunch meeting with the business dean, marketing department chair, and the marketing faculty mentor the alumna mentioned during the qualification visit. The faculty mentor retired a few years earlier but, at the dean's request, had participated in many similar meetings.

The dean and department chair had not previously met the alumna, but they intentionally limited their participation in the conversation because she was clearly enjoying a rewarding experience with her mentor. They did accomplish two of the goals recommended by the school's development officer. The dean asked if she would be willing to consider joining the Dean's Leadership Council, a group of business executives with ties to the school as either alumni or major recruiter of the school's graduates.

And the department chair asked if they could include her in a section of their website which contained brief profile stories of successful alumni. She quickly agreed to both requests, also saying in response, "I know I'm long overdue in doing something for the school."

Following lunch, the alumna presented a guest lecture in one of the business school's largest undergraduate marketing classes. She was introduced by her mentor, which she described to the class as a great honor she hoped they each would also experience some day. She also revealed additional feelings about the school at the end of her lecture when she took questions. A student asked what prepared her most for success. She cited her parents, who she noted were also both alumni. She also made note of the guidance and influence of her faculty mentor, and she shared that playing volleyball had taught her the importance of teamwork. Serving as team captain was her first significant leadership role, and she applied many of the same leadership skills in building her business.

Following the lecture, the alumna made her way across campus to the athletic facilities. The volleyball team would be playing later in the evening, and she addressed them at their pre-game meeting. Following her remarks, she made a point to visit individually with the team captain. No one was close enough to hear the conversation, but several players and coaches noticed she wiped away tears while leaving the locker room.

Prior to the game, the athletic director (AD) hosted a private dinner, which included the alumna's parents and the athletics gift officer. The purpose, as the AD said, was not only the occasion of her visit, but also to thank her parents for being long-time basketball season ticket holders.

During dinner, the AD shared plans for a new multipurpose athletic facility as part of an upcoming university campaign. The facility was to be attached to the basketball stadium and provide training and academic space for all student-athletes. The plans also included a new practice area for men's and women's basketball, and a dedicated competition space for volleyball. This in particular would be a substantial improvement over the current facility where the alumna also had played in the early 1990s.

The AD took care to mention that the project was still conceptual and had not been formally approved by the trustees. As such, fundraising had not begun. The alumna was visibly interested and asked numerous questions. She also mentioned that she would be returning to campus more frequently as a new member of the business school's leadership council. She asked to be kept informed as the project moved through the approval process. They then adjourned to watch the volleyball match.

While the richness of detail in this summary is admittedly limited, it illustrates a number of critical outcomes with specific implications for future cultivation—several of which were accomplished by faculty (and staff) partners. A gift may appear imminent for athletics, however, commitments of time to the business school were also made. The alumna also shared a revealing cultivation trigger by saying she felt overdue in doing something for the business school.

Business and athletics now had the necessary information to build a deeper strategy based on the campus visit's positive outcomes. As a first step, several faculty members could take a brief moment to send follow up emails to reinforce the alumna's emotional bond:

- The faculty member teaching the marketing class where she spoke could pass along positive feedback from the students.
- The department chair could thank her again for agreeing to the website profile, while also proposing a meeting with faculty members to discuss marketing industry trends on her next return trip.
- The faculty mentor could share a personal message of gratitude and pride over her career accomplishments, and offer to reconnect again on a future visit to campus.

These suggestions may seem insignificant, however detailed and coordinated follow-up distinguishes great development programs that fully utilize faculty partnerships. An astute development officer would even offer to provide initial drafts of each email to ensure that the faculty send them, and would include these details in the contact report recording the day's events and interactions. Additionally, the development officers in this scenario would also follow up by debriefing with the respective faculty and staff participants, enabling exchanges of feedback and observations to inform their overall engagement strategy.

Utilizing the President, Provost, and Governing Board

Almost all college and university leaders and board members understand their responsibility to help engage major donors for philanthropic support. Faculty and academic leaders who seek assistance from these individuals will likely face highly coordinated processes well before any donor meetings are arranged. These structures, however painfully meticulous, are necessities.

Each of these potential partners requires information about the proposed use of gift funds and the potential donor and this information often must be presented in a particular manner. Most importantly, a clear rationale is needed to involve the president, provost, or trustee. Sections on the three partners address their possible contributions to securing transformational philanthropic support for academic units.

Presidents

Paradoxically, college and university presidents report that fundraising activities constitute the greatest or near-greatest amount of their time (American Council on Education, 2017; Bornstein, 2005; Selingo, 2013), while at the same time, fundraising is represented as a top area that new presidents feel least prepared to address (Bornstein, 2005; Jackson, 2012; Jaschik & Lederman, 2019). Over time, this learning curve will certainly flatten as more presidents enter the role with major gift experience acquired as deans, provosts, or in other positions.

For now, fundraising responsibilities may still feel new to many presidents, but the necessity of being the "fundraiser-in-chief" has been growing for more than a century. Even 100 years ago, the president was expected "to be a financial builder whose legacy was to leave the institution with increasing wealth, especially in the form of an ever-expanding endowment" (Thelin & Trollinger, 2014, p. 22). This expectation has only grown for contemporary presidents, and the distinctions that once existed between private and public institutions in this regard have disappeared.

Presidents' fundraising efforts are highly visible. Consequently, faculty and academic leaders may view the chief executive as the primary actor who can secure transformational gifts. After all, "No other institutional officer can create the vision, establish university-wide priorities, or make the case for support as effectively as the president" (Hodson, 2010). This truism faces two obstacles for anyone seeking their president's assistance. First, there is only so much time in the day. And second, there are many donors in a president's portfolio who are competing for attention.

For these reasons, academic leaders need respectful working relationships with their institution's chief development officer (CDO)—the CDO is typically responsible for prioritizing the president's time for strategic fundraising activities. In many cases, a president's closest working relationship is with the CDO, second only to the provost, chief of staff, or executive assistant. One survey of public comprehensive university presidents found more than 91% met or spoke with their CDO once a week or more, and nearly 20% spoke together daily (Jackson, 2012).

Institutions structure presidential involvement in various ways. Regardless, academic unit leaders may be able to expedite their requests through several simple approaches and considerations. Recognizing that presidents understand the importance of philanthropy and are invested in academic units' fundraising success, all the recommendations share the goal of assisting the CDO and their team in determining the unique effect of presidents' involvement on donor readiness:

- For best consideration, only request assistance with potential donors capable of a gift amount within the top quartile (or higher) of the institution's largest gifts. A president may be willing to get involved for smaller gifts, but it could take much longer and could mean spending the unit's "capital" prematurely.
- Try to determine in advance if engaging with the president will be important to the donor. Some people and organizations may be truly honored, while others may be indifferent and would respond better to another approach.
- Identify if the potential donor has known ties to members of the governing board. Because presidents report to the board, they will always want to inform a board member of a fundraising meeting with someone they know.
- If planning an upcoming campaign, determine if the donor or the gift purpose (or both) will catalyze and inspire similar donors or gifts. Campaigns require gifts that generate broader excitement and momentum and presidents need to help make these happen. (More on campaigns in Chapter 12.)
- Utilize standing events or other scheduled activities the president regularly attends. These could include fine arts performances and exhibitions, award receptions, distinguished lectures, and major sporting events (home and away). Time may be available before or after the event for one-on-one meetings.

Additionally, it is important to recognize the necessary role of a president as chief strategist for top donors with multiple interests across campus. Such donors certainly have well-established relationships with individuals inside particular units and must never sense internal competition or strained relations resulting from their generosity. This applies to alumni and friends as well as corporate and foundation donors. Institutional priorities must drive solicitation strategy, and the president (and their team) have the tools, information, and skills to diplomatically facilitate planning processes for donors with interests and passions spanning multiple areas.

Provosts

Chief academic officers, like so many others in higher education, are increasingly becoming more involved in fundraising activities out of both necessity and interest (Bateman, Fugate, & Houpt, 2015). As a traditional stepping stone to the presidency, it is understandable that the provost role would provide an avenue for enhancing academic expertise with ample fundraising accomplishments.

Given the intensely internal nature of the role, provosts may be unable to allocate as much time to development and fundraising activity as presidents or deans. Situations in which a provost is called on as a fundraising partner, therefore, need to be carefully chosen. Provosts can be especially effective in sharing a vision with donors of bold, cross-disciplinary ideas that advance the core mission of the institution or address major objectives of a strategic plan. These types of complex initiatives require a champion, like a provost, who can speak to the synergies created by such endeavors and how mobilizing the resources of multiple programs amplifies their collective impact. Whether the provost is the best person to solicit the gift is dependent on many other factors including the depth of their relationship to the donor, and their own comfort level and experience with gift solicitation.

Provosts can also bring wisdom and perspective to fundraising situations through their previous leadership experiences as department chairs or deans, or both. This value can be amplified when their experience at an institution spans a decade or more, which is not uncommon. A study of provosts in the 60 universities that are members of the Association of American Universities found that nearly two-thirds were internal hires, having served as dean or associate dean immediately before their appointment (June & Bauman, 2019). This longevity gives provosts extensive knowledge of institutional history, which can be particularly helpful in building relationships with older alumni, articulating the impact of past gifts on the institution, and in explaining how donors' institutional-level gifts for academic purposes would be implemented.

Governing Boards

Although board characteristics are well documented, the study of their giving and advocacy for philanthropic support is limited (Drezner & Huehls, 2015; Proper, 2019). It is known that members of governing boards, most notably at private institutions, have long been engaged as donors and vital partners in institutional campaigns and other fundraising activities.

Public institutions have also increasingly adopted this practice, transitioning trustee expectations to include a more prominent component of institutional advancement (Nicklin, 1995; Zeig, Baldwin, & Wilbur, 2018). The handicap many public institutions face in fully making this transition is the appointment method of new trustees. In many states, the governor appoints some or all public college and university governing board members. At some public institutions trustee appointments occur through public election. In either case, these incoming trustees are not always assured of having significant financial capacity. Even if they do have the capacity, there still may be an unwillingness to give or lack of appreciation for the importance of philanthropy.

For most leaders of academic units, partnerships with governing board members for fundraising are limited to select cases where the potential donor is directly connected to a board member. This could include situations where the potential donor is known personally by the trustee, or when the prospective donor is a company or foundation. Trustees may also serve on the boards of major corporations or foundations and as a result, could be in a position of influence with their decision-making process for gifts and grants.

While partnerships with governing board members may be infrequent, academic leaders should still be aware of this possibility. Many colleges and universities are becoming more regimented in their onboarding processes for new appointees as well as in evaluating individual member performance. This movement means governing board members are becoming better oriented to their roles as active participants in philanthropy, as donors and advocates (Association of Governing Boards, 2018; Dana, 2008; Masterson, 2018).

WORKING WITH ADVISORY BOARDS AND COUNCILS

External advisory boards or councils are a traditional partnership entity for academic units. These are most often utilized by deans at the school- or college-level, and are not uncommon at the department level. They are also increasingly found in other campus units including research centers, libraries, student affairs divisions, diversity and inclusion offices, and athletics. Virtually any unit can form a volunteer group, but establishing one does not ensure it will be a useful or productive vehicle for increasing philanthropic support.

Best practices for a successful advisory board are highly similar across academic units, as well as throughout the nonprofit sector (BoardSource, 2016; Olsen, 2008). Most importantly, the purpose of the group needs to be clearly articulated and include the scope of work, expectations for meeting attendance, and gift requirements. Term limits should also be established, along with clear policy on the appointment process and continuation through additional terms. Relatedly, membership is increasingly being examined annually through performance reviews. Methods for this vary widely from self-reported reviews to assessments conducted with the board chair. Regardless of the form, this process is viewed as increasingly necessary to ensure effectiveness and rotate off inactive or uncommitted members.

Host units also need to invest the time to select and appoint a chair, conduct a thorough orientation for new members, and develop meeting agendas and relevant materials. In between meetings, regular communication must take place to elevate the board's awareness of challenges, opportunities, and achievements within the unit.

Something easily overlooked is the affirmation value an advisory board can bring to an academic unit. The members should be a group of people who faculty and staff, as well as alumni and other external constituents, would be proud and honored to see associated with their unit. Their involvement, clearly displayed on the unit's website, affirms to the world that they fully believe in the mission and leadership of the educational enterprise (e.g., see Cornell University, n.d.; University of Iowa, n.d.; University of Illinois Chicago, n.d.).

It is also important to coordinate with the central development office or institutional foundation regarding the process of appointing new members or repurposing or restructuring an existing advisory board. Many institutions have policies in place related to these and other aspects of maintaining an advisory board. Larger university systems' governing boards may also have specific protocols and processes for such groups (e.g., see University of Texas System, n.d.).

Well-conceived and organized advisory boards serve as one of the most valuable fundraising activities for academic units and therefore should be viewed as critical partnerships with development. Units that lack a dedicated development officer can engage with the central development office to provide research assistance in identifying potential new members and to collect information regarding existing institutional relationships with the candidates. Central development staff can also ensure that notations are added to individuals' donor records indicating their board membership and related interactions. These vital data points must be documented to make development staff aware of the relationships of these people with the campus unit. It is also critical to improve the validity of future wealth screening or data analysis since volunteering is a powerful indicator of affinity.

INVOLVING ALUMNI VOLUNTEERS

Beyond serving on an advisory board, colleges and universities provide ample opportunities for volunteer service by alumni and others. These include service on alumni association and foundation boards, guest lectures and other interactions with classes and students, hosting local or regional alumni events, and assisting with recruiting and admissions efforts. Alumni may also serve as internal champions within large companies that employ many other alumni.

Whatever options a campus or unit may provide for alumni to volunteer, these opportunities require careful management and ongoing attention in order to ensure positive experiences for alumni and productive outcomes for the academic unit. Establishing accountability is paramount. Any alumni serving in a volunteer capacity must know who they can turn to for questions, guidance, and feedback. In many cases, a development officer is the logical choice for this assignment. However, too much responsibility can detract from the officer's primary role of managing a portfolio of current and potential major gift donors.

As an alternative, volunteer management can be used as a professional growth opportunity for other administrative staff within academic units. For example, an alumni mentoring program might be managed by student affairs staff. Working in partnership with development, this arrangement can help inform more administrative staff about alumni and external constituents' value to the unit beyond monetary contributions. This approach also increases the number of unit staff alumni interact with, thereby increasing the potential for relationship building in addition to the dean and development staff.

More than just filling a need, asking someone to volunteer is also an effective strategy in cultivating financial gifts. Known as the time-ask effect (Liu & Aaker, 2008), asking someone first to donate time and later to give financially has been shown to result in bigger contributions of both. The basis of this model holds that thinking about time activates emotional well-being and beliefs tied to personal happiness, while thinking about money suppresses emotional goals and activates contrasting goals of economic utility.

Deans, department chairs, and faculty members alike should consider this approach with alumni or other individuals who have not previously given to the school, especially if there is evidence that they volunteer with other organizations. An example of this strategy appeared earlier in this chapter when the dean and marketing department chair asked the marketing alumna and prospective major gift donor to become more involved with the school. This strategy was the result of advance preparation with the development officer, which is always recommended and can help to explore the many ways to engage alumni with major gift potential as volunteers first.

Coordinating with Students

Involving students in development activities within academic units can take two forms, both with distinct dividends and challenges. First, a few students can be instrumental when selectively engaged to interact with prospective major donors, as well as with existing donors for stewardship purposes. Second, many students can participate in activities designed to extend their emotional bonding with their alma maters while also educating them about the importance of philanthropy. When all goes as planned, academic units benefit because alumni of these activities are more likely to understand how philanthropy works and to become donors and volunteers who are active readers of alumni publications and participants on institutional social networking platforms.

Students and Prospective Major Gift Donors

Just as faculty members can be instrumental in raising major gifts without making the solicitation, students also possess the power of influence in the donor engagement process. Caution must always be exercised to restrict confidential donor information from students (and vice versa). In other words, students do not need to know about donors' capacity to give and donors do not need to know students' GPAs in order to have meaningful interactions. Care must also be taken to never put students in difficult or uncomfortable situations by asking them to misrepresent their experiences or allowing them to feel pressured in relation to closing a gift. Rather, the best approach is to make sure students are carefully chosen to represent the unit and well-prepared for interactions with major donors. Then, students can simply be paired with donors with overlapping interests or similar experiences and encouraged to be themselves. The scenario earlier in the chapter exemplifies this in the meeting of the alumna and the volleyball team, and particularly the conversation with the team captain.

Whenever possible, consider engaging students as living evidence of what philanthropy can accomplish, create, or make possible, particularly in areas beyond what would be possible otherwise. For example, consider a prospective donor with a defining appreciation for the fine arts. They may be intrigued by a department chair's vision of sending more fine arts students to study in Europe, practice in artists' studios, and visit great museums. However, they may be emotionally moved by one student's presentation about participating in the program and its profound effect on their perspectives on art, culture, and history. Imagine as well that the student had never traveled abroad, was a first-generation college attendee, Pell Grant recipient, and dean's list honoree every semester.

Introducing prospective donors to students like this can be more compelling than anything a faculty member, development officer, or even the president could convey in making the case for support. Engaging students in this way requires a highly selective process, and as such entails considerable oversight and coordination by the development officer, support staff, and, depending on the situation, a faculty member. Students should be fully informed about expectations and understand that they are in no way being asked to solicit gifts. When successful, these experiences advance an academic unit's causes, and also leave an indelible imprint on the minds of the students, hopefully to be remembered years later if they are in a similar position to give.

Broader Student Philanthropy Programs

One of the main schools of thought on why alumni give is based on their satisfaction with the educational experience they received (Drezner & Huehls, 2015). As noted in Chapter 1, *U.S. News & World Report* includes alumni giving participation as a proxy for alumni satisfaction in their ranking methodology (Morse & Brooks, 2020). Together with the notion that early interactions with philanthropy can lead to more engagement later, this thinking has driven the creation of many new student-focused activities intended to enrich the student experience through exposure to philanthropy (Paradise, 2015). As a result, student affairs and institutional advancement offices are increasingly forming partnerships to provide a new element of the student experience that results in more graduates entering their post-college years with a greater appreciation for philanthropy and civic engagement (Miller, 2010; Puma, 2013). This also brings a welcome dimension to add to the longstanding practice of a senior class gift, traditionally the only student-focused philanthropic activity on many campuses. While well-intended, senior gifts suffer from the limitation of time–in this model students are in their final year before engaging in philanthropy (Frezza, 2019).

Academic units can be supportive of institution-wide activities that engage students in philanthropic activities, and they can pursue their own. In large academic units, such as a school of arts and science, business, or engineering, deans may sponsor a student volunteer organization focused on leadership development. In addition to meeting periodically with the dean and other academic leaders, members of this group could be selectively utilized to speak at on-campus events attended by alumni, business executives, or community leaders. They could be asked to support development events such as guest lectures and afforded the opportunity to meet the speakers and other VIPs in attendance. And they could be given regular duties around advisory board meetings as a way to allow them to interact with the same external constituents multiple times a year and possibly over several years.

There are certain to be variations to this approach that could be applied to academic units of any type or size. Confer with faculty and other leaders in the unit, as well as development and student affairs staff, to generate ideas that best serve the unit's needs while also providing meaningful experiences for students.

Stewardship efforts provide avenues for individual student involvement with major donors as well as broader student engagement with philanthropy. For example, major donors with endowed scholarships should always receive information about the recipients, and when possible should have opportunities for personal interaction through campus visits or virtual meetings. More generally, a student organization, in coordination with the development office, could sponsor an event for writing thank you notes to scholarship donors at all levels. This shows students the importance of donor support while also making donors feel their giving is truly impactful.

Stewardship approaches can be strategically applied to many different donor constituencies including young alumni, consecutive-year donors, parents, planned giving donors, and faculty and staff. Stewardship activities in general are an ideal entry point for academic units with a limited history of student involvement in development. The key is to commit to engaging students in a meaningful way that enhances their academic experience and, hopefully, carries over into their alumni years. This type of approach answers the call that many student affairs professionals have been advocating: "Institutions must face the fact that the origin of alumni satisfaction begins with the student experience" (Hurvitz, 2013, p. 139).

CONCLUSION

This chapter has discussed partners who may assist in achieving fundraising objectives. Most importantly, the emphasis is ensuring newcomers understand that fundraising is a team sport. There will always be examples of gifts secured through the lone efforts of a gift officer, dean, or professor. But no institution can realize their full fundraising potential by adopting individualism as an operational approach across its academic, administrative, and athletic units.

This team perspective may be the chief variable that enables weak fundraising schools to begin experiencing sustained progress, as well as high-performing schools to rise to even greater ambitions. Lambert (2019) suggests this in observing higher education's future and the importance of strategic planning, engagement, communications, fundraising, and leading. "Advancing our institutions requires harnessing all these skills with the right external partners as well as effective corralling and partnership with internal colleagues" (p. 5).

Introducing internal and external partners to philanthropy and showing them the unique ways they can help will create awareness and understanding, as well as greater ownership of development and fundraising outcomes. This further builds on the team perspective of fundraising, as individual performance becomes secondary to the collective success of the team. To emphasize this, sage fundraising managers often apply their own version of the quote from Harry S. Truman, "It is amazing what you can accomplish if you do not care who gets the credit" (Truman Library Institute, n.d.). Academic leaders who similarly advocate this perspective toward fundraising initiatives advance the cause along with their own vision and goals.

ACTIONABLE STRATEGIES

1. If you have no written policies for your advisory board members, draft some using the guidelines in this chapter and share them with your board chair. Confer with your chair and development director on an annual evaluation process to determine how those who do not meet expectations will be approached.

2. Explore whether your development staff is tracking and recording volunteer activity in your unit. This data is invaluable and should be documented in constituent records. Develop a system to ensure volunteer activity, such as advisory board membership, speaking in class, and serving as an event host, is recorded in individuals' records.

3. Pick one of the internal or external constituencies discussed in this chapter. Review the ways in which your unit currently asks them to participate in development programs. Develop a short list of ideas for how they could be further utilized to help achieve one or more goals of your development plan.

Section III Case Study: A Model Volunteer Structure for Engaging New Alumni Leaders

Advisory boards are a common volunteer engagement tool utilized by deans, department chairs, center directors, and other leaders of academic units to build relationships with alumni and community/industry leaders. The impact and effectiveness of these entities vary and can be hampered by marginally defined roles and expectations, limited support from the academic unit, and inexperienced (but well-meaning) appointed leaders.

An alternative model to this traditional body is a volunteer structure that is narrowly focused in mission and scope, and charged with achieving very specific outcomes. The Dedman School of Law at Southern Methodist University (SMU) implemented this approach in 2017 with the creation of an Emerging Leader Board (ELB). The 32 initial members were drawn from the law school's alumni association, and all members graduated within the past 20 years (Southern Methodist University, 2017).

This new initiative by the school's dean, who was appointed to the role three years earlier, was viewed as a way for the school to give back to alumni—rather than alumni giving back to their school—through a new opportunity for service and leadership (Collins, 2020). The ELB also complements a larger effort to bring greater diversity to the student ranks—where demonstrable progress has been made. Students of color represent 33% of the school's total enrollment in 2020, up from 18% in 2014. The ELB was envisioned to similarly reflect this overarching commitment to equity and diversity. Currently, gender representation among ELB members is nearly equal, with 17 women and 16 men. And ethnic diversity is represented among the multiple Black, Hispanic, and Asian members (Southern Methodist University, n.d.a).

The ELB meets formally twice per year, including one combined meeting with the school's Executive Board. This body is populated by approximately 70 members representing a traditional mix of older, highly-accomplished alumni and other leaders from the legal profession, many of whom are also major financial supporters of the school and the university.

Between meetings, ELB members are actively involved in a number of activities that directly benefit current students. One is the Mustang Exchange, a mentoring program that pairs students with alumni and non-alumni legal professionals for career networking and counsel (Southern Methodist University, n.d.b). Another is the Inns of Court, modeled on the centuries-old professional association for barristers originating in London (Southern Methodist University, n.d.c). First-year law students are organized into groups of approximately 30, with their "inn" also including faculty advisors, career services staff, and a number of upper-class students. ELB members often represent the "alumni community fellow" that is also assigned to each inn and participates in the meetings, which are mandatory for students.

The ELB is also a fundraising mechanism for the law school, serving in multiple ways (Beard, 2020). While giving is not specifically required for membership, the expectation is expressed through the welcome letter provided to new members. Beyond individual giving, ELB members volunteer to lead fundraising efforts for a variety of initiatives. One activity is a silent auction event supporting a student organization, the Association of Public Interest Law. Funds raised provide summer stipends for students to work at local nonprofit organizations or in the public sector. Another is the Law Firm Challenge, an annual fundraising competition among firms that employ SMU law alumni. ELB members who work in commercial law firms regularly serve as challenge ambassadors to increase giving participation among alumni colleagues in their firms.

This model for working with younger alumni leaders is applicable in many types of academic units. Schools of law, business, and engineering are natural settings for this type of board. Such programs could also benefit other professional schools including nursing, education, public affairs, and social work. Schools located in or near major metropolitan areas with a high proportion of alumni residing in the area could replicate this model as well.

Importantly, this model holds promise for recognizing and engaging alumni who have been historically excluded from development and fundraising strategies (Drezner, 2013). This model of a community of participation builds connections with a diverse range of promising younger alumni and does so in highly personal ways. This will certainly influence their philanthropic habits and choices into the future. Moreover, current students and other young alumni deserve to see a variety of role models, including philanthropic ones. As Greeley (2013) observes, "The long-established image of the university donor as an older, White, male is no longer applicable to today's changing alumni base" (p. 189). Alumni programming within schools and colleges, like the Emerging Leader Board, expose students (and faculty and staff) to a much different—and far more diverse—picture of supportive alumni.

Key Lessons

- **Recognize the value younger alumni can bring.** ELB's members are still building their careers, so most are actively engaged as leaders in professional societies, service organizations, and community initiatives. Their value as connectors and advocates mirrors their more senior counterparts serving on the Executive Board, and both are strategic assets for the school's dean.
- **Be deliberate in facilitating engagement with other leaders.** The Dedman School regularly involves associate deans and select faculty in ELB meetings and related activities to help educate members more deeply on the school's inner workings. Their interactions with the Executive Board also help create a potential pathway for current and future ELB members to transition upward to this board (two have done this already). Creating a diverse pipeline of alumni leadership is expected to benefit the future composition of the Executive Board, as well as other leadership opportunities in the school.
- **Don't miss a teaching opportunity.** ELB meetings regularly include brief updates from the development staff on the school's broader alumni engagement activity and plans, as well as giving data and trends (similar to the recommended data points in Chapter 13). Exposing this cohort of alumni leaders to the school's structured approach to philanthropy will yield positive dividends as their ability to make larger gifts grows over time.

References

American Council on Education. (2017). *American college president study 2017*. Retrieved June 13, 2020, from https://www.aceacps.org/duties-responsibilities-dashboard/.

Association of Governing Boards. (2018). *The AGB 2018 trustee index*. Retrieved July 24, 2020, from https://agb.org/knowledge-center/resources-by-format/reports-statements/page/2/.

Bateman, B. W., Fugate, W. R., & Houpt, J. B. (2015). The academic ask: Partnering academic affairs and institutional advancement. In J. Martin & J. E. Samels (Eds.), *The provost's handbook: The role of the chief academic officer* (pp. 145–155). Baltimore, MD: Johns Hopkins University Press.

Beard, A. (2020, September 18). Director of Development, SMU Dedman School of Law (A. Conley, Interviewer).

BoardSource. (2016). *Advisory councils: Nine keys to success.* Retrieved July 24, 2020, from BoardSource. https://boardsource.org/advisory-councils-nine-keys-to-success/.

Bornstein, R. (2005, November 4). The nature and nurture of presidents. *The Chronicle of Higher Education.* Retrieved July 25, 2020, from https://www.chronicle.com/article/the-nature-and-nurture-of-presidents/.

Collins, J. (2020, September 25). Judge James Noel Dean and Professor of Law, SMU Dedman School of Law (A. Conley, Interviewer).

Cornell University. (n.d.). *Advisory council.* Retrieved July 24, 2020, from The College of Arts & Sciences. https://as.cornell.edu/advisory-council.

Dana, E. H. (2008). Why college trustees? In A. Walton & M. Gasman (Eds.), *Philanthropy, volunteerism & fundraising in higher education* (pp. 583–586). Boston: Pearson Custom Publishing.

Drezner, N. D. (Ed.). (2013). *Expanding the donor base in higher education: Engaging non-traditional donors.* New York: Routledge.

Drezner, N. D., & Huehls, F. (2015). *Fundraising and institutional advancement: Theory, practice, and new paradigms.* New York: Routledge.

Frezza, D. H. (2019). Annual giving. In M. Worth & L. Matthew (Eds.), *Advancing higher education; New strategies for fundraising, philanthropy, and engagement* (pp. 71–82). Lanham, MD: Rowman & Littlefield.

Greeley, L. (2013). Creating an engagement model of advancement for young alumni. In N. D. Drezner (Ed.), *Expanding the donor base in higher education: Engaging non-traditional donors* (pp. 187–205). New York: Routledge.

Hodson, J. B. (2010). Leading the way: The role of presidents and academic deans in fundraising. *New Directions for Higher Education: Perspectives on Fundraising, 149,* 39–49.

Hurvitz, L. A. (2013). Building a culture of student philanthropy. In N. D. Drezner (Ed.), *Expanding the donor base in higher education: Engaging non-traditional donors* (pp. 138–151). New York: Routledge.

Jackson, R. L. (2012). *The American public comprehensive university: An exploratory study of the president's role in fundraising* (Docotral dissertation, Western Kentucky University). Retrieved July 25, 2020, from https://digitalcommons.wku.edu/diss/18.

Jaschik, S., & Lederman, D. (2019). *2019 survey of college and university presidents.* Washington, DC: Inside Higher Ed and Gallup. Retrieved July 25, 2020, from https://www.insidehighered.com/news/survey/2019-survey-college-and-university-presidents.

June, A. W., & Bauman, D. (2019, January 13). The provost's path: How more than 200 scholars reached the provost's office, and where they went next. *The Chronicle of Higher Education.* Retrieved July

23, 2020, from https://www.chronicle.com/article/how-more-than-200-scholars-reached-the-provosts-office-and-where-they-went-next/.

Lambert, M. T. (2019). The present and future of higher education. In M. J. Worth & M. T. Lambert (Eds.), *Advancing higher education: New strategies for fundraising, philanthropy, and engagement* (pp. 3–11). Lanham, MD: Rowman & Littlefield.

Liu, W., & Aaker, J. (2008, October). The happiness of giving: The time-ask effect. *Journal of Consumer Research, 35*, 543–557.

Manke, K. (2020, February 29). College of natural resources receives $50 million naming gift. *Berkeley News*. Retrieved July 20, 2020, from https://news.berkeley.edu/2020/02/29/college-of-natural-resources-receives-50-million-naming-gift/.

Masterson, K. (2018, March 18). 8 tips to get new trustees up and running. *The Chronicle of Higher Education*. Retrieved July 23, 2020, from https://www.chronicle.com/article/8-tips-to-get-new-trustees-up-and-running/.

Miller, T. E. (2010). The context for development work in student affairs. *New Directions for Student Services, 130*, 3–8.

Morse, R., & Brooks, E. (2020, September 13). *How U.S. News Calculated the 2021 Best Colleges Rankings*. Retrieved September 25, 2020, from https://www.usnews.com/education/best-colleges/articles/how-us-news-calculated-the-rankings.

Nicklin, J. (1995, May 19). Trustees are being asked to show commitment with donations. *The Chronicle of Higher Education*. Retrieved July 22, 2020, from https://www.chronicle.com/article/trustees-are-being-asked-to-show-commitment-with-donations.

Ohio State University. (2020, July 9). *Professor Emerita donates $7.5 m to EHE, largest individual gift in college's history*. Retrieved July 20, 2020, from https://ehe.osu.edu/news/listing/professor-emerita-donates-largest-individual-gift-college-history/.

Olsen, G. A. (2008, February 22). The importance of external boards. *The Chronicle of Higher Education*. Retrieved July 23, 2020, from https://www.chronicle.com/article/the-importance-of-external-boards/.

Paradise, A. (2015). *Student philanthropy: The foundation for engagement as lifelong donors*. Washington, DC: CASE. Retrieved August 30, 2020, from https://www.case.org/resources/student-philanthropy-foundation-engagement-lifelong-donors.

Proper, E. (2019). Give or get off: The role of trustees in college fundraising. *Philanthropy & Education, 3*(1), 1–22.

Puma, M. (2013). Fostering student affairs and institutional advancement partnerships. In N. D. Drezner (Ed.), *Expanding the donor base in higher education: Engaging non-traditional donors* (pp. 171–186). New York: Routledge.

Schervish, P. G. (1997). Inclination, obligation, and association: What we know and what we need to learn about donor motivation. In D. F. Burlingame (Ed.), *Critical issues in fundraising* (pp. 110–138). New York: John Wiley & Sons.

Selingo, J. J. (2013). What presidents think: A 2013 suvery of four-year college presidents. Washington, DC: *The Chronicle of Higher Education*. Retrieved July 25, 2020, from http://www.maguireassoc.com/wp-content/uploads/2015/08/Chronicle-Presidents-Survey-for-Education-Counsel-2.pdf.

Shaker, G. G. (2013). Faculty and staff as prospects and donors. In N. D. Drezner (Ed.), *Expanding the donor base in higher education: Engaging non-traditional donors* (pp. 123–137). New York: Routledge.

Shaker, G. G. (2015). *Faculty work and the public good: Philanthropy, engagement, and academic professionalism.* New York: Teachers College Press, Columbia University.

Southern Methodist University. (n.d.a). *Emerging leader board.* Retrieved September 18, 2020, from https://www.smu.edu/Law/Alumni/Emerging-Leader-Board2020.

Southern Methodist University. (n.d.b). *Mustang exchange: Mentor. make a difference.* Retrieved September 18, 2020, from https://mustangexchange.chronus.com/about.

Southern Methodist University. (n.d.c). *Program overview: Inns of court.* Retrieved September 18, 2020, from https://www.smu.edu/Law/Students/Inns-of-Court-Program/Program-Overview.

Southern Methodist University. (2017, November 17). *SMU Dedman School of Law launches emerging leader board.* Retrieved September 18, 2020, from https://www.smu.edu/News/2017/law-leader-board-17nov2017.

Thelin, J. R., & Trollinger, R. W. (2014). *Philanthropy and American Higher Education.* New York: Palgrave Macmillan.

Truman Library Institute. (n.d.). *Truman quotes.* Retrieved August 30, 2020, from https://www.trumanlibraryinstitute.org/truman/truman-quotes/page/5/.

University of Illinois Chicago. (n.d.). *Advisory board.* Retrieved July 24, 2020, from College of Engineering. https://engineering.uic.edu/about/advisoryboard/.

University of Iowa. (n.d.). *Advisory board.* Retrieved July 24, 2020, from College of Education. https://education.uiowa.edu/about-college/advisory-board.

University of Texas System. (n.d.). *Rule 60302: Advisory Councils of an Institution.* Retrieved July 24, 2020, from Regents' rules and regulations. https://www.utsystem.edu/board-of-regents/rules/60302-advisory-councils-of-institution.

Walton, A., & Gasman, M. (2008). Volunteerism: Service to campus and society. In A. Walton, & M. Gasman (Eds.), *Philanthropy, volunteerism & fundraising in higher education* (pp. 363–369). Boston: Pearson Custom Publishing.

Zeig, M. J., Baldwin, R. G., & Wilbur, K. M. (2018). Leveraging an overlooked asset: The role of public university trustees in institutional advancement. *Philanthropy & Education, 2*(1), 53–74.

PART IV

Executing Fundraising Plans and Initiatives

CHAPTER 11

Align Your Strategic Plan

.

The chapters in this section provide applications for the concepts, ideas, and research findings presented in previous sections. Each chapter addresses a core development activity and all share the duality of being the most critical for academic leaders to understand, and the most often overlooked, downplayed, or simply disregarded.

When done well, these development activities benefit an academic unit in dollars raised and also by elevating the importance of philanthropy in the eyes of internal and external constituents alike. Harnessing this intangible quality of perception is often what distinguishes high-performing fundraising schools, departments, and other academic units from those that continue to struggle with unmet goals, flat or declining gift volume, and turnover among development staff.

This section's first chapter addresses strategic planning. It is not intended to serve as a comprehensive resource on the process of conducting a strategic plan for an academic unit or an entire college or university. This topic is well-addressed in the scholarly literature, and there are an abundance of experiential perspectives and process models. For the latter, see an insightful four-part series by Perlmutter (2019a, b, c, d) in *The Chronicle of Higher Education* that looks sequentially at this process through the stages of preparation, management, implementation, and follow through. Similarly, there are extensive resources on strategic

© The Author(s), under exclusive license to Springer Nature   165
Switzerland AG 2021
A. Conley and G. G. Shaker, *Fundraising Principles for Faculty and Academic Leaders*, Philanthropy and Education,
https://doi.org/10.1007/978-3-030-66429-9_11

planning specifically for fundraising, including Sargeant and Jay (2014), Seiler (2016), and Lindahl (1992).

This chapter is intended to help academic leaders understand why and how to engage development directly in an academic unit's strategic planning process from the beginning so that philanthropy can meet its full potential and enable the plan's ambitious goals. Conversely, failure is likely when development joins only when the need is urgent and after the plan is finalized. To state the obvious, development strategic planning should follow the priorities established by unit strategic plans; assuring that the two go hand in hand is a sign of a high-performing fundraising program and high functioning collaboration between the academic and development leaders.

Engaging Development in the Planning Process

Sound planning takes place when existing resources are aligned to the strategic plan, and tactics necessary to execute the plan are feasible within the institution's resources (Goodman & Salem, 2015). This feasibility includes knowing where existing and potential donor support aligns with the plan's major goals. And this is where development can make the greatest contributions to the planning process and needs to be included.

At the institutional level, Ziedenstein (2019) notes development perspectives provide an internal reminder to look outward:

> The first role of the chief advancement officer in university strategy development is to ensure that external stakeholders are brought into the process in the appropriate way. External stakeholders, such as key donors and influential alumni, not only provide an off-campus point of view but also will be crucial at some point in funding elements of the planning effort. (p. 30)

While there could be discussion and debate over what is considered the most appropriate way to incorporate external opinions, overall this hardly seems an objectionable statement.

As one looks more deeply, however, this practice is observed far less in strategic planning efforts within schools, departments, and large research centers than at the institutional level. Unit gift officers and development teams are often limited to participating in interviews with external planning consultants or responding to a survey instrument along with other unit staff. While development personnel may be viewed as important members of the unit, their perceived role as contributors to the academic direction and future is often limited.

This practice is not entirely without merit as most development staff do not hold terminal degrees, nor are they likely to teach, research, or serve on academic committees for promotion and tenure, curriculum, or others requiring faculty expertise. However, they do possess what is among the most important elements of a strategic plan's success. They know their largest donors' interests, values, and motivations for giving. Moreover, gift officers likely know potential donors' interests or they know how to utilize research resources that can provide these insights.

Time is a critical element in the strategic planning processes. Knowledge derived from development expertise is imperative for recognizing when and how a grand plan (and its elements) may become realistic. If additional resources are required to fund the objectives underlying some or all of a plan's goals, it will take time to raise these funds. Involving development from the beginning enables fundraisers to understand the rationale and finer points guiding the inclusion of these goals and objectives. With this information, they can make connections to specific donors and potential donors who possess matching interests. Planning committees that engage development later in the process, or after its conclusion, delay what are already lengthy undertakings with most donors.

Another aspect of time is essential in relation to gift support for a strategic plan. In addition to identifying interest among donors for specific plan aspects, gift officers may also advise caution when there is potentially little or no interest. A hypothetical scenario shows the importance of this insight and input.

A school of arts and sciences is considering a strategic plan goal of expanding graduate degree programs in the physical sciences. Specific objectives would include hiring five new assistant professors and two tenured professors. And another objective is to grow enrollment of graduate students in biology, chemistry, and physics by set amounts for the next five years. The provost will provide initial funding for the new faculty lines because the initiative reflects an institutional priority. A limited amount of funding will be provided for fellowships to recruit graduate students. The draft strategic plan reflects this support and includes a proposed action item to secure additional endowed graduate fellowships from alumni and others.

Data on the school's history of gifts for graduate fellowships, whether anemic or robust, and assessment of future donor potential in this area should be provided to the planning committee as this goal and action item are being explored. Bypassing this step and simply including this item within the strategic plan will not ensure a windfall in endowed graduate fellowships. Careful consideration must be given in all situations where philanthropic funding is necessary for specific purposes. By using development data and consulting with fundraising staff, planning committee leaders also empower development with the most time to match donor interests with institutional needs and to begin the process from a place of collaboration.

This kind of dedicated attention is also necessary in academic units that lack development officers. Development staff from the central office or foundation should be invited to be active participants in the strategic planning. Even with limited experience working with the unit's donors, such staff can leverage their development research resources to collect historical data and investigate potential sources of major gifts as elements of the plan emerge.

ALIGNMENT EXERCISE: MATCHING DONOR INTERESTS AND STRATEGIC NEEDS

Among the greatest benefits of a fundamentally sound development program is the utility of applying core fundraising activities to new situations and needs as they arise. This includes those goals that result from strategic planning, as illustrated by an alignment exercise described here.

Referring first back to the donor management matrix in Chapter 8, leaders of academic units should have current knowledge of, and engagement with, their top donors and potential donors. These are the entities in the 1A box of the matrix. In addition, each individual or organization should have an engagement strategy with specific actions planned leading toward near-term gift discussions. If this approach is being followed, these matrices can be considerable assets in strategic planning processes.

The exercise illustrated in Fig. 11.1 uses a hypothetical academic school to explore development readiness as it is approaching a strategic planning process. Most leaders of academic units can identify their key priorities, many of which will ultimately become the core of a strategic plan. In this exercise, these priorities are reflected in the middle row in response to the statement, "In three years, the school will…"

The school's five largest existing donors are identified in the row above the leader's priorities. These would be considered 1A donors in the matrix

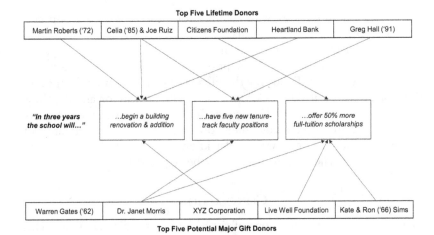

Fig. 11.1 Strategic planning development readiness exercise

since they have the greatest financial capacity and affinity and established relationships with the school. The top five potential major gift donors are in the bottom row. These may include past donors who it is believed have not yet given to their likely capacity. These may also include potential donors who are being cultivated but are not yet ready to give. Many of these also come from 1A in the matrix, but may also be 2A or 1B.

The value of this exercise for strategic planning rests in drawing lines from the top and bottom rows to the priorities that align with each donors' specific interests and values. Some may have multiple interests as demonstrated through past gifts or through philanthropic or other conversations (that were dutifully recorded in the database for use in future situations like this one). In some cases, the interests of a potential donor may be unknown, as illustrated by the one name in the bottom row with no connecting lines.

This illustration can be modified to include more names in rows, as well as additional strategic priorities. It can also be used during the actual strategic planning process to explore emerging goals' viability from a philanthropic perspective. Using this tool effectively is contingent on many of the development functions and processes noted throughout the earlier chapters. If this exercise proves ineffective, it is likely an indicator that more relationship building with external constituents is needed—specifically with the very same individuals and organizations whose support is needed to enable the strategic plan's success. If the chart is empty of donors or potential donors or the priorities and donors do not connect, challenges are ahead. Funds for the plan could still be raised from other donors. However, if they lack the highest gift capacity or affinity, these will likely be smaller gifts. Consequently, the process will require more time to raise more gifts from more donors. Or, if the donors are not represented because they are not yet known to the development team, more time than allocated will also likely be required.

Conclusion

Despite criticism and questions of the value of strategic planning (Eckel & Trower, 2019; Ginsberg, 2011), this traditional visioning tool will continue to be utilized by colleges and universities, and the major academic units within them. These exercises require considerable investments of energy and attention from a broad range of participants. While the end result may represent the collective vision and aspiration of the unit or institution, a plan without resources behind it is equivalent to a wish list.

Successful plans have demonstrated that the goal-setting process must be tied to reliable budget resources (Fain, 2007). Excluding or limiting the participation of development misses vital opportunities for securing new or supplemental resources for the plan's goals and objectives. The case study in this section provides an example of an academic unit in a major public research university that embraced this approach. By engaging development staff and also an advisory board and key donors in a totally new way, the resultant plan successfully matched the leader's vision with the philanthropic resources, from the start. The plan ultimately inspired gifts that enabled the school to pursue the objectives necessary for achieving its ambitious goals.

Actionable Strategies

1. Before embarking on a new strategic plan, have candid conversations with some of your top donors. Ask them how important it is for them to know that an organization has a strategic plan before they

choose to make a gift. Ask if they have ever read a strategic plan from your college or university, or any other organization they support.

2. If you have a development officer for your unit, quiz them on core information they should know. This would include data about enrollment, graduation rates by degree and major, research expenditures, and your physical space including facilities' total square feet and composition of instructional and research space. To be positive contributors in your strategic planning process, they must have the same grasp of this baseline information as the academic leadership team since some (or possibly all) of these measures may relate to plan priorities.

SECTION IV CASE STUDY: A STRATEGIC PLAN INFORMED AND INSPIRED BY PHILANTHROPY

Kansas State University (KSU) announced in May 2019 a $20 million gift designated for the College of Business Administration (CBA) to advance its strategic plan (Kansas State University Foundation, 2019). Looking behind the headline reveals a story most academic leaders wish they could tell about a strategic plan that inspired gifts like this one. While the donor had a lengthy giving history, including a $5 million gift a decade earlier to endow the deanship (Kansas State University Foundation, n.d.), the real story is how CBA intentionally took what many view as a staid academic tradition and used it to engage those with the capacity to fund transformational goals.

The process in this case began as many do, with the appointment of a new dean. CBA's marketing department chair of 10 years was named interim dean in 2015 and permanently appointed the following year. An outside planning consultant was hired and began conducting internal interviews with all CBA faculty and staff in early 2017.

These interviews also included several executive committee members of the Dean's Business Advisory Council. The full council totals more than 60 members, with 12–14 typically appointed to the executive committee (Kansas State University, n.d.a).

CBA had previously conducted strategic planning, but the goal in this case quickly emerged to create a plan like they never had before (Gwinner, 2020). The Strategic Planning Leadership Team, a group comprising the dean and associate deans, department heads, initiative leaders, and a faculty senate representative, committed early on to creating a plan that would serve as a living document. The mission, vision, and core values would remain relatively stable, but the goals would be under constant review and revision.

The advisory council embraced the concept of a plan that would be brief but focused, and identify not just goals to advance the college, but specific tactics for achieving them. As a reflection of their collective business experience, they proposed including timelines for the tactics to hold key groups and individuals accountable for progress. The leadership team agreed; everyone considered accountability essential to achieve the plan and prevent it from being quickly forgotten.

The final plan was presented to the full advisory board in fall 2017 and adopted by the college later that year. The plan retained the sought-after brevity, with just three focus areas; reinventing student experiences, expanding external collaborations, and strengthening foundations for enterprise sustainability and growth (Kansas State University, n.d.b).

It was no coincidence that many of the goals underlying these focus areas align with the interests and beliefs of CBA's top donors. But rather than a case of the tail of philanthropy wagging the academic dog, many of these goals would have been included regardless. CBA benefitted by actively engaging these donors in the planning process and enabling them to see first-hand each goal's importance. They did this rather than waiting until after the plan's completion to introduce its already-established goals by way of seeking gifts to accomplish them.

In particular, the seeds for the $20 million gift in 2019 were planted before the initial interviews in early 2017 and continued through the executive committee meetings and ongoing individual conversations with the donor (Willems, 2020). Everything started with an open exchange of ideas, and CBA never "pitched" specific projects for the donor to consider that could just be incorporated into the plan. The result was elements in the plan that both the college needed and the donor believed in.

For example, part of the gift is designated to fund a new Center for Financial Analysis, which reflects the donor's advocacy for data-driven analysis and decision-making in business. As a Midwestern public business school, CBA also wanted elements of the plan to help build its brand. The donor shared the same belief, so another part of the gift is designated to fund the creation of a strategic marketing director position. This would be a first for CBA as the college's marketing activity was limited mainly to providing internal support, such as websites, admissions collateral, and similar administrative needs.

Another objective to be funded by the $20 million gift is a new digital learning repository. This resource will include recordings of multi-course programming for wider distribution to full-time students and continuing and executive education classmates. Content will also be made available to alumni, targeted industry segments, and the business community in Kansas and beyond.

Others who were engaged in the planning process from the beginning were also inspired to give to the priorities. Another alumnus serving on the executive committee committed $500,000 in matching funds for new endowed scholarships. These support students in accounting, the donor's major. But the scholarships also target out-of-state students to address the strategic plan's objective for building a stronger image and brand to enhance CBA's ability to recruit top students from anywhere. Within 18 months, the full $500,000 had been applied in matches to 15 endowed scholarships established by other donors.

It should also be noted that 2016 marked not only the new dean's appointment, but also the completion of the college's new 160,000 square-foot facility. Initiating a strategic plan shortly after these events was prescient in helping to realize the largest gifts of numerous longtime CBA supporters. Engaging them in the planning process, rather than soliciting them after it was over, helped create a strategic plan that is doing far more than simply sitting on a shelf until it is time for the next one.

Key Lessons

- **Dream big and let others help you dream:** The dean may set the vision for a school, but it should be a collective vision informed by many voices. Use the strategic plan to empower others to share their perspective of what the school can become.
- **A plan is just a wish list unless there is financial support behind it:** Everyone acknowledged that the final plan had to identify credible sources of support for those goals that required resources beyond CBA's budget.
- **Engage alumni early and often:** Consistent involvement created true ownership among the alumni who participated in the planning process. They brought valuable industry insight and ideas, and

it inspired many to provide financial backing to activate the plan components that resonated most with them.

References

Eckel, P., & Trower, C. (2019, February 14). Stop planning. *Inside Higher Ed*. Retrieved July 31, 2020, from https://www.insidehighered.com/views/2019/02/14/colleges-need-rethink-strategic-planning-opinion.

Fain, P. (2007, October 5). Vision for excellence. *The Chronicle of Higher Education*. Retrieved July 31, 2020, from https://www.chronicle.com/article/vision-for-excellence/.

Ginsberg, B. (2011, July 17). The strategic plan: Neither strategy nor plan, but a waste of time. *The Chronicle of Higher Education*. Retrieved July 31, 2020, from https://www.chronicle.com/article/the-strategic-plan-neither-strategy-nor-plan-but-a-waste-of-time/.

Goodman, C. A., & Salem, H. (2015). *Getting the most out of univesity strategic planning*. Santa Monica, CA: RAND Corporation. Retrieved July 29, 2020, from https://www.rand.org/pubs/perspectives/PE157.html.

Gwinner, K. (2020, June 30). Edgerly Family Dean, KSU College of Business Administration (A. Conley, Interviewer).

Kansas State University. (n.d.a). *Dean's Business Advisory Council*. Retrieved July 28, 2020, from College of Business Administration. https://cba.k-state.edu/alumni-partners/advisory-councils/business/.

Kansas State University. (n.d.b). *Strategic plan 2018–2022*. Retrieved July 28, 2020, from College of Business Administration. https://cba.k-state.edu/about/strategic-plan.html.

Kansas State University Foundation. (n.d.). *Massachusetts couple establishes first endowed deanship at k-state*. Retrieved July 28, 2020, from https://www.ksufoundation.org/why-i-give/2011/edgerley.html.

Kansas State University Foundation. (2019, May 3). *Transformational gift advances college strategic plan*. Retrieved July 28, 2020, from Innovation & Inspiration: The $1.4 Billion Campaign for K-State. https://inspire.k-state.edu/your-support-in-action/campaign-news/EdgerleyCBA2019.html.

Lindahl, W. E. (1992). *Strategic planning for fund raising*. San Francisco: Jossey-Bass.

Perlmutter, D. D. (2019a, September 18). Admin 101: How to manage the strategic planning process. *The Chronicle of Philanthropy*. Retrieved July 29, 2020, from https://www.chronicle.com/article/Admin-101-How-to-Manage-the/247126.

Perlmutter, D. D. (2019b, August 6). Admin 101: How to plan for strategic planning. *The Chronicle of Higher Education*. Retrieved July 29, 2020, from https://www.chronicle.com/article/Admin-101-How-to-Plan-for/246796.

Perlmutter, D. D. (2019c, November 25). Admin 101: How to properly wrap up a strategic plan (and why that matters). *The Chronicle of Higher Education*. Retrieved July 29, 2020, from https://www.chronicle.com/article/Admin-101-How-to-Properly/247572.

Perlmutter, D. D. (2019d, October 22). Admin 101: Tips on carrying out your strategic plan. *The Chronicle of Higher Education*. Retrieved July 29, 2020, from https://www.chronicle.com/article/Admin-101-Tips-on-Carrying/247365.

Sargeant, A., & Jay, E. (2014). *Fundraising management: Analysis, planning and practice* (3rd ed.). New York: Routledge.

Seiler, T. L. (2016). Plan to succeed. In E. R. Tempel, T. L. Seiler, & D. F. Burlingame (Eds.), *Achieving excellence in fundraising* (4th ed., pp. 27–35). Hoboken, NJ: John Wiley & Sons.

Willems, G. (2020, June 23). President & CEO, KSU Foundation (A. Conley, Interviewer).

Ziedenstein, D. (2019). Strategy as the foundation for advancement. In M. J. Worth & M. T. Lambert (Eds.), *Advancing higher education: New strategies for fundraising, philanthropy, and engagement* (pp. 25–33). Lanham, MD: Rowman & Littlefield.

CHAPTER 12

Campaigns

Fundraising campaigns are a long-standing strategy within US higher education. As noted in Chapter 2 with Harvard's 1641 initiative, *New Englands First Fruits*, campaigns have served all manner of institutional aims. While campaigns were mostly limited to private institutions into the mid-twentieth century, they have since become part of the institutional legacies at public flagship institutions, regional state universities, and community colleges. It is increasingly rare to find a college or university that has never undertaken a fundraising campaign in some form.

This chapter provides essential fundamentals for conducting successful campaigns for academic units. These fundamentals apply if a campaign is part of an overall institutional effort or exclusively within a single unit. In cases where more depth and breadth of information on campaigns are needed, useful resources are available from Schroeder (2019), Worth (2017), Nichols (2002), and Gearhart (1995). Additional campaign resources written for the nonprofit sector and applicable to higher education include Lysakowski (2018), Conley (2016), Pierpont (2011), Lindahl (2008), and Dove (2000).

Long-serving faculty and academic leaders at institutions that have completed campaigns witness the mechanics of these efforts and the longer-term outcomes. At their core, campaigns are more than just attempts to raise specific dollar amounts in fixed time periods. Tactical

177

matters are important, but as O'Brien (2005) notes, it must always be remembered that,

> ...the ability of this model to raise funds, although effective, pales in comparison with its ability to be a catalyst for organizational change. By forcing an organization to develop a sustained focus on vision and values, major campaigns can transform institutions. (p. 30)

Campaign Fundamentals

Campaigns take many forms, but the most prevalent campaign vehicle to emerge in higher education over the past three decades is the comprehensive campaign. This term has come into favor over the legacy term of capital campaign, as "capital" implies physical structures, such as new construction or renovation of existing facilities. The term capital also is associated with capacity-building by raising greater endowment resources or similar funds for long-term uses and priorities.

The comprehensive campaign moniker is more accurate, as it encompasses these types of gifts as well as the gifts to academic, athletic, and other units (Worth, 2017). Each of the major units typically has a dollar goal. These add up collectively to the overall institutional goal. These efforts also count all funds raised through annual fund activities including direct mail, phone solicitations, and digital efforts such as giving days. And they count planned gifts, such as new bequests, along with gifts-in-kind of donated equipment, artwork, and software. The comprehensive campaign essentially counts all possible gifts in all forms received during the campaign timeframe. CASE (2009) provides guidelines for counting gifts and organizing campaign standards that are used by many institutions for structuring their campaigns.

Many of the fundamentals highlighted here and in other contemporary campaign resources were first developed and implemented in the early 1900s as Americans reached a turning point in the acceptance of mass philanthropy. With regional and national drives aimed at World War I relief efforts and larger societal issues of poverty and illness, giving took on a broader American identity. "Philanthropy would not be a mere pastime nor an exclusive obligation of the wealthy; rather, it would be a widespread activity in which the majority of Americans would participate" (Thelin & Trollinger, 2014, p. 150).

These efforts increasingly utilized campaign features still present today, which include careful planning and organization, committed volunteers, prestigious leadership figures, recognition and publicity, matching gifts, accurate records and reporting, and a definite time limit (Cutlip, 1965 [1990]). Colleges and universities began adopting this model in hopes of replicating the widespread enthusiasm that would inspire gifts from many rather than a few alumni and constituents.

Two illustrations are used here to explain the central features of successful campaigns. The first, in Fig. 12.1, is a sample campaign progress chart. Visual representations of a campaign's progress also emerged in the early 1900s with the advent of modern campaign techniques and have continued to be used, especially in higher education (Cutlip, 1965 [1990]). However, most illustrations fail to identify the campaign's end, which diminishes the sense of urgency to take action. The treatment displayed here also effectively illustrates if a campaign is ahead of schedule or behind.

This sample represents a six-year campaign with a goal of raising $50 million between January 1, 2014, and December 31, 2019. It presently depicts the total raised with one year remaining. It also shows the "quiet

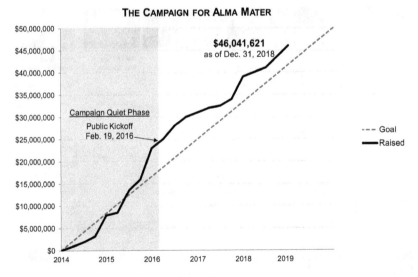

Fig. 12.1   Sample campaign progress chart

phase," spanning the first 25 months, where nearly half of the goal was raised before the public launch. Much of the first year was slightly behind schedule; the line representing the amount raised is below the line depicting the goal. This is not atypical for the quiet phase when campaign-oriented and new fundraising efforts are focused entirely on securing significant lead gift commitments.

The value of using this type of illustration is the visual reinforcement of time. During a campaign's quiet phase, this tool can be a powerful reminder for campaign volunteers, development staff, and leaders within the academic units that large, lead gifts must be secured early to be in a position to publicly launch the campaign. This tool can also be replicated for individual units, such as academic departments and centers within a school, to illustrate smaller dollar goals that are part of a larger campaign effort.

Understanding the structure and purpose of the campaign progress chart is necessary for a greater explanation of the key fundamentals of a campaign. Figure 12.2 provides a visual representation of the major phases of campaigns and a number of the critical actions that take place within each phase. This illustration is modeled on the same campaign

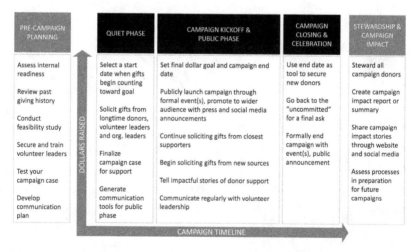

Fig. 12.2 Campaign phases and key actions (Conley, 2016) with permission from the publisher

progress chart to reinforce the importance of time and the proper sequence of major steps in campaign planning and execution.

Given campaigns' complexity and multiple moving parts, important steps are sometimes taken out of sequence particularly when planning activities are rushed or diminished. This can have a profoundly negative impact on timing since campaigns are exercises conducted within a fixed timespan and some steps may require three to six months or more to complete. Planning also involves the governing board, president, deans, volunteer leaders, and others who already cope with significant demands, making delays detrimental to the entire schedule and scope of a campaign.

The subsequent sections highlight the five campaign phases and the rationale for the major actions identified in each. These are summarized for the benefit of academicians, but the amount of labor and expertise required of development leadership and staff is significant and much more than these brief treatments suggest. Development staff should partner with academic leaders and their faculty throughout these phases to provide institutional context and insight beyond the major points identified here.

Pre-Campaign Planning

As noted in Fig. 12.2, this phase largely occurs before any gifts are counted toward a campaign dollar goal. Exceptions are made recalling that donors make major gifts when the timing is right for them, and not simply when they are asked (or when a campaign begins). Early, unexpected, and very large gifts that correspond to an anticipated campaign's priority areas can accelerate the planning process and be counted toward the eventual dollar goal—they may even influence the amount of that goal. Most gifts, however, will be realized after this critical planning stage and institutional leaders, the governing board, and longtime donors' engagement in activities that bring into focus the top institutional needs and a vision for the institution's potential.

Assessing internal readiness at this stage means many things, including examining historical giving data, staffing levels for gift officers and support, and budget resources for travel, events, digital and print media, and similar expenses. But for academic leaders, the priority at this stage is agreement on needs within their units. This is a necessity for comprehensive campaigns as well as stand-alone efforts for a single unit. The existence of a formal strategic plan can help inform and guide the formation of a campaign's priorities; however, the absence of one does not preclude establishment of goals and objectives (Ziedenstein, 2019).

Academic leaders and their faculty need to articulate a consistent vision of the unit's direction and the campaign's contribution to realizing this vision. Campaigns can have a transformational effect, but not without the discussions that help create a unifying voice: "Without this kind of dialogue, resources are often secured for less significant or even the wrong purposes, and the real benefits of these resources may be marginal or misguided" (O'Brien, 2005, p. 37).

Additionally, an initial inventory of key needs and opportunities should be developed across major divisions within the unit, along with estimated costs. These should all tie back to the strategic plan or shared priorities and include input from department chairs and leaders of administrative units such as student affairs, diversity and inclusion, instructional technology, and others. The initial outcome will appear to be a grossly unrealistic wish list, but this is to be expected as "every initial list of priorities created by an institution in the first planning stage far exceeds the donor capacity, staff, budget, and historical fundraising levels of the organization" (Schroeder, 2019, p. 115). To help educate process participants and keep expectations realistic, these inventories should be explained as beneficial to gift officers and development research staff throughout the campaign duration. New donors are continuously discovered and a general awareness of needs is helpful when discerning their interests for potential campaign gifts.

Once an agreed vision is developed and defined and a working inventory of needs is collected, a case for support can be drafted, typically with the guidance of experienced development staff. Consultants engaged to lead campaign planning or for its communications efforts may assist with the case. Regardless of the approach, the working document is shared internally, as well as with select external audiences.

Campaign plans are extensive in scope and document the vision, needs, and draft case, with the intention of collecting feedback and inspiring interest. One of the most important feedback exercises relates to setting the campaign dollar goal. This is typically informed and developed through personal interviews with a representative population of potential major donors. Ideally, these donors have the capacity and willingness to (eventually) commit some of the largest campaign gifts. In the meetings, which are often conducted by an external consultant, a potential gift amount is tested. This is not a solicitation but rather an assessment of the possibility of a comparable gift based on the draft case for support. Donors are assured these meetings are confidential, and the results are reported to the institution in aggregate to help determine if the initial campaign goal is realistic.

These meetings can also identify other major campaign donors and volunteer leaders. Institutions may direct their consulting partner to ask select participants about their interest in serving on a campaign leadership council, and whether they know others who should be considered. Identifying potential volunteer leaders at this stage is critical, as is determining the most effective volunteer structure.

Lastly, the communications plan requires consideration at this point. Like many major tasks in this phase, this activity will likely be directed by the central development or foundation team in collaboration with the institution's marketing office. However, academic leaders would do well to think ahead about reaching their alumni (both local and far from campus), corporate supporters, and various external constituents with ongoing messaging about the campaign. Early attention to internal communication is also useful, as it is vital to keep faculty, staff, and students informed and to invite them to be donors and volunteers as well.

Relatedly, academic leaders must use the pre-planning phase to begin crafting the messaging required to sustain interest and momentum through the campaign. Websites, newsletters, and other formal vehicles are valuable tools, but many academic leaders underestimate the value of their own remarks about the campaign's purpose and accomplishments. These should be incorporated, in the appropriate form, into standing appointments and events including faculty meetings, faculty and staff orientations, holiday receptions, presentations to student groups, speeches to community organizations, and any like opportunities that arise. Confidence in an organization's leadership is a critical motivator for giving. Articulating a powerful vision and campaign case is an excellent opportunity to build this confidence among potential donors.

Quiet Phase

The lead responsibility for most of this phase's main actions (see Fig. 12.2) rests with development staff and leadership. The central responsibility for academic leaders is also the one that is the most often misunderstood.

Sequential solicitation is the process where the very first solicitations for campaign gifts are meticulously planned and executed. In institution-wide campaigns, these often include the involvement of the president, board chair, senior campaign volunteer, deans, or athletic director, all depending on the interests of the potential donor. Rosso (1991) characterizes sequential solicitation in two major components, top-down and inside-out. The first principle describes the process of approaching the largest (and top) potential donors before any others who may support the campaign. Understanding this is particularly important as inexperienced academic leaders sometimes believe soliciting their alumni population en masse is the right catalyst for beginning a campaign:

> [Sequential solicitation] forces a focus on the larger gifts and discourages a preoccupation with the smaller gifts at the bottom of the gift-range chart. Small gifts are graciously received, but they do not contribute as much to the desired outcome as do the larger gifts. (Rosso, 1991, p. 92)

The gift range chart projects the gifts needed at different levels to reach the desired goal. The accumulated knowledge and experience of previous campaigns have shown that success is highly dependent on securing a small number of gifts at the highest levels. Emphasis has traditionally been placed on the top 10–20% of donors whose gifts may account for 70–90% of all dollars raised. Over time, this phenomenon has become even more pronounced and much funding now comes from as little as the top 1% of donors. A long-running study of higher education campaigns conducted by CASE (2017) found that the top 1% of donors accounted for 64% of all campaign giving in 2006, and this figure increased to 79% by 2015. These figures reinforce the importance of the top-down practice in sequential solicitation. Failure to secure lead gifts from this vital donor population during the quiet phase could seriously jeopardize the entire campaign timeframe and even the campaign itself.

Also during this phase, the amount sought in the campaign should be referenced as a working goal, or even a range. This is imperative for academic leaders, development staff, and volunteers alike. Despite the implied secrecy of the term, the quiet phase is often known to large numbers of faculty, staff, and closely-connected alumni and friends. Flexibility is necessary as one or more donors at the top of the gift range chart may give far more than anticipated. As a result, the goal, duration, or both could be altered, a process which will be easier to manage

Table 12.1 Sample gift range chart

Gift Amount	Gifts Needed	Potential Donors Needed	Total	Percent of Goal (%)
$10,000,000	1	4	$10,000,000	20
$5,000,000	2	8	$10,000,000	20
$1,000,000	5	20	$5,000,000	10
$500,000	10	40	$5,000,000	10
$100,000	20	80	$2,000,000	4
$50,000	35	140	$1,750,000	3.5
$25,000	75	300	$1,875,000	3.75
$10,000	100	Many	$1,000,000	2
$5,000	200	Many	$1,000,000	2
		(Major Gift Goal)	$37,625,000	75.25
<$5,000	Many	Many	$12,375,000	24.75
		(Campaign Goal)	$50,000,000	100

with widespread understanding that finalization will occur just prior to the public announcement.

To further illustrate projecting a campaign goal, consider Table 12.1 depicting a gift range chart for the fictional institution illustrated in Fig. 12.1 with its $50 million goal. The institution's development team created an initial gift range chart during pre-planning that utilized historical data including the number of gifts at different levels over the previous decade. They combined this with knowledge of existing and potential donors and interpretations of likely campaign supporters and gifts.

The feasibility study interviews provided newly gathered qualitative and quantitative data pertaining to the top potential donors. This allowed the construction of this revised chart, which was used to guide the sequential solicitation process during the quiet phase.

Many approaches can be employed when constructing a gift range chart. A long-standing technique to use as an initial step is the rule of thirds (Seymour, 1966). This states that the top 10 gifts likely provide a third of the goal, the next 100 gifts provide the next third, and all the rest will provide the final third. Refinements to the table can follow as information about donor interest is obtained (especially at the highest levels). Considering the probabilities of gifts at the upper levels of the chart is vital for the mathematical development of a realistic gift chart (Dove, 2000). This knowledge can assist, for example, in determining an appropriate ratio of potential donors needed. Table 12.1 reflects a ratio of four to one for all gift amounts.

The second of Rosso's (1991) sequential solicitation principles, inside-out, refers to the need for widespread support within an organization before external constituencies are solicited for campaign gifts. In an academic unit, this means gift commitments at any level by the dean, department chairs, senior administrative staff, and development officers. This also includes gifts from members of advisory boards, with the exception of any in the upper levels of the gift range chart.

While top-down focuses on major gifts, inside-out emphasizes gift participation. Units pursuing campaigns need to convey the commitment of leadership and staff through their own philanthropy, with recognition that gift sizes must be personally, not organizationally, determined. Academic leaders and internal constituents should be encouraged to make pledges to be paid over the full duration of the campaign. The full value of these multi-year pledges counts toward the comprehensive campaign's running total. This multi-year pledge approach is preferred over simply making an annual gift since this allows for greater progress toward the goal earlier in the campaign.

Together, top-down and inside-out are powerful instructional tools to explain the mechanics of an ambitious, multi-year campaign. Utilizing them in the sequential solicitation process during the quiet phase generates momentum needed to launch the public phase. This approach helps generate a contagious enthusiasm that will inspire others to join the effort.

Campaign Kickoff & Public Phase

The public announcement of a campaign is the realization of the extensive pre-planning efforts and successful lead gifts secured through sequential solicitation. It is an opportunity to recognize and thank the early donors, as well as campaign volunteers who have shared their hopes and vision through the investment of their time and advocacy.

The forms of announcing a campaign are nearly infinite and are driven largely by institutional culture and budget resources. Black-tie galas may be appropriate for some, while informal campus-based events that center on students may fit elsewhere. Some campaigns have launched with nothing more than a simple press conference for local media. Virtual events of various kinds also seem a likely approach for future kickoffs.

For comprehensive campaigns, institutions' development leadership often collaborates with the president and senior academic leaders to determine the most meaningful and fitting kickoff celebrations. A key aspect of this process is finalizing the dollar goal and the official campaign end date. These two points may be fluid earlier in the quiet phase even as initial lead gift discussions take place with potential donors.

Long after the celebration of the public announcement subsides, nearly all campaigns reach a point where interest wanes or outright fatigue sets in. Keeping volunteers engaged, development staff motivated, and academic leaders focused on the continued need for solicitations further into the gift range chart all can be challenging. This reinforces the importance of a robust communication plan.

Delivering positive news and updates throughout the campaign is critical, but especially during the public phase's latter stages. Closing in on the goal is always a worthy subject that can be returned to repeatedly, but is not enough on its own. A significant inventory of stories should be developed about new gifts as well as the impact of gifts completed earlier in the campaign and already in use. Gift announcements can be held for particular moments in the campaign, and some donors may be willing to embargo their announcements to help create a steady sequence of significant campaign stories. This contributes to a sense of perpetual momentum through the campaign closing, which can help achieve those final giving benchmarks.

Campaign Closing & Celebration

Like the kickoff, the closing of a comprehensive campaign can take many forms and academic leaders may not have a significant role in determining how it will end. What academic leaders can influence is the use of two highly effective methods of securing campaign gifts only available at this late stage.

By collaborating with development staff, academic leaders can discern which major donors were solicited, but did not give, during the quiet phase. Perhaps the timing was not personally or organizationally (for companies or foundations) conducive for giving at that time. These refusals are easily forgotten as the campaign carries on and new donors are solicited. As long as the instances were characterized as "not now" rather than "not ever," these conversations should be revisited on the chance of changed conditions. Showing these potential donors the unprecedented levels of support realized during the campaign can be compelling, especially when presented as an invitation to be part of a historic institutional moment.

This same principle can apply to making final campaign solicitations through annual giving appeals and events. In one campaign study, Lindahl (2008) found potential donors highly likely to give when the campaign was within 95% of goal, noting the presence of an "end-of-the-race mentality" and donors' self-image of gifts at this stage providing a final burst across the finish line. Highlighting metrics such as number of gifts, alumni donors, and first-time donors can help create the image of a growing giving community. Joining this community and achieving the campaign goal can inspire people who believed their gift was not large enough to make a difference earlier in the campaign. This technique is especially important to broaden the total base of donors at all levels and enable the possibility of a larger campaign goal next time.

Stewardship & Campaign Impact

The placement of stewardship in this final phase is somewhat misleading as stewardship should be practiced throughout every campaign stage. Its inclusion following the campaign's formal end is a reminder of the considerable opportunities to sustain the transformational gift support experienced during the campaign. This can be achieved by carefully and strategically keeping donors engaged and informed about the outcomes of campaign gifts.

Stewardship following a campaign is not just saying thank you to donors, nor is it simply publishing names in an honor roll. Rather, stewardship is "making certain donors' gifts are used wisely, used for intended purposes, managed well in endowments, have an impact..." (Tempel & Seiler, 2016, p. 432). From this perspective, stewardship activities take many forms and should continue for many years following the campaign. Academic leaders need to schedule time for it as they did for various development activities during the campaign.

Post-campaign stewardship efforts should be planned and approached with two categories of donors in mind. First, major gift donors need to see the evidence, suggested in the definition, showing that gifts are being used for the intended purposes and resulting in demonstrated impact. This process is time-intensive, but responsibility does not rest solely with the dean or academic leaders. Much of the organizational effort to coordinate these communications will be driven by development staff including gift officers, data analysts, endowment compliance, marketing, and donor relations. Development teams must continue partnering with academic leaders as they did during the campaign to ensure no major gift donor is forgotten.

The second stewardship category is the thousands of donors who made smaller gifts. This population's size makes it nearly impossible and totally inefficient to convey thanks and appreciation individually or even through large events. Instead, most institutions convey messages of impact and thanks through broad communication channels post-campaign. Academic units should complement institutional efforts with cost-effective approaches directed to their donor population. The goal is to generate high levels of confidence that these gifts are making a meaningful difference for the unit's priorities. Digital communication vehicles now make this task far more achievable than ever before and should be the cornerstone of campaign communication plans from pre-planning to post-closing.

The final action point in this stage is to review internal campaign processes to identify what worked well, and what needs improvement. Most colleges and universities undertake extended formal institutional reviews, but individual units should do the same, even informally. The outcomes should be documented in a brief report and saved for application to future campaigns.

The Role of Academic Leaders in a Campaign

The success of current and future campaigns is increasingly dependent on academic leaders who understand the importance of planning, as well as professionally executing major tasks within each campaign phase. Development professionals will take responsibility for much of the time-consuming minutiae. They are not substitutes, however, for academic leaders and their vital campaign role: "The unit head must be perceived as leader of a community that has envisioned, researched, debated, decided, and unified around common aspirations. Only then can we, the fund raisers, begin to plan a comprehensive campaign" (Nichols, 2002, p. 155).

A summary of select campaign roles for academic leaders closes this chapter. This complements the insights shared in Part 6 of the *Don't Fear*

Fund Raising series, which focuses on engaging faculty in campaigns. Acknowledgment of these leadership and fundraising principles prepares academic units for the transformational potential of successful campaigns.

- During pre-planning, begin to envision potential gift discussions. Think about how to start a gift conversation, connecting the known interests of a donor with specific campaign goals (reviewing Chapter 7 may be especially helpful here). As the case for support is refined, consider how to articulate its central principles in ways that resonate with various audiences while still retaining its core focus.
- Do not panic if the quiet phase begins slowly. Early gifts can be difficult to secure, but momentum can be quickly generated after closing the first or second lead gifts. Mention these gifts in subsequent solicitations since research shows donors are influenced by others who give to further the vision.
- Be prepared to explain to faculty that a campaign cannot focus on everyone's area of interest or research.
- When the campaign launches, ensure all academic unit leaders and campaign volunteers can articulate the case for support similarly and convincingly.
- Realize that prominent namings are not a campaign goal; rather, they are recognition opportunities that can facilitate achieving a vision for the future. Focus on how the funds within these types of gifts address campaign priorities.
- Approach every donor meeting fully prepared, especially during the quiet phase. The top of the gift range chart is sparsely populated, and campaign goals cannot be achieved without successfully securing these gifts.
- When talking about the campaign to any audience, speak less about the dollar goal and more about the impact the campaign will have on the next five years, and the next 25 years. (Recall in Chapter 2 the importance of knowing institutional philanthropic history. This campaign will add to that historical legacy.)
- When appropriate, recognize gift officers as well as the larger development operation. Campaigns are intensely staff-driven efforts that raise the profile of the entire institution. Expressions of appreciation by highly-visible academic leaders are remarkably powerful in building a greater campus-wide esprit de corps.

CONCLUSION

Comprehensive campaigns are most readily recognized as effective vehicles for meeting immediate and near-term needs, while strengthening an institution's overall position for the future. Development leaders recognize another valuable, but often unmentioned benefit. After conducting multiple successful campaigns, development leaders have discovered that higher fundraising totals can be sustained well into the post-campaign years. This allows them to enter the next campaign's pre-planning from a position of strength and to consider much greater goals.

Research based on data from major consulting firms reinforces this point. An illustration in the book, *Leading the Campaign*, shows gift revenue in an expected trajectory without a campaign (Worth, 2017). When actual campaign gift revenue is included, a substantial "campaign premium" is revealed through significantly higher totals. As Worth notes, the immediate years following a campaign's end may see moderate declines, "But it typically does not return to its precampaign level, producing important postcampaign value in the form of permanently higher annual and capital support" (p. 16).

If presidents and boards reduce development resources once a campaign ends, however, the campaign premium can be negatively impacted. Once the goal is achieved and funding set aside for the campaign is exhausted, multiple staff positions may be cut and expenditures significantly reduced for travel, events, and marketing. While a staffing and budget analysis should always be part of a post-campaign evaluation, short-term cost savings can have significant long-term repercussions on future gift revenue. This is a consideration at the institutional level but should also be applied within individual units.

ACTIONABLE STRATEGIES

1. If your unit has conducted previous campaigns, identify key features of your unit that exist today because of those efforts. These could include new or renovated buildings, endowed scholarships and fellowships, faculty professorships and chairs, and academic programs or research centers. An inventory of "campaign impact" is a valuable tool in preparing the case for future campaigns by demonstrating tangible outcomes, even if the campaign gifts were received years or decades ago.

2. Using the items from #1, ask your development officer to give a brief presentation at a faculty meeting. This demonstration of campaign impact is vital, as future campaigns (with inevitably higher goals) require the involvement of more volunteers and advocates. Your faculty could be a crucial link to new campaign donors but must be confident about campaigns' value, understand how fundraising within a campaign works, and envision how they can play a contributing role. (If your unit has no campaign history, these two exercises can still be conducted highlighting other examples of donor support.)
3. Construct a gift range chart for a potential campaign to support a unit priority. For the top two gift levels, are you able to identify enough prospective donors needed to raise those gifts? Use this tool to show faculty and other academic leaders in your unit that successful campaigns take more than one potential donor at these top levels.

References

Conley, A. (2016). Capital campaigns. In E. R. Tempel, T. L. Seiler, & D. F. Burlingame (Eds.), *Achieving excellence in fundraising* (4th ed., pp. 243–258). Hoboken, NJ: John Wiley & Sons.

Council for Advancement and Support of Education. (2009). *CASE reporting standards & management guidelines* (4th ed.). Washington, DC: CASE.

Council for Advancement and Support of Education. (2017). *2015 CASE campaign report*. Washington, DC: CASE.

Cutlip, S. M. (1965 [1990]). *Fund raising in the United States: Its role in America's philanthropy*. New Brunswick, NJ: Transaction Publishers.

Dove, K. E. (2000). *Conducting a successful capital campaign* (2nd ed.). San Francisco: Jossey-Bass.

Gearhart, G. D. (1995). *The capital campaign in higher education: A practical guide for college and university advancement*. Washington, DC: National Association of College and University Business Officers.

Lindahl, W. E. (2008). Three-phase capital campaigns. *Nonprofit Management & Leadership, 18*(3), 261–273.

Lysakowski, L. (2018). *Getting ready for a capital campaign*. Arlington, VA: Association of Fundraising Professionals. Retrieved August 4, 2020, from https://afpglobal.org/sites/default/files/attachments/2018-12/AFPRea dyReferenceCapitalCampaign2018.pdf.

Nichols, S. (2002). Unit-based campaigning. In F. A. Hilenski (Ed.), *The unit development officer's handbook* (pp. 153–159). Washington, DC: CASE.

O'Brien, C. L. (2005). Thinking beyond the dollar goal: A campaign as organizational transformation. *New Directions for Philanthropic Fundraising: Reprising Timeless Topics, 47,* 29–42.

Pierpont, R. (2011). Capital campaigns. In E. R. Tempel, T. L. Seiler, & E. E. Aldrich (Eds.), *Achieving excellence in fundraising* (3rd ed., pp. 81–91). San Francisco: Jossey-Bass.

Rosso, H. (1991). *Achieving excellence in fund raising.* San Francisco: Jossey-Bass.

Schroeder, F. W. (2019). The art and science of comprehensive campaigns. In M. J. Worth & M. T. Lambert (Eds.), *Advancing higher education: New strategies for fundraising, philanthropy, and engagement* (pp. 113–127). Lanham, MD: Rowman & Littlefield.

Seymour, H. J. (1966). *Designs for fund raising.* New York: McGraw-Hill.

Tempel, E., & Seiler, T. (2016). Stewardship and accountability. In E. Tempel, T. Seiler, & D. Burlingame (Eds.), *Achieving excellence in fundraising* (4th ed., pp. 431–438). Hoboken, NJ: John Wiley & Sons.

Thelin, J. R., & Trollinger, R. W. (2014). *Philanthropy and American higher education.* New York: Palgrave Macmillan.

Worth, M. (2017). *Leading the campaign: The president and fundraising in higher education* (2nd ed.). Lanham, MD: Rowman & Littlefield.

Ziedenstein, D. (2019). Strategy as the foundation for advancement. In M. J. Worth & M. T. Lambert (Eds.), *Advancing higher education: New strategies for fundraising, philanthropy, and engagement* (pp. 25–33). Lanham, MD: Rowman & Littlefield.

CHAPTER 13

Measuring Impact

Aligning strategic priorities with donor interests and conducting successful campaigns are two unparalleled opportunities for academic leaders to build legacies of successful fundraising. This applies to the units they oversee and their own professional experience and growth.

This chapter addresses a core function with direct connections to the previous two chapters. High-performing fundraising organizations evaluate the effectiveness of their programs and staff in ways that extend far beyond measuring dollars raised. Academic leaders can use the insights provided here when assessing the overall health of their development and fundraising efforts. This deeper perspective is necessary for moving away from the long-running practice of judging success solely on dollars, which has afflicted not just higher education but the entire nonprofit sector.

> For decades, fundraising performance has been measured by two simple criteria: "How much did you raise?" and "How much did it cost?" These two are essential components, yet judgements based only on a cost-benefit ratio can be misleading since it offers no details on solicitation activities and their results. (Greenfield & Brown, 2016, p. 329)

This practice is even more damaging when the amount raised is evaluated based on unrealistic goals, including those set for individual gift officers assigned to work with academic units. Consistently unmet dollar

© The Author(s), under exclusive license to Springer Nature   195
Switzerland AG 2021
A. Conley and G. G. Shaker, *Fundraising Principles for Faculty and Academic Leaders*, Philanthropy and Education,
https://doi.org/10.1007/978-3-030-66429-9_13

goals may not be as much an indication of gift officer performance as they are of expectations that are not grounded in data and evidence. When changing personnel is considered the most expedient solution to improve overall fundraising performance, it becomes a perpetual and self-inflicted cycle.

Sound goal-setting for gift officers takes many factors into account in addition to the academic unit's fundraising potential or the most urgent needs of the coming year. These are indeed important, but should be balanced with enabling factors. These include considerations about the gift officer including length of tenure in their position as well as within the institution, total major gift fundraising experience, and the composition of their assigned portfolio of donors (Grabau, 2012).

Measure More Than Dollars

As noted several times in this book, academicians' skills can be applied to development and fundraising. These include evaluation. For example, evaluating the health of academic degree programs encompasses review of a wide array of student enrollment and assessment data to discern trends, as well as faculty measures such as teaching loads, course evaluations, and research productivity. Rarely do one or two data points provide a complete picture of an academic enterprise at a point in time.

This same principle applies to development. Various data need to be tracked over time to supplement the basic measure of dollars raised. As defined in the Chapter 1, fundraising is the act of asking for a gift and development is all the things necessary for improving the likelihood of success when those requests are made. Measuring the productivity of development efforts exclusively by dollars raised fails to accurately assess performance and often drives development staff toward counterproductive practices that harm the long-term fundraising potential for a school, college, or unit (Peters, 2019).

Recent evidence of gift officer performance can help set baseline expectations that can be refined with institution-specific considerations. In a study of more than 240 institutions covering the five-year period of 2013 to 2018, individual major gift fundraising officers accounted for an annual average of $724,569 in gifts (EAB, 2019). The study further segmented the findings by institutional type and public or private sector. For privates, average fundraiser revenue at research institutions was $970,536, master's was $537,649, and baccalaureate was $697,996. For publics, research was

$866,085 and master's was $372,070. (There was no figure for public baccalaureate.)

This study also classified institutions as "High ROI" and "Low ROI" based on a number of tracked measures. Gift officers at High ROI institutions closed an average of 12.6 major gifts annually, with about 8.1 valued between $25,000 and $100,000 and the remaining 4.5 above $100,000. By comparison, gift officers at Low ROI institutions closed 6.9 gifts, with 4.7 at $25,000 to $100,000 and just 2.2 above $100,000.

These figures provide initial benchmarks for individual gift officer performance; however, this approach is not singularly effective. Measuring the total number of face-to-face meetings is another common metric, but development programs often track additional measures to assess performance. For example, the number of qualifying visits gift officers conduct with newly-identified major gift prospective donors is helpful to document as it ensures that the officers are not visiting the same individuals repeatedly. Some programs also set a fixed percentage of visits that must be for qualifying purposes.

Relatedly, programs may also track the number of prospects a gift officer disqualifies. Gift officers need to be engaging individuals with major gift capacity and interest in connecting with the institution. If a gift officer quickly determines a lack of one or both of these main factors, documenting this in the database prevents others from attempting contact in the future. This activity does not lead to increased gift totals; however, it is necessary within the development process. As such, development staff should not be admonished for disqualifying prospects and these efforts should be recognized.

Another important metric for academic leaders relates to collaboration. Development programs are increasingly adding some form of measurement and acknowledgment when gift officers from different units work together on cultivation and solicitation efforts (Peters, 2019). These instances often center on one donor who has clearly demonstrated interest in engaging and supporting multiple units or programs across an institution.

RECOMMENDED ACADEMIC UNIT METRICS

For a comprehensive perspective on an entire academic unit's philanthropic performance, a wide range of data should be tracked annually to supplement the evaluation of individual gift officers. Measures of dollars and donors provide an effective starting place. Reviewing a full decade of data identifies outliers and allows for extended calculations of compound annual growth. Most often this unit-level data should be available from the central development office or foundation.

Dollars

In addition to cash received, pledges of cash through multi-year commitments and planned gifts provide insight into future cash flow. Measuring the raw number of gifts by different categories can reveal weaknesses and opportunities. Options for measurement include annual evaluations of:

- Total giving: The value of all pledges and cash received;
- Total cash: From the total giving sum, the amount of cash received;
- Total number and dollar value of new planned gifts;
- Total number of gifts by amount (create 3 to 5 bands of gift amounts to identify trends in gifts by amount);
- Total number of new endowments (by dollar value and purpose).

Donors

Measuring donors helps reveal misplaced confidence in fundraising performance in those cases where dollar totals appear to be strong, but are derived from a very small number of large gifts. Items to document include:

- Total number of gifts and dollar value by source: Alumni, other individuals, corporations, foundations;
- Total number of first-time donors by source (same sources as above);
- Total number of consecutive-year donors (under five years, 6–10, 11–20, 20+);
- Retention rates by donor source (track first-time donors and donors of $1,000+).

These measures will provide a strong baseline of information and should be used to inform the annual development plan (see Chapter 9). For example, if a school has a low retention rate among alumni giving at least $1,000, the plan could include a strategy for this population, such as special outreach and testing of new stewardship approaches. Many additional metrics can be added as time goes on to align with unit priorities.

Taking an objective, data-driven approach to assessment and planning brings transparency to processes that gift officers often find incongruous with their own knowledge and observations of alumni and donor populations. Academic leaders should certainly have high aspirations (and expectations). There must be a partnership perspective with development officers, however, driven by realistic success metrics and continuous improvement. Retaining productive gift officers in their roles is essential. The EAB (2019) study cited earlier found that for every year a gift officer stayed with a university, they raised an additional $106,000. Over time, this premium can enable an academic unit to achieve many priorities and an entire institution to realize continuously stronger gift revenue.

Comparing Performance with Peers

Tracking and interpreting institutional fundraising data reveal weaknesses and growth opportunities; however, it does not provide comparative insights beyond campus. Given the competitiveness within academic disciplines to recruit the best students and most accomplished faculty, fundraising benchmarks among peers would be as helpful to know as any of the most common metrics in academic rankings. But fundraising figures at school and department levels are typically not shared beyond an institution's own internal reporting procedures. Colleges and universities regularly produce publicly-distributed annual fundraising reports. Most do not include individual academic unit gift totals or numbers of donors, although there are exceptions (e.g., University of Washington, n.d.).

One potential source for fundraising data at peer schools is the accrediting body or agency for specific academic disciplines. For example, business schools are accredited by AACSB. An annual survey conducted by AACSB for its members was recently expanded to collect fundraising data, allowing business schools to compare their fundraising totals directly with peers (Nelson, 2018). AACSB also regularly hosts fundraising and development conferences for deans, business school administrators, and development staff.

While other accrediting bodies may not offer formal services or sources of information about fundraising, development professionals in some fields have organized their own efforts. For example, schools of engineering, technology, and computing are accredited by ABET. While ABET does not provide survey or conference services like AACSB, there is a development staff-driven organization called the Engineering Development Forum (EDF). This group has hosted an annual conference since 1992 open to engineering development staff, deans, and interested faculty (Engineering Development Forum, n.d.). EDF also conducts occasional benchmarking studies of fundraising performance.

Similar organizations exist for other disciplines and areas including the Academic Library Advancement and Development Network (n.d.) and the National Association of Cancer Center Development Officers (n.d.). And there are smaller groups organized around even tighter commonalities, like the business schools in the SEC Conference (University of Mississippi, n.d.). The lifespan of some of these organizations may be limited and development staff can help keep up with these organizations by building relationships and collecting data from like units. And, broader associations, such as the Council of Colleges of Arts and Sciences (CCAS), periodically feature development-specific programming for deans and leaders and always provide opportunities to build informal connections with academic peers.

Lastly, for comparison's sake, it is important to determine if a development program is well established within the academic unit or still relatively new. Some colleges and universities may have the appearance of a successful program, but formal development activity may be limited within some academic units. This disparity is especially common among public institutions within the smaller academic units, such as schools of education, nursing, public health, or fine arts. Many of these schools begin with a shared development officer responsible for supporting multiple units. If fruitful, it may lead to a full-time gift officer for the unit, but this can take many years.

Hiles (2010) provides guidance regarding measuring the quality of development programs that are in the start-up phase compared to well-established programs. He notes, "the two most important elements of a successful start-up program are being able to build infrastructure support while building relationships with current and future donors" (pp. 54–55). While this advice is addressed to institutional development programs, the same principle applies for academic schools and units. Building infrastructure requires time and attention, but must be undertaken in conjunction with donor engagement activities and efforts.

Hiles notes established programs face different challenges. Central among them is guarding against complacency by actively tracking and analyzing the metrics of annual fundraising outcomes, regardless of how good they are. Also, just as the development plan should be reviewed repeatedly throughout the year so too should the development team receive continuous feedback regarding performance, not just via annual review. And lastly, academic leaders must serve as role models by conducting quality, strategic visits that lead to solicitations for important gifts. Deans in particular can send powerful messages to development teams and faculty by being proactive in engaging donors. It is also necessary to communicate details about closing big gifts, as well as promising leads and new discoveries. These forms of leadership attend to dynamics inside the organization as well as externally and will elevate the entire unit's awareness, appreciation, and participation in development activities.

Conclusion

This chapter reveals ways to measure and follow fundraising performance beyond just total dollars raised. But academic leaders need to do more than regularly analyze the recommended quantitative data. As part of their role model responsibility, it is especially important for academic leaders to look beyond their own wishes, focus on the larger cause, and always demonstrate empathy for donor interest. This requires embracing campus-wide collaboration whenever appropriate and understanding that unit timeframes and metrics may mean nothing to donors.

Deans and department chairs also need to create conditions where their gift officers are not viewed as individual operators but team-focused partners (Warwick, 2006). Discussions about expectation setting, goals, and measures of success should be transparent and explainable through historical data, predictive analytics, and job duties and time allocations. Access to and engagement with faculty members and research staff can also be a critical step that helps unlock a cultivation trigger with a potential donor. Successes are often the result of the work of many, and academic leaders should continuously encourage openness and collaboration between development and the unit's faculty and staff.

Overall institutional knowledge can help move gift conversations forward, and since every individual is different, the information needed to keep moving forward can come from nearly any corner of a college campus including admissions, physical plant, government relations, and research and sponsored programs. When this type of interaction is discouraged and gift officers are instructed instead to spend all their time on the road, institutions risk setting unreachable goals, embarking on unfundable projects, or setting otherwise unsound expectations that cannot be supported by the donor pool (Warwick, 2006). Institutional culture toward fundraising may not be easily detected within performance metrics, but they are certainly influenced by it. And these metrics cannot experience sustained improvement without the active support of academic leaders who recognize the connection.

In closing, this approach to measuring success reinforces the argument of fundraising becoming an established profession (see Chapter 4). Professionals in other fields are not judged by a sole criterion, and fundraisers should not be measured exclusively by how much they raise. Bloland and Tempel (2004) use established professions like medicine and law to reinforce this point, as they note how some forms of surgery have low success rates, or certain legal cases may not often be won, but physicians and attorneys still enjoy high levels of prestige and honor.

> In fundraising, the bottom line appears to be so objective and concrete that it may obscure the significance of the fundraising professional's skill and knowledge. Success in raising funds is so important that it threatens to be the primary or only real measure used, even though it may have relatively little to do with typical professional characteristics. (p. 13)

ACTIONABLE STRATEGIES

1. Working with your development director, review the performance metrics identified in this chapter. Which are tracked for your unit, and which could be incorporated to better evaluate the impact of your development activities? Develop an action plan to add these new metrics into your unit's annual development plan.
2. If you currently do not have access to any peer benchmarking data, reach out to a counterpart at a peer institution. Ask how they measure the impact of their development program and explore if they would find it beneficial to share data around the metrics highlighted in this chapter.

REFERENCES

Academic Library Advancement and Development Network. (n.d.). Retrieved August 8, 2020, from University of Florida, George A. Smathers Libraries: https://www.uflib.ufl.edu/aladn/.

Bloland, H., & Tempel, E. (2004). Measuring professionalism. In L. Wagner & J. P. Ryan (Eds.), *New Directions for Philanthropic Fundraising* (43), 5–20.

EAB. (2019). *Optimizing advancement's ROI: Insights from EAB's advancement investment and performance initiative.* Retrieved June 3, 2020, from https://eab.com/research/advancement/on-demand-webconference/optimized-advancements-roi/.

Engineering Development Forum. (n.d.). Retrieved August 8, 2020, from Engineering Development Forum: https://engineeringdevelopmentforum.org/.

Grabau, T. W. (2012, Spring). Major gift metrics that matter. *Colloquy*, pp. 36–40. Retrieved August 8, 2020, from https://www.ats.edu/uploads/resources/publications-presentations/documents/major-gift-metrics-that-matter.pdf.

Greenfield, J. M., & Brown, M. S. (2016). Budgeting for and evaluating fundraising performance. In E. R. Tempel, T. L. Seiler, & D. F. Burlingame (Eds.), *Achieving excellence in fundraising* (4th ed., pp. 321–336). Hoboken, NJ: Wiley.

Hiles, T. S. (2010). Determining the success of fundraising programs. *New Directions for Higher Education; Perspectives on Fundraising* (149), 51–56.

National Association of Cancer Center Development Officers. (n.d.). Retrieved August 8, 2020, from https://www.naccdo.org/.

Nelson, C. (2018, December 21). *2017–18 BSQ finances module: A look at business school fundraising practices.* Retrieved August 8, 2020, from AACSB: https://www.aacsb.edu/blog/2018/december/2017-18-bsq-finances-module-a-look-at-business-school-fundraising-practices.

Peters, N. (2019). Structuring and managing the advancement staff. In M. J. Worth & M. T. Lambert (Eds.), *Advancing higher education: New strategies for fundraising, philanthropy, and engagement* (pp. 231–242). Lanham, MD: Rowman & Littlefield.

University of Mississippi. (n.d.). *SEC Business School Conference 2019.* Retrieved August 10, 2020, from University of Mississippi University Development: https://give.olemiss.edu/sec-business-school-conference/.

University of Washington. (n.d.). *Report to contributors.* Retrieved August 8, 2020, from University of Washington: https://www.washington.edu/giving/recognition/report-to-contributors/.

Warwick, J. (2006, March). Beyond metrics. *Currents*, pp. 16–23.

CHAPTER 14

Losing Oneself in a Great Cause

Organizational leadership requires myriad skills, including versatility, self-awareness, strategic thinking, and commitment to the cause. As Hodge (2016) writes, every nonprofit needs a visionary who embodies the mission. In complex higher educational institutions, there are multiple such people who advocate for school and units' specific missions. Academic leaders do this inside their institutions and externally as well. Doing so for philanthropic purposes is likewise based on vision for furthering the educational purpose. Becoming a student of philanthropy simply provides the grounding to put one's efforts to their best use.

The evidence presented throughout this book shows the elevated state of inquiry related to higher education philanthropy and the ways in which it is helping to advance fundraising practice. Similarly, the inclusion of case studies, donor examples, and situational scenarios provides models for applying research findings and fundraising principles to current and future opportunities. With these resources in hand, academic leaders possess more avenues for bringing their vision to life for donors and encouraging their support. Add to that the ability to inspire others through one's personal passion for the cause and a powerful combination is formed and ready to be practiced, refined, and perfected.

The following recommendations reinforce some of the most important principles in the book for academic leaders to employ in their fundraising

© The Author(s), under exclusive license to Springer Nature   205
Switzerland AG 2021
A. Conley and G. G. Shaker, *Fundraising Principles for Faculty and Academic Leaders*, Philanthropy and Education,
https://doi.org/10.1007/978-3-030-66429-9_14

and development activities. These are applicable for new and recently appointed academic leaders, as well as those who are more established but seeking insights on achieving stronger engagement and fundraising outcomes.

Advancing the Cause of Higher Education

Academicians who take on administrative leadership roles are invaluable to the enduring legacy and operational success of colleges and universities. Development is certain to be a management responsibility that will only continue to grow in importance. New and established leaders alike can make development and fundraising effective tools for their successful service based on the following recommendations.

Understand Where Charitable Dollars Come From

As discussed in Part I, academic leaders, faculty members, and even development professionals must always remember that nearly 90% of all charitable giving in the USA comes from individuals (Giving USA Foundation, 2020). Research insights on high net worth individuals also explain why soliciting this population for major gifts is different than raising small, annual gifts. This is effectively stated by Heil and Bate (2011).

> Gifts from high-net-worth donors are never transactional: they come only as a direct result of developing and implementing a strategic set of steps focused on building the relationship between the donor and the organization. These steps must be both based on the emotional involvement of the donor and developed over a lifetime of giving. (p. 180)

Gift opportunities from foundations and corporations are also important and not to be overlooked. However, odds for success can be greatly improved by prioritizing partnerships with development staff to identify individuals who may have both the capacity and interest for a gift.

Stay Focused on Strategic Donor Engagement

This recommendation directly complements the first. Part II highlighted research on how donors think about philanthropy and decide to give. Always remember to focus on the importance of the donor interface. Personal time with donors is critical, but not just to build stronger relationships. These interactions must be deliberate and focused in moving toward a discussion about a gift. Lively (2017) notes that major gift staff needs to always make forward progress. "Each meeting must be purposeful. In other words, gift officers should always execute a strategy that moves the prospect closer to a gift discussion" (pp. 38–39). When academic leaders take this same strategic perspective toward every meeting, the cultivation period can be dramatically reduced, resulting in greater frequency of reaching donor readiness and more opportunities to secure major gifts.

Position Development as a Core Operational System

Parts I and III focused on the operational tenets and tactics of managing development in the academic unit. Thoughtfully creating and effectively overseeing operational systems is a core management tool of a productive and efficient academic unit. As one dean observed following their time in the role, "Systems and processes are the heart and soul of how institutions continue to function long after you have stepped down" (Butin, 2016, para. 16). Make development a core operational system so these processes function in the current period and continue through leadership changes. If systems are already in place, explore opportunities for improvement using lessons from this book. Too many academic units experience repeated starts and stops in their development efforts when leaders depart. This confounds donors, volunteers, and internal partners who all want to help.

Remember that Raising Money is a Team Effort

The identification model in Chapter 6 centered on the principle of engagement and emotion working together. Graduates of a particular academic program (i.e., a community of participation) may share a common identity, but their feelings and memories (i.e., frameworks of consciousness) may not rest solely in their classroom experience. Students interact with a range of faculty and staff, so remember to engage the entire unit in development. The goal here is for everyone to understand they might play a role in securing future gifts. Jung and Lee (2019) noted this in a study of giving to a large arts administration department in a public research university: "Involving the whole unit is crucial to success as many parts of the unit have been influential in students feeling more emotionally attached even after they graduate" (p. 244). This does not mean everyone needs to be prepared to solicit gifts, only to understand how fundraising works and where they may fit in. And, as discussed in Chapter 10, do not forget to consider that external partners can be on the team, too.

Guard Against Complacency and Fear of Change

Even as development programs appear to be on steady footing and donors are dedicating a significant amount of their support to academic units specifically (Shaker & Borden, 2020), it is important to be ahead of the curve. Experienced leaders, as well as those who join units with existing development efforts, need to take new approaches to some aspect of existing activities. Engaging in professional development activities focused on fundraising, reading books like this one, following industry media stories about innovations in philanthropy, talking with donors about how their gifts came about—all can spark ideas. The case studies in Parts I, III, and IV provide real examples of deans who embraced aspects of their development efforts in new ways, with unprecedented results. Changes—even minor ones—can bring positive results immediately and over time. Both results serve development well, beyond just the additional funding they may secure. When results are positive, expectations rise—among faculty and staff, donors and volunteers, and even the gift officers themselves.

Looking Ahead

The beginning of Chapter 1 featured three quotes on philanthropy's role and impact on higher education, dating from 1988, 1999, and 2010. These quotes were included to provoke serious thought regarding the quickly evolving perspectives of private support among educational scholars, driven by changing external conditions and internal influences.

Conditions are certain to continue shifting—globally, regionally, and locally in ways that cannot be fully anticipated. Global pandemics and environmental concerns are affecting day-to-day life in profound ways and will bring repercussions for years ahead. Adverse economic conditions, political and public policy shifts, technological advances, and powerful social forces that challenge perspectives on racial equity, social justice, and inclusiveness will almost certainly remake societies. Each of these impacts college campuses in countless ways, but all portend new financial pressures and will almost certainly come with a need for greater resources.

Amidst this backdrop of continuous change, the principles in this book are timeless and allow for flexibility in their deployment. The strategies and tactics that relate to these principles can be developed over time, but all will be ineffectual without a vision for the unit's future and the momentum and commitment to achieve it. Development staff and their senior managers are primary partners in supporting academic leaders in this endeavor, but they cannot carry this charge alone. Deans, presidents, and all other academic leaders need to provide the transformational leadership for this effort:

> Within a philanthropic context, academic leaders must convince both internal (professional fundraisers, faculty, staff, and students) and external (alumni and other donors) stakeholders of their long-term vision of the institution. Success is only achieved if all of these constituents partner in the efforts. (Drezner & Huehls, 2015, p. 68)

Conclusion

The articles from the *Don't Fear Fund Raising* series by David Perlmutter that follow in Part V reflect many of the principles, recommendations, and donor scenarios found throughout this book. The dean and career academician who wrote the series speaks as a peer who has transitioned from full-time faculty member into academic leader.

The transformation included self-realization that development and fundraising were an essential function of the role, but one for which there was no formal preparation. This echoes Hunsaker and Bergerson's (2018) finding that, "While deans are expected to engage heavily in fundraising, this expectation alone does not translate into the competence and skill necessary to complete the task" (p. 77). A comparable level of fundraising confidence to Perlmutter's can be achieved by partnering with development professionals to apply this book's principles and by working through its actionable strategies. In other words, one does not need to be a natural fundraiser to succeed in development; rather, a combination of commitment, willingness to learn, practice, and collaboration can go a long way in achieving this goal.

Lastly, success in fundraising is not limited to a given year, and obsessing over metrics—whether monthly, quarterly, or annually—detracts from the need to focus on the donor. Academic leaders come and go (as do development staff) but a donor's bond can remain constant. Observations of Booker T. Washington (1900) are again useful to explain why this focus on donors—and not just dollars—matters.

As noted in his autobiography, Washington was frequently asked about his rules for raising funds for Tuskegee Institute. He named just two. The first was to do everything possible to make the institute's work known to potential supporters, and the second was "not to worry about the results" (p. 181). For Washington, the primacy of the cause, engaging potential donors around it, and demonstrating his passion for that purpose drove his efforts in a way that simply securing dollars for the school did not. He describes his perspective as such:

> In order to be successful in any kind of undertaking, I think the main thing is for one to grow to the point where he completely forgets himself; that is, to lose himself in a great cause. In proportion as one loses himself in this way, in the same degree does he get the highest happiness out of his work. (p. 181)

The great cause of education is what attracted most academicians to this, their chosen profession. The ability to make a difference in the lives of others and for society as a whole is a driving force for many faculty (Shaker, 2015). For those who take on fundraising responsibilities, therefore, the greatest happiness will be derived not by how much is raised, but from the impact each gift creates and the good it achieves.

ACTIONABLE STRATEGIES

1. Think back to your perceptions about fundraising and institutional advancement prior to reading this book. Has the book challenged any long-held assumptions? If so, share this information with a peer and explore their assumptions about fundraising. Ask about their perceptions of development and fundraising. Do they consider this administrative function in your unit a top priority, or simply another layer of bureaucracy in your institution's overall administration? Use findings from the book to explain to them what made you look at this topic or issue differently.

2. With the "Looking Ahead" section of this chapter in mind, discuss current conditions and emerging events with other academic leaders (or faculty) in your unit. Decide how these may relate to the need for additional resources and how philanthropic contributions could be used to help.

References

Butin, D. (2016, January 13). So you want to be a dean? You'd better be skilled at risk management and compromise. *The Chronicle of Higher Education.* Retrieved September 8, 2020, from https://www.chronicle.com/article/so-you-want-to-be-a-dean-234900.

Drezner, N. D., & Huehls, F. (2015). *Fundraising and institutional advancement: Theory, practice, and new paradigms.* New York: Routledge.

Heil, M. K., & Bate, S. (2011). High-net-worth donors. In E. R. Tempel, T. L. Seiler, & E. E. Aldrich (Eds.), *Achieving excellence in fundraising* (3rd ed., pp. 173–182). San Francisco: Jossey-Bass.

Hodge, J. M. (2016). Major gifts. In E. R. Tempel, T. L. Seiler, & D. F. Burlingame (Eds.), *Achieving excellence in fundraising* (4th ed., pp. 225–242). Hoboken, NJ: Wiley.

Hunsaker, R. C., & Bergerson, A. A. (2018). The fundraising role of academic deans: A qualitative study. *Philanthropy & Education, 2*(1), 75–96.

Jung, Y., & Lee, M.-Y. (2019). Exploring department-level fundraising: Relationship-based factors affecting giving intention in arts higher education. *International Journal of Higher Education, 8*(3), 235–246.

Lively, D. (2017). *Managing major gift fundraisers: A contrarian's guide.* Washington, DC: CASE.

Shaker, G. G. (Ed.). (2015). *Faculty work and the public good: Philanthropy, engagement, and academic professionalism.* New York: Teachers College Press, Columbia University.

Shaker, G. G., & Borden, V. M. (2020). *How donors give to higher education: Thirty years of supporting U.S. college and university missions* (Research Dialogue, No. 158). TIAA Institute. Retrieved August 27, 2020, from https://www.tiaainstitute.org/publication/how-donors-give-higher-education.

Washington, B. T. (1900). *Up from slavery: An autobiography.* Garden City, NY: Doubleday & Company, Inc. Retrieved June 12, 2020, from https://docsouth.unc.edu/fpn/washington/washing.html.

PART V

A Dean's Perspective

Foreword

Like most academics taking up fundraising, I went from 0 to 100 or, more colorfully, was thrown into the deep end of a lake without any training or preparation. When I became director of a school within a college of arts and sciences, suddenly I was expected to raise money from alumni (and occasionally non-alumni donors) and to package proposals for local and national foundations. I discovered quickly that some of the traits and training that had helped me succeed as a professor, such as my research, teaching, learned society service, and peer engagement, were helpful in the transition to this new responsibility.

This did not mean, however, that I didn't have a lot to learn. In fact, the biggest thing I had to learn was that I had a lot to learn. I was some 20 years into becoming an expert in my academic field; now I was an intern in a new area. Further, I found it surprising that there was a notable lack of literature written with academics (and, more important, the academic *mentality*) in mind about fundraising. Certainly, very good workshops and some books and articles about academic fundraising were available. But I definitely perceived a gap in the literature for "us."

The demographics and psychographics of those who become development professionals are often different than those of the people who become academicians and campus leaders. The first development professional with whom I worked was a graduate of our communications program and a cultured, intelligent, and perceptive person who was a terrific fundraiser. His mentoring was invaluable: I feel we became a great team. But the knowledge and insight chasm remained.

Now, writing almost 15 years later, I see an improving situation. As noted throughout this book, recent decades have seen remarkable growth in formal academic programs and courses about philanthropy and the nonprofit sector. This is complemented by more rigorous research and study of complex issues and problems in this field, disseminated through peer-reviewed books, journals, and professional conferences. Finally, it appears the professional world of fundraising is evolving in the same way the fields and disciplines we are all part of did many decades ago.

I was overjoyed, then, when Drs. Conley and Shaker expressed their intention of writing a book specifically for faculty and academic leaders that laid out in a thoughtful and practical manner the fundamentals of fundraising grounded in not just their own experience, but extensive empirical evidence and theoretical context. I was further impressed—and humbled—to learn of their intent to include my series, *Don't Fear Fund Raising*, as the concluding section of their book. I wrote these seven articles between 2013 and 2016 for *The Chronicle of Higher Education* to share my own insights and observations on fundraising. And as the authors shared with me, many of my tactics and recommendations directly align with the principles they would be writing about in their book.

I am proud to make my small contribution to this work because I think it is important for academics not to fear fundraising. That fear is real: the fear of compromising one's integrity and status and values; the fear of failure; the fear of floundering out of our long-established areas of competence. My series, now combined with this book, reassures all those new and maybe not so new chairs, directors, deans, and even presidents that fundraising should not be feared. "Institutional advancement" is a profession, art, and science; it has to be learned, practiced, understood, and executed with diligence. When this is done well, the benefits are tremendous not just for our students, programs, and institutions, but also for our donors.

I believe that *Fundraising Principles for Faculty and Academic Leaders* will be a landmark work and will be valuable for anyone either thinking about becoming a leader or who are already leads in any type of institution, from community colleges to Ivy League universities to state research institutions. Moreover, it's a very timely volume because, as of this writing in 2020, more than ever we need effective fundraising for America's public and private universities.

David D. Perlmutter Ph.D.
Professor & Dean
College of Media & Communication
Texas Tech University
Lubbock, USA

CHAPTER 15

Don't Fear Fund Raising

INTRODUCTION, DONORS ARE NOT YOUR STUDENTS; YOU DON'T HAVE TO STICK TO THE LESSON PLAN

Originally Published: July 22, 2013

To paraphrase the opening line of Peter Mayle's popular travel memoir, *A Year in Provence,* my life as fund-raiser-in-chief for the journalism school at the University of Iowa began at dinner.

It was the summer of 2009, and I had just become director of the school. It was my first face-to-face contact with a donor, an alumnus of the university who, appropriately, wanted to help start a program that could train undergraduates for careers in philanthropy, specifically as professional development officers—that is, fundraisers. I felt that this wonderful, original concept—and its focus on oral and written communication skills, persuasion, and public relations—would be a great fit with our program.

After minimal small talk, we got down to business: Our idea was to create an interdisciplinary certificate program in "Fundraising and Philanthropy Communication." I covered such issues as the timeline and the basics of curriculum design. Following advice from the development officer, I spoke the language of "return on investment": The donor's money would produce timely, measurable results that would help students through defined outcomes.

© The Author(s), under exclusive license to Springer Nature Switzerland AG 2021
A. Conley and G. G. Shaker, *Fundraising Principles for Faculty and Academic Leaders*, Philanthropy and Education, https://doi.org/10.1007/978-3-030-66429-9_15

By dessert we had dealt with all his queries and concerns. A few weeks later he made the commitment and donated $100,000 to our new venture. Since then he and several other major donors have committed more to the program, which is now up and running, based at the Iowa journalism school, serving more than 50 students and 14 other departments. Last year we were even able to make a tenure-track hire in philanthropy communication with a focus on social media.

My story is not unique. Anyone considering a career in college administration must learn to practice the art and science of working with donors. In eras of tight budgets, especially at state institutions, many department heads and even faculty members are being recruited and instructed (or begged) to join the effort. For example, in the spring of 2013 at Iowa, the College of Liberal Arts & Sciences convened a meeting to start training department chairs in more depth to support fund raising efforts in a capital campaign. I was asked to give a talk because of my experience in reaching out to donors. My theme: Don't fear fund raising.

I also passed on one major observation to the audience: My 20 previous years of teaching and research in higher education both augmented and undermined the skills I needed for donor development. People making the transition from full-time educator to part-time money raiser should appreciate the similarities and differences between those professions:

You will be a beginner. By the time your faculty career has progressed so that you are qualified to be a department administrator, you may have accumulated years of experience, titles, and status as a scholar and teacher. Your new job carries the designation of chair, director, or dean. You are, in a word, a "senior" in academe.

Then, suddenly, you are a freshman again. Almost every administrator I know recalls being dropped into fund raising and development without having taken any classes or workshops and often without even having participated in fund raising at a preadministrative post—as was my case when I started at Iowa as director of its School of Journalism and Mass Communication. In my job interview, I had emphasized that I was "willing to learn" and enthusiastic about donor and alumni outreach.

So when the promotion comes, be ready to go back to school as a pupil. I read books and articles, both scholarly and popular, on fund raising and development. I took excellent training workshops. Most of all, I considered myself to be an apprentice to the experienced advancement professionals at our university foundation.

You are speaking for everyone. A basic tenet of good administration is: Don't play favorites. You may have a longtime research track in one area of your discipline, but you will fail as a department chair if you appear to be championing that subfield above all others. Likewise, when you start fund raising, you represent everyone and everything that your department does. You need to be able to explain and show the value of disparate kinds of teaching and scholarship, programs, and projects to nonacademics. You are also providing, to borrow the language of accounting, a subcertification that a particular cause is worth supporting—even if that cause was, until you boned up on it, alien to you.

Being a spokesman (or spokeswoman) highlights the personal-trust factor in donor relations. To donors, you are the face, voice, and character of your program. They want to hear what its accomplishments and challenges are—candidly, accurately, and without cant or spin. Officially and legally they are potentially giving money to your department for some good outcome to help your students or faculty members, but in a very personal sense they are giving the money to you—that is, trusting you with it, as its solicitor but also as its steward. As a university-foundation representative explained to me, "They see us as salespeople; they see you as the CEO of the company. For any big business deal, they want to meet the guy or woman in charge, not just the sales force."

You must show that you will pay attention to how their money is allocated and watch over its continuing benefits.

Learn to listen as well as pitch. Faculty members in some disciplines, such as anthropology and journalism, are trained to be good listeners, and most professors like a good conversation.

But working with donors involves many nuances that the novice may not pick up on right away. Donor meetings are rarely PowerPoint-aided lectures; at a lunch or coffee meeting, donors may have no agenda, and the academic fund raiser's role is to listen more than to guide. Many donors, for instance, prefer not to discuss donations at length. The amount and the kind of donation can be brought up, agreed to, and dispensed with over a few minutes at the end of a two-hour lunch—typically by the development officer who often joins you for the meeting.

Such donors prefer to declare how much they love their alma mater, or reminisce about their wonderful professors, or assert how a program contributed to their professional success. Indeed, in cataloging the more than 100 donor meetings I have participated in since my first such dinner, I could find enough material to write up an oral history of Iowa's journalism school.

The point is to hear donors out. You may come into a meeting with a prepared "ask." But they are not your students, and you don't need to stick to the lesson plan.

Learn the language of "return on investment." Donations to universities are often made with idealistic intent. A family whose wealth was gained in the insurance industry that wants to endow a chair in violin to honor a mother who always loved classical music is, in fact, trying to create some higher good without any accounting chart attached to it. And older donors may simply want to "give back" to their old school.

Modern donors, however, typically define "good" through the metric of "return on investment." They want to know what measurable outcomes we project. For example, in outlining the new program in philanthropy studies to the potential benefactor, I eventually laid out a timeline and a grid—dates, actions, personnel costs-projecting what would happen each semester for the next two years. I detailed those actions: surveying what was taught in philanthropy education across American universities and colleges, redesigning courses, cross-listing courses in business and law and several other disciplines, starting a student club, applying for approval of the certificate program, and so on.

In short, we told the donor: If you help us, we will make these specific things happen. We are accountable. The worst thing to say to donors is, "Don't worry; we'll take care of it." They want to know more and in detail.

You are a matchmaker, so think about value for both sides. What you and your faculty consider to be the department's priorities should not be forced on potential donors. Yes, you should speak enthusiastically about your greatest needs (phrasing them as "greatest potential areas for success") and your goals. But as a friend of mine who has raised hundreds of millions of dollars for political causes put it, "Don't forget that it's their money and their passion."

Listening, however, doesn't just mean sitting back while a donor recalls the joys of his freshman year. It means finding out what cause really excites him and translating that into something that benefits your program. For instance, if he says he really appreciated a professor who motivated him during his undergraduate days, you can demonstrate how endowing a professorship in the same area will help attract or maintain faculty talent to benefit current and future students.

You are, thus, a form of matchmaker in several senses of the word. You want to connect good money with good causes, but sometimes you must say no to ideas that can't work, would be unacceptable to your faculty, or would raise ethical issues. Sometimes what donors consider priorities can't or shouldn't be imposed on a department. In academe, forced-fit gifts are as unsustainable as forced marriages. You are the interlocutor and interpolater between worlds and must make the initial judgments and the long-term projections about what can and cannot work out.

Think long-term as well as short-term. Another dimension of fund raising is making contacts that may benefit your department financially, but not necessarily right away. Professors are probably "medium term" thinkers as professions go. University researchers plan multiyear projects; they certainly enter into tenure tracks lasting six years. But development work can extend decades, even across generations.

For example, many alumni help the institutions they care about through legacy bequests. My job with such donors is to keep them updated about our progress, ask their advice, and (implicitly) communicate that their future munificence is (and will be) well appreciated. In other cases, I may talk to people whose giving plans are uncertain; we simply want to keep in contact until they decide that they want to give, even if that decision is a long way off. One foundation development officer put it this way: "Sometimes the return on investment of our time will come to our successors."

You are part of a team. Faculty members, of course, are used to working on committees, and many researchers collaborate on projects. But the grit of scholarly productivity often involves solitary thinking, data analysis, and typing.

In contrast, no fund raiser works alone. As the donor who gave us that $100,000 pointed out to me, his own contribution came at the tail end of many contacts with the campus foundation. Although I was the latest and chief "maker of the case," I was part of a group effort of faculty members, consultants, alumni, students, staff members, development professionals, and, of course, the significant intellectual contribution of the donor himself.

An illustration comes from another chapter in the building of our philanthropy communication program. Our major benefactor visited the school after the program had started. We brought together the program coordinator, key development officers from the foundation, myself, and, most important of all, a student who had signed up for the certificate. We marshaled all the facts (the analytics and metrics, in business parlance): what actions had been taken, progress on the curriculum, number of students signed up for the program, support from other donors. I asked our terrific graphics-and-design professor to put together a one-page newsletter presenting these facts clearly and attractively.

The totality of our presentation was useful, I think, but the student was the real star. Her enthusiasm and her narrative—about how she looked forward to a career helping philanthropic causes, including health research—were infectious. At the end of the meeting, our benefactor committed another major donation to the program. Yay, team!

As a newcomer to fund raising, you will be propelled into a time machine where you feel like an undergraduate again, exploring and learning a novel field with new protocols, rules of engagement, and sometimes counterintuitive wisdom. But don't fear fund raising: Ethically and pragmatically practiced, it is a stimulating adventure that is also patently necessary for the survival of higher education.

PART I, THE INS AND OUTS
OF ASKING 'FRIENDS' FOR MONEY

Originally Published: April 1, 2014

Before I became a department chair, I had no experience with fund raising and held all the usual stereotypes and fears that faculty members tend to have about "asking people for money."

But my field is political communication, so I did know something about the fund-raising enterprise. One of its fundamental dilemmas is encapsulated in this campaign tale: The aides of a first-time politician ask him to solicit donations from a list of his well-to-do friends. He is flummoxed: "I can't call these people. They are my friends; how can I ask friends for money?" The next day the aides give him a second list, this time of wealthy potential donors he doesn't know. Again he balks: "I can't call these people. They are strangers; how can I ask strangers for money?"

If you are (or are hoping to be) a department chair, dean, or senior administrator, you will engage in fund raising. Even faculty members now are sometimes expected to help make the case to donors. But few of us have any formal preparation for the task, and so fears abound: Will I fail at it, and be humiliated? Will I become the pawn of outside interests?

Many of our trepidations revolve around "the ask"—the actual request for money. In fact, when I talk to academics who are thinking about becoming administrators, the No. 1 reason they hesitate is "I can't imagine asking people for money."

At one time, I couldn't either. I've been fund raising actively now for five years, first as a chair and now as a dean. In a new series of columns over the coming months, I will offer perspectives and techniques intended to ease your transition as a faculty member moving into this new financial realm.

Fund raising involves a particular kind of friend making. Since getting involved in annual campaigns and major-donor solicitation, I have met many interesting and, yes, friendly people. Some have become friends.

Although I left the University of Iowa almost a year ago for a new position in Texas, I still regularly converse and meet with the friends I made fund raising in Iowa—but I no longer ask them for money. In several recent cases, however, they have offered me unsolicited help in my new job because they happened to know graduates of my new university or had connections to the charitable foundations with which I now collaborate. Their assistance is a bonus, but I would have hoped to stay friends with them anyway.

Nevertheless, it is important to make a distinction between the kind of friend everyone has and the friend you make in your role as an academic fund raiser. The former would be nonplussed indeed if, during a fishing trip, you asked: "Could I get $3-million for an endowed chair?" The latter, on the other hand, would not be surprised by that "ask"— depending on your timing, groundwork, and sense of their readiness to commit to the cause.

The friendship you have with donors should be an honest one. People who are major supporters of disciplines like music, engineering, or history tend to be achievers. They are accomplished artists, retired scientists, business leaders. They did not climb the jungle gyms of career and life by being naive and unsophisticated. They know your job is to advocate for your department or college, which is typically housed in their beloved alma mater, and they understand that raising money is vital.

At the same time, many donors view you as assisting them. I have had major donors say "thanks for helping us find the best way to help the university" or "I really appreciate your taking the time to make this happen." They genuinely appreciate those who allow their passion for a particular project or cause to see fruition.

Cultivate your "people reading" talents. If you've survived the multiple crucibles of a doctoral program, the academic job hunt, tenure and promotion, and, above all, teaching classes, then you've learned something about how to gauge what other people think about you. Most academics stepping into administration, and thus fund raising, are not clueless about reading body language and verbal signals. Such skills are invaluable in fund raising because timing and nuance are all-important—as they are in many a regular friendship.

A professional fund raiser told me about his decade-long relationship with someone who had a high "capacity" to give—that is, he had the wherewithal to give heavily to the department from which he had graduated but had yet to do so: "Mr. Black will give one day, but the timing is not right for him due to family and professional circumstances. We both know that and accept it." Pushing Mr. Black to give big too early might well spoil their relationship and undermine the future prospects of a major gift.

Development officers once described a particular alum to me as someone who "did not like to talk about money." And he didn't. So we spent our time together talking about our university, higher education, and many other topics. At some point, however, he felt comfortable enough with me, and confident enough that a gift was going to a good cause, that he decided the time was right to bring up money. If I had pushed him too early I don't think the outcome would have been better, and it could have been a lot worse.

The academic fund raiser must work hard to treat donors as unique individuals. They each have singular capacities for giving, family commitments, and passions and interests. You can't force a relationship with them. No matter how pressing the needs of your department or college, you will find that there is a right moment to ask for money and it can't be rushed, although it can be missed.

Building a gradual friendship with someone will allow you to sense when they are ready to give and when they are not.

Don't forget why you are there. When you visit donors, if all you talk about is their money, you will alienate them. On the other hand, don't forget the reason you came in the first place. If you are traveling to meet donors, your institution is investing its money and your time. Everyone understands the benefits may not be immediate. In the case of legacy gifts, the monetary rewards of the relationship may not appear for decades. As one fund raiser put it: "You might be helping your successor's budget."

Nevertheless, you are not being paid just to enjoy travel, meet interesting people, and dine out. You should always keep in mind the hungry mouths back home and precious resources being expended on your sojourns.

Ethical protocols can help. The Texas Tech Foundation, for example, has a rule prohibiting the acceptance of personal gifts from donors. Such precepts remind you (and them) that the relationship, however friendly, has a business component.

Always be ready with projects for their passions. Sometimes the donation comes before the relationship. I have met alumni for the first time when they cut to the chase and said, "I want to help your scholarships." They were clear in what they wanted to do and which part of the institution they wanted to support. Sometimes the contact file you read before meeting a new donor will include notes like, "Ms. White was a scholarship student and wants to help current students in need."

Be ready before your meeting with details of how scholarship donations apply at different levels.

More typically, you will secure a donation from someone you have met many times and built a relationship with, so you've had time to assess their passions and interests. Every time you meet with them, come armed with ideas, projects, or programs that match their focus.

The point is to be prepared if an opportunity arises, because it can pass away just as soon. I've heard sob stories from academics who, caught off guard by a donor's surprise offer, said "I'll get back to you," only to find the next day the prospect had changed his or her mind.

Development folks often do the actual asking. A final perspective on dealing with the "friend" donor will be one on which I elaborate in essays to come: Academics rarely fund raise alone, nor should they.

You are part of a team. At the University of Iowa, I worked with a development officer who happened to be a graduate of our school and who raised money for other departments besides mine. Here at Texas Tech, where I am a dean, I work with a development officer and several staff members who are dedicated exclusively to fund raising for our college. At both universities, a central foundation employs many lawyers, researchers, and development personnel with different tasks, including regional coverage and special gift management.

In the case of the actual ask, it is much more typical for the solicitation to be made by a development officer, sometimes with you there, sometimes independently. A prospect may proffer: "I owe so much to Professor Higgins, who encouraged me to stay in school; I'd like to do something in his name. How can we make that happen?" At that point, as an academic administrator, I could talk about a named professorship or scholarship in honor of Professor Higgins and about its value to students. The development officer, though, might talk about details such as minimum level of gift, how endowment investment works, and legal niceties of donor intent.

The circumstances vary but never in my now five years on the road talking to donors have I ever felt truly alone and uninformed. The simple mantra I always keep in mind: No matter how much fund raising I do, I will always be an amateur. The development officers are the professionals, and the best results are obtained when we work together.

There is nothing demeaning, frightening, or overwhelming about being an academic involved in fund raising. Obtaining support from private donors is vital to the success of higher education, wherever you teach and whomever you serve. Our communications college, for example, gives away some $400,000 in scholarships each year because of the generosity of our friends and the hard work of the dean, department chairs, and development personnel before me.

The personal rewards for you, however, should be underscored as well. I have met many good people and learned so much about my institution, and the current state of the industries our students aspire to join, that I feel fund raising has made me a better administrator and teacher. So don't be afraid to ask friends for money, and while searching for it look forward to making friends.

PART 2, MATCHING DONOR PASSION
TO YOUR DEPARTMENT'S NEEDS

Originally Published: July 14, 2014

An acquaintance who was a department chair at a small liberal-arts college described one of the nightmare-come-to-life scenarios of every academic administrator faced with fund raising. He had met an alum with "a very high capacity"—the development term for wealth available to give—who was ready to make a major gift. The catch was that the donor embraced "fringe phenomena" (let's call them leprechauns here to protect his privacy). His ambition was to finance an endowed chair in leprechaun studies—not as in folklore but as in scientific fact.

To their credit, my friend, his faculty, the college foundation, and the upper administration stood tall and politely turned down the proposed gift.

The anecdote, although unusual, typifies a common apprehension of academics who are thinking about becoming administrators and thus entering the world of fund raising: the danger of selling out, of being pushed around by outsiders whose money drives the department and its constituencies to places they don't want to go.

So if you are a department chair, director of a center, or dean of a college, what should you do if you find that what the donor wants is not what you need?

Remember your mission. We recently hired a new development officer for our College of Media & Communication here at Texas Tech. In interviewing the candidates, I emphasized that we are not in the business of making money. We are a nonprofit dedicated to: (a) the discovery, creation, and dissemination of ideas and knowledge; and (b) the preparation of students for successful careers and thoughtful citizenship. But to achieve those ends at the highest level possible, we need to raise a lot of money from private sources.

That is a distinction with a difference. One way to keep on track as an academic involved in fund raising is to remember that loyalty should be to the mission, not the money. The latter is a tool to achieve the former.

That said, it's not always easy to stay mission-focused. As a December 2013 article in *The Chronicle* on department chairs highlighted, an average day on the job may consist of reviewing schedules, preparing assessment plans, dealing with personnel issues, filling out forms, recruiting, answering email, fielding complaints … and trying to find money to support the program.

The big picture—the department's intellectual and pedagogical goals and priorities—may get lost in the hourly minutiae. Nevertheless, when a windfall dangles before your eyes, you need to make a hard-headed calculation of whether it can work and if it really will help.

Know what you want—in detail. One of the great benefits of thinking about development is that it prompts careful consideration of the department's future by you and your faculty: What are your exact goals and needs? How much money would help you achieve them?

If you think that can be done in a single afternoon meeting, just try it. Most people who become professors are passionate about, and inwardly directed to, their own area of expertise in research and teaching. That's as it should be to maximally benefit students and scholarship. But when it comes to picking out, say, the department's five top-priority areas for outside funding, having 25 professors all advocating for their passions as the obvious focus may lead to gridlock or, worse, dissipation—as in, "OK, we are agreed: We have 25 maximum priorities!"

Still, the conversation is vital. Every department should set realistic goals and needs, and then choose which ones are the actual priorities. If you hope to get private money for your "tops" list you must:

- Create justifications for the goals and needs that you can easily explain to lay outsiders.
- Attach a price tag to the goal or need. What amount of money is required to make it happen, and to make it last?

The exercise may well be painful, but the result will help you stay on mission.

Accept that some of your department's priorities will be more attractive than others to donors. When I interviewed for the deanship I now hold, I was asked, "What are your priorities?" My answer was that I thought there were organic priorities that made sense for the college already, one of which was increasing research, teaching, and community service in Hispanic media. The college already had an about-to-be-named Hispanic Media Center that did great work and even edited an influential journal. Our city itself has a large and growing Hispanic/Latino population.

And Hispanic media in general—from news to digital gaming to advertising—is booming in jobs, venues, and research. In short, with continuing outside help, the college can become a leader, perhaps *the* leader, in this area. It was a slam dunk for the faculty to agree that it should be a priority. And it was one (the center did get a naming gift) that was attractive to donors.

Finding a project that makes sense to a department's internal and external constituencies is not usually so simple. Take, for instance, a common challenge in donor relations. The kind of gift most alumni tend to think about first, since it most obviously connects with their own experience and "helps students," is scholarships for undergraduates. Yet when I participated in a meeting of department chairs at the University of Iowa a few years ago, and we were asked to name our two top fund-raising goals, all of us listed "Ph.D. student support" and "faculty-research support." None of us were opposed to enhancing undergraduate scholarships, but in tight budget times we were most concerned with the survival of our doctoral programs and the retention of productive faculty members.

Be willing to shift gears. Don't be hypnotized by your agenda. Keeping your priority list handy does not mean you should ignore out-of-the-box opportunities.

When I started as an administrator, at the University of Iowa, two foundation officers—who were both graduates of our journalism program—came to me with an idea from a donor. He was not a graduate of our program, but he was trying to find a home for a certain concept: Nonprofits desperately needed more professional help in raising money, so why not create a training program for undergraduates interested in becoming development officers?

At the time, I was just venturing into fund raising myself. I certainly knew that we had no such program or any variation of it within our university. And it was an intriguing idea, because the basic skill sets to work in development included effective communication skills we were already teaching: data analysis, listening, reading, writing, and speaking. I also liked that our journalism program could make this new offshoot a standout, something that few other programs offered.

Fast forward three years: With major gifts from the original donor and others, a lot of help from professionals, and hard work by faculty, the program became a success.

Recast and redirect, gently and thoughtfully. Consider the "undergraduate scholarships" default mode of most donors versus the other needs and priorities of your department. While I have never attempted to talk donors out of helping undergraduates through scholarships, I have tried to persuade some of them that:

- Our national reputation is often tied to the prestige and accomplishments of doctoral students and research faculty.
- While helping young people go to college is admirable, you also want top faculty members and graduate assistants teaching them.
- Undergraduates can gain increased applied skills and cognitive development by getting experience with research. And again, the best professors and graduate students are necessary for that outcome.

The point is: A donor's passion is achievable via many vehicles.

Leave doors open. Sometimes a donor's idea will not work at a particular time but will be worth retrieving if circumstances change. A dean in the sciences at a major research university told of a retired faculty member who loved his home department, had done well in life because of personal thriftiness and several lucrative patents, and wanted to create an endowed chair in his subfield. The catch: The area of research he had in mind—his own—was not one that was a focus of the department anymore. Creating a chair in that subfield would, the dean and the faculty worried, be of only short-term benefit.

Wisely the dean (and the department chair) did not just say "No, thanks" and walk away. He continued the conversation with both the donor and the department. Finally, some years later, a group of faculty members made the case that the college needed to invest in a new and exciting area of research. The dean explored the topic, and they all agreed that the new area was, plausibly, a pathway of research derived from the old specialty of the retired professor.

What happened next was truly win–win: The emeritus benefactor recognized the relationship between his passion and the revised idea. He gave; everybody was happy.

If you are an academic administrator involved in fund raising, you are your department's face, voice, and character to the wider world, and the interlocutor, especially between faculty and donors. In dealing with donors whose ideas don't match your department's, don't give up easily or force a fit. Just as with good teaching and research, a little creativity and playing with alternative scenarios can help fund raising move forward.

PART 3, LEARNING HOW TO BE
THE PUBLIC FACE OF YOUR DEPARTMENT

Originally Published: September 29, 2014

When I got involved in fund raising as an academic, a wise development officer noted a key difference in the way donors saw him and me. "I am a salesman," he said. Most donors, being business people, understand sales, he explained, and have no problem evaluating sales pitches.

But before they give a substantial amount of money to an organization, he added, they really want to know and develop confidence in its leadership: "*You* are the public face of the unit. They need to trust you and believe in you."

In other words, donors certainly want to see facts, figures, plans, and prospects, but faith in the person who presents them is paramount. As an academic, you're used to going it alone and representing your own scholarly interests until you take on an administrative role and have to start fund raising. So how do you become an ambassador for your department's causes and win the trust of disparate potential donors?

Be in command of the facts. As the public face of the department (or college), you must know a lot about what you are advocating for. Don't go on the road until you:

- Are knowledgeable about your program's and your university's basic numbers and statistics. Nothing is more embarrassing than asking for help to create a scholarship and then drawing a blank when the donor inquires, "So, what does tuition run nowadays, with room and board?"
- Have handy, perhaps in aesthetically pleasing pamphlet or flier form, a menu of some of the top projects or programs for which you seek support. That list should reflect the consensus of the faculty, not just your own preferences.
- Understand the history—quantitative and qualitative—of the department. You don't want to be surprised by a donor bringing up a major problem from the past that you don't know anything about.

At the same time, if you really don't know how to answer a particular question, don't try to fake it. It is perfectly acceptable to reply, "Hmm, that's a good question. Let me find out about that."

Be able to translate academic jargon and processes. Part of your job as the public face of your department is being able to describe what it does in ways that outsiders can understand and appreciate.

A dean acquaintance described how he was seeking money for an endowed chair from a donor who, like most people outside higher education, knew nothing about academic hiring. Basically the donor had said, "If I give you the money next week, could we find somebody and hire them by the end of the month?" The dean quickly and clearly explained the process of approvals, committees, ads, interviews, and faculty votes. In a nutshell: "It is complicated and takes a relatively long time, but we do it this way so we can hire the best possible person."

Be positive. Another piece of advice I appreciated from development folks is this: "Nobody pours money into a sinking ship." Appeals for exceptional emergencies or to stave off disaster can work ... once. In the long run, people will help you if they think investment will mean better times, not just keeping the wolf from the door for a semester. Indeed, research on charitable giving shows that sustainable positive outcomes get more donations than "woe is me."

You need to be positive in personality to bear the positive message. If you are dour and grievance-laden, then academic administration and fund raising may not be for you. You may well have a long list of complaints you yearn to share with the world (e.g., "The conference-room ceiling leaks!" or "The head of the promotion-and-tenure committee is a supervillain!"). Keep them to yourself.

Positive does not mean delusional. The donors want to know that you are a shrewd evaluator of the challenges your institution faces, and they will appreciate sensible solutions. They can tell when someone is being a Pollyanna.

Understand the donor's background and interests as best you can. As dean, I replaced someone who had retired after being dean since the college's founding at Texas Tech and had been at the university for 30 years in one capacity or another. As a development administrator put it to me, "Almost every donor knows your predecessor on a first-name basis. It's going to take you years to get close to that." That's why I have been writing, calling, and, above all, traveling as much as I reasonably can.

I am helped, as you should be, by the memory, notes, and files that were kept about past development efforts. Procedurally, every time anyone from the university foundation or the college meets with a donor, there should be a "contact report" added to that donor's profile. Important points from past conversations should be available, and you should be familiar with them—as in "very concerned about access to college for needy students" or "strongly grateful to Professor Sellmeyer, who was his mentor."

Don't be afraid to ask for help. The retired dean of our college is my go-to for advice and background knowledge. I have also found that donors themselves are good sources of advice about the passions and concerns of their friends.

Of course, humans are complex, and surprises crop up all the time. In the give-and-take of conversation, you will learn that donors have multiple interests or interests that no one expected. Go with the flow, and take notes. You never know when a seemingly tangential aside or thought bubble may prove significantly useful months or years down the road.

Be presentable. If you are already a chair, dean, or director, or are about to become one, you probably have some inkling that the dress codes, manners, and ways of speaking in your peer group are different than for faculty members. Consider: Would you write a big check to somebody who was wearing flip-flops? Well, maybe you would, as a faculty member. But in the business world—the one in which most donors have spent their postcollege lives—"unkempt" translates as "unprofessional."

Context and setting matter, of course. When visiting New York in winter, I pack my blue suit, school tie, and black shoes. In California I go tieless (but with a university pin) and sport pastels. If I am meeting an 80-year-old donor and spouse for the first time at a fancy restaurant, I dress up. If I am staying at his house and we are old friends, a polo shirt and sandals may be fine. In time and with experience, you will learn which sartorial aspect fits which occasion and audience.

Become a good listener. An acquaintance recalled that when he became department chair, he found that one big difference from being a faculty member was that he had to "hear out" his colleagues. It's true: At faculty meetings, anyone can daydream, play World of Tanks online, or catch up on correspondence—except for the chair, who will incite resentment if she or he seems distracted. Likewise, in your office you should not seem bored if a senior professor comes to complain about his teaching schedule. Pay attention; it's part of the job.

It's no different dealing with donors. They are most likely achievers, people who have done well in their careers. They are meeting with you out of courtesy and are generally disposed to hear you out, but not just to hear you. They have ideas, reminiscences and stories, questions, and propositions that you should courteously consider.

Don't do it just to be polite or because you hope it will result in money. Do it because it's good for you and your department. Alumni in particular can provide external feedback on the quality of the education you are providing or on industry trends. Their ideas for helping your department may be ones that have never occurred to you. Listen and learn.

One of the misimpressions that people who don't work with donors have is that the enterprise involves a lot of "kissing up." Well, no. Grovel to donors, over-flatter them, and they will soon lose respect for you and lose faith in your causes. Most donors want to work with someone they can grow to admire and trust, not a sycophant.

Nevertheless, you should be, to borrow a phrase from Samuel Johnson, "most able" to make yourself "agreeable to those with whom there was business to be done." It's not difficult, and the rewards are personal satisfaction and the accelerated progress of your academic program.

PART 4, WHY IT'S IMPORTANT TO BE
PEDANTIC ABOUT DONOR INTENT

Originally Published: December 1, 2014

A gift to your department can seem so straightforward, like the first time a donor told me, "I want to endow a scholarship for a student." Easy enough, I thought. Then a development officer explained that in accepting this seemingly simple gift, we had to satisfy tax laws, foundation rules, departmental mission and priority, and "donor intent."

That last criterion was the one that needed the most painstaking definition. What did the donor mean by "student"? An undergraduate, a graduate student, or either? A student already in good standing in our major or a first-year recruit? Could the student be a double major or just minoring in our field? Would requirements include a certain GPA in high school or college? Was there a geographic condition on the gift—that the recipient come from a particular high school or the donor's home state? Would the scholarship rest on objective academic merit, faculty recommendation, or "need"? How would each of those be defined?

And so on.

Why so much attention to detail? Because it's your obligation as a good steward of any funds you raise (more on that in future essays in this series). But there are other reasons to be meticulous about donor intent. You, as the academic on your fund-raising team: (a) are ethically liable to fulfill donor intent; (b) will be regularly audited by your college or university foundation to ensure that you are following donor intent; and (c) will shape relationships with other donors by how you honor the wishes of any one of them. Put another way, the more attentive you are at the front end of a gift, the less trouble you will encounter on the long (theoretically perpetual) back end.

Over the years, I have compiled a growing checklist of tips to make sure of satisfying a donor's wishes.

Know the rules. Money raised for academic purposes at colleges and universities, whether private or public, is governed by a host of entities and legal requirements. One rule that comes up on occasion: Under tax laws, a private gift cannot directly benefit the benefactor, other than as a tax deduction. So, for example, a donor cannot provide a scholarship that then goes to his granddaughter. Somewhat more hazy is the question of influence. I once had to explain to a donor of a professorship that he could not sit on the committee to choose the recipient. Instead, I worked with him on some faculty-friendly criteria for what kind of candidate would be selected.

Another common restriction is when institutions set a minimum for certain types of gifts. For example, one university may require a gift of at least $1-million for an endowed chair, while another may set the floor at $3-million.

Likewise, how much you have to give to win "naming rights" (whether for a brick or a garden or a laboratory) will vary, as will the way terms like "scholarship," "fellowship," or "assistantship" are defined.

The more familiar you are with those rules, the better you will be able to safeguard donor intent.

Read the will. Reading the fine print is as vital for established gifts—especially if you are new to your job—as it is for recent ones. Two days after becoming director, and thus chief academic fund raiser, of a journalism school, I attended a meeting to review the previous year's spending from one of our largest endowment accounts. I still shiver at the memory. The money had been given 70 years before, and the donor had no living relatives; the account was represented by a law firm as trustee. The school had been spending the money for a long time—decades—to support full-time lecturers. But the lawyer, who was new to the account, had actually read the will and pointed out that the "intent" was to finance "lectures," not "lecturers." That single consonant affected some $100,000 of yearly spending. Oops.

From then on, I vowed never to remain ignorant of existing accounts. I read everything, not just the summary in the scholarship file. And I do not hesitate to ask the dumbest (sounding) questions. Some examples:

- When a scholarship specifies that the recipient be from a particular high school, and that school has since split into two, should we check to determine whether the donor now prefers one school or would consider either one?
- When a graduate fellowship has been designated for an "international doctoral student," does that mean a non-U.S. citizen whose B.A. or M.A. came from an overseas institution? Or can the student be a non-U.S. citizen educated in the United States?
- A fund is slated to "pay for the technology in [named laboratory space]." But could that cover mobile technologies, such as clickers and iPads?

In short, be pedantic. Better to be picky and sure than end up being reproached because you misunderstood what the donor specified.

Always work in consultation with the development office. The good news about fund raising is that you are never alone. Almost every college and university has a development office. Academics can get into trouble when they go rogue and solicit or, even worse, accept gifts without adequate consultation with the professionals. You may not always see eye-to-eye, but they are the experts on the restrictions under which you operate.

In finding out what donors intend and noting it precisely in writing, you rarely have to invent new descriptors and phrasing. Very likely the foundation folks have seen and heard it all before and will have carefully parsed phrases at hand that fit the intentions of most donors. For the really complicated or tricky gifts or requests, the experts will help you develop novel but appropriate responses.

Don't rush the closing. In the fund-raising world, tales circulate of "deathbed bequests"—when a donor decides at the last minute to bestow a legacy. I know of one such incident. The gift in question, however, was last-minute only in being made final: The foundation reps and the donor's lawyers had been working on the wording for months, leading up to the moment of giving.

I know from experience that the heady rush of a proffered gift can sometimes lead to an urge to close the deal as soon as possible. Maybe the donor will change his mind, you worry. While the gift process should not be drawn out—a donor can indeed be alienated if things seem to drag on—the importance of the event should encourage all parties to plan carefully. A few faulty or unclear phrases conceived in haste will cause no end of problems later.

Make sure everyone's on the same page. A common minefield becomes apparent when what you, your faculty, and your department want is out of sync with what the donor wants. Sometimes the split is a chasm. A dean I know in the sciences discussed a donor who was interested in endowing a chair in a subfield that almost all of the dean's research-faculty members considered irrelevant and without intellectual merit. Whatever his own opinion, the dean wisely declined the gift. No munificence is worth creating an imbroglio between the administration and academics.

That doesn't mean you as an academic leader should not take the opportunity to lead. In one case I know of, several donors had expressed interest in establishing a particular program at a department in the social sciences. None of the faculty members there were interested in it themselves. But the chair persisted, and over time they came to appreciate that a modest program in that area would attract more majors, increase the profile of their department, and support some of their other ambitions. They ended up embracing the gift.

Donor intent is rarely a mystery. But you, as the academic representative on the fund-raising team, must make sure that everyone, including the donor, agrees not only on what the outcome of the contribution will be but also on how it will be managed year after year. After all, we are raising money for the future as well as the present. We hope that students, faculty members, and the program will benefit from our work long after we have retired, not just in the next fiscal year. So sweat the details of donor intent, and everyone will win.

PART 5, HOW TO BE A GOOD STEWARD ONCE THE GIFT HAS BEEN GIVEN

Originally Published: March 9, 2015

When department chairs, directors, deans, and others embark on academic fund raising for the first time, they naturally focus on "the ask"—that is, on getting the gift. Equally important, however, is the long tail of fund raising: the stewardship of gifts.

There's a lot to absorb about how you satisfy the many legal, ethical, and procedural requirements of a donation, oversee the munificence over time, and keep donors (or their heirs or trustees) apprised of its progress. And it's crucial that you do learn because:

- It's your job. You, as lead academic officer of your department or college, hold the legal and fiduciary obligation to steward gifts responsibly.
- It's the ethical thing to do since the gift is in your charge.
- For some donors, an initial donation may be a "test gift." Handle it well, and more will very likely come your way.
- Your reputation as a good steward will help you become more successful in fund raising in the long run.

Being a good steward of donations means spending a lot of time thinking ahead.

Check with the experts. I am, and always will be, an amateur when it comes to fund raising. It's a part of my job as a dean, but the development folks are the professionals in this arena.

At a large institution, the development officer assigned to help your department is merely the "local" representative of a much larger and varied group of pros. The university development office will have individual experts on wills, contracts, taxes, corporate giving, grant writing, financial reporting, and so on. Almost any question you have about a potential gift can be answered by people who are specialists. Then, too, there will be the senior foundation managers, who most likely possess decades of experience. Even at small colleges, you will find experts who can answer your fund-raising questions.

It is unlikely, then, that you will ever find yourself alone in the wilderness, unsure about a gift or a stewardship issue. Difficulties crop up when the lure of the gift tempts chairs and deans to jump too quickly into an agreement. Your mantra whenever you are offered a donation should be: "Let me check with the foundation on that!" Yes, uttering those words will cause delay, but most donors are men and women "of affairs" and understand the importance of laws and contract wording.

You will sidestep 99 percent of potential roadblocks if you avoid trying to secure and oversee a gift on your own.

Manage expectations at the front end. Spend enough time fund raising and you will eventually have a story to tell about the "one that got away." In my case it was a very, very large potential gift to create a center a few years ago. Many meetings and lots of conversations resulted in an impasse.

I wish my successor at that university luck in making the gift work in the future. I don't begrudge the lost opportunity, however, because I have heard of many seemingly wonderful gifts that ultimately led to stewardship disasters—with unhappy donors, mortified deans and chairs, disappointed provosts, and angry professors. The lesson: Only close the deal if you are fairly sure the terms will work properly.

Case in point: At a small liberal-arts college, a department chair and dean secured a donation for an endowed chair in a particular subfield. Both administrators saw warning signs ahead: The subfield was very narrow; the focus was not connected to anything already taught in the department; the donor was impatient to see "immediate transformative results." In short, the planning was not thorough, the donor was not well briefed, the faculty were unenthusiastic, and the expectations all around were too high. Outcome: Three years of failed searches for the position, infighting among the faculty, a scolding from the president, and an irate donor.

Work out what to expect from the gift with an actual timetable and metrics of "success." The plan must be plausible to everyone, not just to you.

Report a problem; offer a solution. The average major donor is sophisticated about money and realizes not every investment turns out well. You can get into trouble over stewardship of gifts if you misrepresent their outcomes as more successful than they really are. If you are candid about a challenge that arises—and, crucially, if you have a suggested fix to offer—more often than not the donor will be understanding and even helpful.

For example, I faced a case once where we had failed, for two years in a row, to award a particular scholarship backed by a donor's gift. Looking into the details, we found the basic problem was that the scholarship was supposed to go to an undergraduate major from a particular county in our state. Yet the county, which had already been sending very few kids to our university, had seen a decline in population. I called the donor, reported the conundrum, and offered several options. Outcome: We revised donor intent to include several more surrounding counties so it still went to someone from his general home region.

Don't shortchange any concern you might have, no matter how minor, about the details of a gift agreement or the donor's intent. Determine what the benefactors mean but also make sure that they *know* what they mean as it translates to an academic setting.

Showcase good news. On the flip side, when you have good news, show and tell it! Foundation officers are always puzzled when chairs and deans fail to let donors know about the benefits wrought by a donation over time, not just right after the giving. A phone call, a letter, a web post or, especially, a personal visit all can help. Set up reminders on your calendar, or schedule regular visits—anything that cues you to communicate with the people who were so generous. If your department holds a scholarship banquet each year, invite the recipients and the donor and seat them together. At the very least, encourage the beneficiary to write a thank-you note.

In one case, for a particularly big gift, I worked with a staff member and a faculty member overseeing the project to create a "newsletter" about it. Initially, the original donor was its entire readership, and that very happy reader later gave even more.

If a gift helps faculty research, why not set up a lunch with the professors and their graduate students, along with a tour of their labs or a signed copy of their books? You can come up with many other ideas. The point is to demonstrate to donors that their gifts are reaping rewards.

Donor trust in you—the chief voice and face of the academic unit—is a crucial precursor to "the ask." Likewise, trust needs to be maintained, year after year, once the gift is given. But don't be distracted by hopes of material rewards alone. Being a good steward is like being a good teacher: Both duties are essential to our profession.

PART 6, HOW TO PERSUADE FACULTY MEMBERS TO BUY IN TO A CAMPAIGN, OR EVEN HELP

Originally Published: September 5, 2016

One of the greatest challenges to successful academic fund raising is obtaining the faculty buy-in. Don't assume that raising money is all about reaching out to people off the campus. You need to actively and sensitively lobby on the homefront, too.

A sea change has occurred across academe as institutions that once depended largely on tuition or state support have had to up their fund-raising game. The smallest liberal-arts college and the largest state university alike now know they cannot move forward—or even survive— without extensive, focused, and professional fund raising. Thrown into the center of that storm are academic administrators and professors with little or no experience in "development" and "advancement."

Hence this series, in which, so far, we have looked at how to: ask friends for money, build donor passion, be the public face of your department or college, understand donors, and be a good steward.

Now let's turn to the many challenges—and opportunities—you face in convincing faculty in your department, school, or college to support fund raising.

Some don't understand its centrality today. At one university where I worked, a survey of faculty members found that more than half were unable to identify *any* benefits of academic fund raising. At that same institution I recall talking to a senior professor who questioned why I would spend my time trying to raise money. We had that conversation in a room named for a donor, just prior to a meeting to review the recipients of our scholarships, all financed by donors.

That was some years back, and faculty awareness on this front has improved since then. When I interviewed three years ago for my dean-ship, I was surprised to hear professors ask me about my fund-raising experience and philosophy. Typically, I heard such questions only from provosts, presidents, and foundation executives.

Many other administrators, however, still have to take the time to explain why and how they seek to raise private donations. Building awareness internally is the first step toward affirming consent and maybe even getting some help.

You can't promise to fund their subfield. Faculty members are properly trained to explore an (often narrow) area of passion. In contrast,

A. CONLEY AND G. G. SHAKER

when you become an administrator you have to put aside favoritism for people, projects, or areas of teaching and study. If you, as a political historian of 19th-century Middle Europe, became dean of a college of arts and sciences and insisted that the chemistry and psychology departments develop tracks focusing on the Hapsburg monarchy, well, your administrative tenure would be short-lived.

Likewise, a major challenge in galvanizing faculty support for a fund-raising mission is found in the spotty nature of what gets funded. A donor may wish to endow a chair in violin. Great, right? Professors of the oboe, existential philosophy, and mollusk reproduction may respond: "How nice." Or they may react: "Why isn't the dean raising money for my area?" All humans are susceptible to envy and jealousy, and on campuses such tendencies are exacerbated by increasingly scarce resources. When people feel they are getting poorer, they are less likely to delight in a neighbor's windfall.

So you have to smooth the way. First, explain the human angle and the context of all major gifts. In the case of the violin-lover, tell the story, as in: "The donor's mother played the violin but, because of war and poverty, was never able to achieve her dream of attending a music program like ours. He wants to honor her memory by helping students." And so on. In short, the donor was focused on violin for sound, personal reasons and unlikely to shift his object of passion to, say, the cello—or biochemistry, for that matter.

Then point out how one gift does not preclude the possibility of another and may even set an example. Development experts contend that publicizing major gifts may inspire other donors to act.

At the same time, be candid with your faculty. Not every cause has an angel—as in: "I honestly have not met anyone yet with a similar passion for [your field] who has the giving capacity of our violin benefactor. But I will keep looking."

Fund raising takes time ... away from campus. When I run workshops for administrators I often joke, "If you spent all the time on the road fund raising that you should, you would face a faculty vote of 'no confidence' within a year." Not a few chairs and deans get so caught up in the external mission that rebellion simmers or erupts back home. Either they leave too many internal matters unattended or, more simply, they are out of the office too often. Being electronically "in touch" is insufficient. Whenever I'm on the road, I try to respond to phone calls or emails as fast as I can but students, staff, and faculty need a dean in residence, not an absentee leader.

As usual, you will have to assess and adjust to local conditions. How much time is typical for a dean to spend fund raising on the road? The current figure regularly cited is 40 percent; for chairs I would say 10 percent, but all variations up and down exist. For some, that much time away would be fine; for others, it would entail career suicide.

If you are starting to raise money in a department with no development tradition, then suddenly being away a lot is too much too soon. Ease into the enterprise, explaining your goals and tactics along the way. Be transparent while trying to be transformational. During busy months on campus I may not travel at all; during the slower summer months, I once took five trips in three weeks.

Donations aren't good news to everyone. You probably have read stories about "controversial" gifts that incited campus disputes. Some landmines are easy to spot. In one such case, a major donor wanted to endow a chair in a "pseudoscience" at a major research university. Fortunately, everyone agreed on the appropriate response: No, thanks.

But trouble can also arise if a gift is intellectually and pedagogically sound but not a good fit for the department or college. A president at a small liberal-arts college revealed that he turned down a gift for an endowed chair because the area was so narrow that it would have been difficult to sustain a program, and the kind of students that populated his college were unlikely even to be interested in the classes taught. He concluded: "It just didn't fit us."

You are, after all, the chief academic fund raiser for your unit. Faculty buy-in begins and ends with their trusting that you truly represent academic interests and are not just trying to rack up big dollar signs. Conversely, it is of no benefit to a donor if a gift collapses because it was locally unsustainable.

Everyone is either too busy or too uninterested to help you. Even if your faculty are aware of the need for fund raising, and fully approve, you may find yourself at a dead end when nobody wants to participate. In reality, few faculty members will have any expertise (or interest) in directly helping to raise money because: (a) They are busy with their research, teaching, and service responsibilities, and (b) to many of them, fund raising is unfamiliar and distasteful, and they just don't feel comfortable doing it.

So how do you proceed? First, don't overreach. Your goal is to get selective faculty members involved—not all of them. Some will never do it; others will never be adept at it and may do more harm than good. Don't scare people by making sweeping statements like, "We are all on the fund-raising team!" There is no team besides you and the foundation; everyone else is a volunteer and should be viewed and appreciated as such.

One winnowing method is to identify professors in areas that are likely to be of maximum donor interest. For example, for the vast majority of donors, their most recent experience with higher education was as undergraduates, so their default "give to" cause is undergraduate scholarships. So for help in raising money for that, turn to faculty members who have won teaching awards or who lead special undergraduate programs.

Consider also personality and temperament. A veteran foundation officer once described a professor who said he was happy to lead a tour of his laboratory for prominent alumni. Within 20 minutes he had offended almost all of them by his officious manner, negative comments about students, and general "I am amazing, so fund me" attitude. Some people should not represent your institution—no matter how talented they may be in their own field.

At the very least, faculty members can help you tell your story. Ask for help in showing how giving—for scholarships, for a lab, for a professorship, etc.—will have a long-term positive effect on students, the department, the college, or the planet. Ideally, a few of those faculty members will then be willing to take on a more active role.

Ultimately, faculty buy-in is not a box you check and move on. You have to be consistent, transparent, and honest in representing your program and its diverse interests. You will never get 100-percent fervent participation, but you will find selective allies who can advance the success of your fund-raising enterprise to the benefit of all.

INDEX

© The Editor(s) (if applicable) and The Author(s), under exclusive   247
license to Springer Nature Switzerland AG 2021
A. Conley and G. G. Shaker, *Fundraising Principles for Faculty
and Academic Leaders*, Philanthropy and Education,
https://doi.org/10.1007/978-3-030-66429-9

Printed in the USA
CPSIA information can be obtained
at www.ICGtesting.com
LVHW011523301223
767723LV00001B/1

9 783030 664282